THE ANGELS

The Epic True Story

...of triumph over tragedy. Stuart Sharp had a vivid imagination and, from an early age, used it in an extraordinary way. From creating his own back yard orchestra at the age of ten, to seeing visions of himself as a world-class composer, author and film maker.

These were compelling images, which included great orchestras recording the music whirling around in his head, and him writing a best-selling book. Just as clear was a film that, one day, would be produced and distributed around the world.

Growing up in a pub, with a dysfunctional family in a deprived post-war era, all this seemed impossible; but the visions persisted. What they did not foretell was the price that he would need to pay, to turn such dreams into reality.

The catalyst that propelled him on his odyssey was the tragic death of his son; and making the decision, to set out on his adventure, was a desperate one. Following his divorce, he lost everything precious to him; ending up living rough in his car and, eventually, on the streets of Shepherds Bush, London.

A penniless non-musician, he moved into a hostel for the homeless; later becoming its night manager. Over the following decades, he rose further from the ashes; and the ovation from the Philharmonia Orchestra of London, following their recording of his Angeli Symphony, was a singular moment in his life.

His journey also took him to the Dark Continent where, against unbelievable odds, he organised and composed the music for one of Africa's most successful concerts – just as his visions had foretold.

The publication of 'The Angels' is the next step forward, towards the completion of his trilogy of dreams.

Stuart J. Sharp

THE ANGELS

Olympia Publishers
London

www.olympiapublishers.com
OLYMPIA PAPERBACK EDITION

Copyright © Stuart J. Sharp 2012

The right of Stuart J. Sharp, to be identified as the author of this work, has been asserted in accordance with sections 77 and 78 of the Copyright, Designs and Patents Act 1988.

All Rights Reserved

No reproduction, copy or transmission of this publication may be made without written permission.

No paragraph of this publication may be reproduced, copied or transmitted, save with the written permission of the publisher, or in accordance with the provisions of the Copyright Act 1956 (as amended).

Any person who commits any unauthorised act, in relation to this publication, may be liable to criminal prosecution and civil claims for damage.

A CIP catalogue record for this title is available from the British Library.

ISBN: 978-1-84897-303-9

First Published in November 2012

Olympia Publishers
60 Cannon Street
London
EC4N 6NP

Printed in Great Britain

There is a wonderful analogy between life goals, and flying a plane

No matter what course you set out for yourself in life, it will rarely
be a straight one; because of the many variables along the way

Before one sets out on a flight to a destination, it looks simple
on a map; just go from A to B. But if you calculate
your course settings like this, you will
never reach your destination

However, once you know the wind speed and direction, at the level at
which you're flying, you can adjust your course settings
accordingly, and have a much better chance
of reaching your destination

When I set out on my new life course, I had no idea of the
turbulence that would beset my journey along
the way. Some events took me way
off course, but they gave me
experience to fly higher

Eventually, although I still went off course, I was
flying so high that I could always see my
destination, even though it was
far off in the distance

All this became clear to me, when
I finally gained my 'wings'

Stuart J Sharp

Dedication

This book is dedicated to the memory of a son I never knew in this world, but hopefully will in the next.

Ben, we will meet again.

Acknowledgments

Jo Dobson: For the courage, dedication and unconditional love showed to my daughters Emma and Kate, following my fateful decision to take a new course in life. This was a journey that seemed, at best, ridiculous; and at worst, madness. I am glad that I got there in the end; and hope that, through this book, they will gain a better understanding of my reasons for doing so. In many respects, it is a rather long letter to them; explaining much that they have never known about me.

Phyl Sharp: My dear, late mother; who never failed to believe in me no matter what trials and tribulations appeared to bring me down. I know that she has been helping me a great deal from her lofty new position. She was a pure spirit. The president of Zambia met her and said to me, "You have inherited the spirit of your mother; and without it, you could not have created history in my country."

Aunt Pat and Uncle Bob: for their constant sacrifice, love and support in my early years

Hilary Hunt: My lovely sister, who has been with me all the way; and knows, more than anybody, the deprivations we shared during the post-war years.

My daughters - Emma and Kate Sharp: Who missed out on so much in my transition from the old to the new Dad. I told you, many times, that I wanted you to remember me as a hard working composer, and not as a hard drinking cook. I tried my best with you, under cripplingly difficult circumstances. I hope that your journeys with me to Africa, where you met the president of Zambia, will never be forgotten. One day, we will smile again together.

Michael Eisner, CEO of The Walt Disney Company 1984-2005: His communications gave me great hope. He expressed a love of my music; and encouraged me to work hard on the screenplay, and never give up. I am truly thankful for his wonderful advice over the years.

Jonathon Brosnan: Another vital supporter of my projects, who has never failed to encourage me. He only knows the words 'Yes' and 'Can do'. He has been a true rock in my life.

Anthony Wade: A brother in arms, who never failed to believe in my dreams, even when they seemed doomed. His kindness, love and, for many years, my fingers on the ivories, have sustained me. Without Anthony's support, it would have been impossible for me to realise my dream of producing the Angeli Symphony. Long may our relationship continue.

Joan Meadowcroft: A wonderful lady who helped me tremendously. A true earth angel.

Allan Wilson: Without the support of my dear friend, I doubt that I would have survived the many onslaughts along my path to finish my symphonies. The way in which he conducted the London Philharmonia Orchestra, when they recorded my Angeli Symphony, was a joy to behold. To him, I am eternally grateful, and hope that we may record my next symphony together.

Khalid Javaid: An amazing man, who has helped me since the day I met him. He gave me a job, when I was struggling and homeless. In many respects, he was the key to my future success. He was certainly the link to my African project and, without his help, the concert would not have taken place.

Rahmat and Jahangir Khan - World champion squash partnership:
They encouraged me to learn squash. Rahmat coached me to play squash the Khan's way. This gave me another skill, from which I could earn cash to send home. I am truly grateful for their input, and squash has kept me fit to this day.

Ruthie Henshall: She believed in my music; and encouraged me throughout the auditions, the duet 'Nowhere without You', and its final recording.

Adam Ellis: An exceptionally gifted music producer, who produced my pop and rock music albums. I am truly grateful for his friendship over the years, along with that of his father, Kevin.

Danny Edgar: Without him, and his inspirational business acumen, I would not have gone on to create the finance necessary to hire great orchestras. His loyalty and honesty gave me the hope to continue.

Oliver Cheatham: He travelled from America to sing my concert theme song in Africa, and was just wonderful.

Keshi Chisambi: One of the most amazing people I have ever met. He was originally my colleague and, later, dear friend who, although totally blind, was the rock behind the organisation in Zambia that produced the concert.

Alan and Silvana Pearson own SAQ International in Melton Mowbray: A big 'Thank you' for your love and support. Without the use of your incredible equipment, I could not have recovered so quickly from my hip operation. I can never forget all the wonderful dinners and laughs we had, and I look forward to many more.

Louise Emmanuel: Finding Louise, who sings the female part of the duet "Nowhere without You" – the book's theme song – was a ten year struggle. This song required someone with the right heart, and not just the right voice. Louise has it all, and it has been a joy to know her.

Jeff Anderson: When I needed a great vocal talent to sing my duet with Louise Emmanuel, Jeff came along at precisely the right time. I was looking for a young artist with a love and compassion for humanity that burned in his soul. Jeff has these qualities in abundance, and I am truly grateful that he also became a friend.

The London Philharmonia Orchestra: I had dreamed about the world's best orchestra recording my symphony. When the day finally arrived, and I heard them begin to play, I thought that I must still be dreaming. Their combined greatness made the incredible occasion joyous and beautiful. Here's to the next symphony, which is in the pipeline. I can't wait to do it all again…

Bryan and Dorothy Shipstone: For their wonderful friendship and encouragement.

Craig Clyde: Without his help and guidance, it would have been impossible for me to contemplate writing the screenplay. He, and his lovely wife Vaunie, showed me great love and respect during my time with them in America. I will never forget this, and am honoured that they consider me a friend.

John Peat: He was my bank manager at the local branch of the Royal Bank of Scotland, and a crucial link in my financial affairs. Taking the time to understand my vision of producing the Angeli symphony, his advice was invaluable, and for this I am most grateful.

Dr Kenneth D. Kaunda, former president of Zambia: His belief, that I would successfully organise and compose the music for a great concert in his country, never wavered. There were many doubters and detractors. He was a true statesman and, without his belief, the concert could not have taken place. His son Kaweche was my link to his father, and to him I owe great thanks.

Ellis and Manny Elias: Ellis sponsored the musical recording of the African concert and song, with the unfailing support of his brother Manny. Without their tremendous efforts, against all odds, the concert could not have been the success that it turned out to be.

Barry and Kath Hayes: Although Barry has now passed on; my thanks to him and Kath for their kindness and loving support.

Eddy Grant: A very dear friend and squash-playing partner, who encouraged me to never give up on my musical endeavours. His many hits, across the decades, inspired me to keep going. He took time out of his busy schedule to visit me when I was recording, and encouraged me to finish the music and the book. Eddy was, and still is, there; pushing me along. I treasure his friendship.

Martin Head: For his love and commitment in helping me with many important pieces of filming, over several years.

Susan and Michael Evans: For their unfailing support.

Yusuf Islam (Cat Stevens): I met him through Rahmat Khan, and he gave me the following piece of advice; which I have never forgotten, and for which I am most grateful. "When you compose a piece of music from the heart, it can get lost in the production. As the composer, the hardest thing is to keep the original feel. Your challenge, if you produce your music, is to never lose the original intention and feel." He was right. It was incredibly hard, and it took so much longer to produce my music; but his wise words stayed with me throughout the productions.

Anne Marie Piercy: Her exceptional attention to the historic detail in my book, along with her insights, made it a pleasure to work with her. To her I send my grateful thanks.

Nick and Celia Charles: For their unfailing support and love throughout the filming and editing of the book's theme video. For Nick's incredible green screen editing, taking many hundreds of hours, I send my heartfelt thanks.

Colin and Hilary Anderson: For their unfailing friendship, and unconditional care, shown to me over the years. Colin Anderson, OBE, is the founder and chief executive officer of ASG Ltd; one of Northern Ireland's longest established and most progressive communications companies. I offer a sincere thank you to him and his wonderful team, for the unique way in which they have helped bring worldwide recognition to my book and music. A most sincere thank you to Hilary Anderson, who has been a rock with her love, kindness and support. Without her special gifts, I doubt that we would all be where we are now.

Michael Stout: Has been a powerful supporter of my book, music and project in Africa. His total commitment to ensure the book's veracity, by working with me over several months, has been a joy; and his skills as a proofreader and editor are second to none. I treasure his loyal friendship, and long may it continue.

Olympia Publishers: For believing in my story, and following it through with total commitment. To the whole team, I extend my heartfelt thanks.

Mr Derek McMinn, MD, FRCS: Affectionately known as 'the father of modern hip resurfacing'; Derek is one of the world's leading hip and knee experts, and inventor of The Birmingham Hip Resurfacing (BHR). Along my journey, I suffered from crippling osteoarthritis, necessitating the resurfacing of both my left and right hip joints. Derek's revolutionary treatment not only got me back on my feet, finally free of pain; but even able to play squash again. For this, I am eternally grateful to him and his team.

To all those not mentioned, who have helped me in any way,
I send my grateful thanks

Stuart J Sharp
www. angeli.tv

Foreword

I first met Stuart Sharp in September 1997 at Abbey Road Studios, where I was conducting a film score. Arrangements had been made for him to hand over a demo tape, of music he had spent several years putting together. A jazz musician friend of mine, Anthony Wade, had worked with non-musician Stuart during those years, to tease the 'Angeli Symphony' out of his head, and into an electronic version of his 'Opus 1.'

I have to admit that I found Stuart's proposal to be an almost impossible challenge. He insisted that London's Philharmonia Orchestra was the only orchestra he would accept to record his symphony. He was totally oblivious to the fact that such an undertaking was usually within the domain of film and music moguls, or firmly established composers. Here was a man, who some years earlier, was a penniless non-musician living in a hostel for the homeless! I am embarrassed to say that his demo tape lay on my desk for a number of weeks before I listened to it.

During this time, I pondered over the unbelievable courage and determination of this man, but could not imagine that his music would, in any way, be of a standard acceptable to one of the world's greatest orchestras; and I did not relish the phone call I would have to make to break the bad news. However, very late one night I put aside an hour to make my critique. The first few bars grabbed my attention to the point where I leaned in closer to the speakers in total surprise and amazement. The piece was so full of anguish, torment, pain and intense musical passion that I felt I was looking directly into this man's heart.

He'd told me of the death of his son, and why he needed to write this wonderful piece; which had me in tears long before the music ended. I have to admit that I was stunned, even more so knowing that this was only a demo! I could imagine the finished, orchestrated score; and the Philharmonia Orchestra recording it. But in the cold light of day, it meant that Stuart would have to finance this enormous challenge himself.

Stuart's wonderfully written book describes the trials, traumas and tribulations which, over many months, eventually brought us to Whitfield Street Recording Studios for the 'big day'. Something I shall never forget, for as long as I live, is that after the first sight-read through of the whole piece, the orchestra gave Stuart a huge, heart-felt round of applause. I have never seen any orchestra, anywhere in the world, give any composer an ovation like that before. It was a very emotional experience knowing that they were moved to do that for Stuart. The best analogy I can give, regarding what Stuart has achieved, would be like me writing a book on brain surgery – I know where my brain is, but I have no idea how it works!

Over the past fifteen years Stuart has gone on to compose and record more great pieces, ranging from Classical to Rock 'n' Roll. Each time he sends me a new recording, I smile at his courage, determination and sheer strength of mind. This is a book that will inspire and motivate people of whatever walk of life, culture and creed. It goes far beyond music, into the realms of achieving the impossible; with faith, sacrifice and an unswerving belief in oneself. It shows that anyone can do anything, if they really want it badly enough. I am sure that 'The Angels' will sell around the world, and launch his wonderful music to a very grateful public.

Allan Wilson
Conductor, orchestrator, arranger

1. The Snow People

1947

The winter of 1947 provided me with a glorious sight. I was three years of age when I saw snow falling for the first time. Enduring endless hours, sitting by the open bedroom window late at night, had paid off. Even the bitter breeze felt good, as it froze my nose and ears until they tingled. I was determined to keep watch until it arrived. When those soft, fluffy flakes fell from the moon-kissed, darkening clouds, I witnessed a beautiful sight. My blackened world of bombed-out houses became transformed into a white glaze of icing on this giant Christmas cake.

Everywhere and everything became quiet. A lone couple fought their way home, through the oncoming blizzard, and noticed my skinny frame silhouetted at the open bedroom window. They pointed at me, and I just stared at them *maybe they're thinking that I might jump out*. The woman hurried to the front door, and banged on it with a God Almighty wallop.

I was feigning sleep, when my mother rushed into the bedroom, then gently closed the old and rusting metal-framed window. It creaked, and she sighed. I could hear her shivering, as she lovingly tucked me in. It seemed an age before I could hear the telltale snores; one low - one high. I was soon nudging my nose against a window, the view from which was transforming into a winter wonderland of pirouetting snowflakes. I dragged the coarse, brown, army issue woollen blanket off the bed, and wrapped it around my shoulders for warmth. I wanted the scene to go on forever. I felt at one with nature, and merged with the thickening cascade of snow descending over the surrounding streets and gardens. It was truly magical, and I did not want to sleep. What was the point, when a new world was unfolding before my eyes?

I began to shiver, and my teeth chattered uncontrollably as I gently closed the window. It creaked annoyingly, and echoed loudly. I felt sure that it would wake my parents, so I hovered for a moment, and listened; one low - one high. Saved by the snores, I was prepared to dive back into bed quickly; but an odd force held me back. I suddenly became fearful, and felt a presence in the room.

A vision of my furious father, filling the doorway, flashed through my mind. I looked nervously over my shoulder, and glimpsed an odd sight from the corner of my eye. I quickly pulled the blanket over my head, as panic began to take control of my body. It took some time to pluck up courage, to peer over the prickly edges of the old worn-out cover; but I had to physically stop myself from screaming *this can't be real...*, instantly covering my head again

An attractive lady and a young boy stood motionless by the bedroom door. They stared, impassively, straight at me; and I could almost see through them. I was frozen with fear, and closed my eyes, praying that they would disappear. They were so white *maybe they're snow people.* I waited for what seemed an eternity, wishing hard for them to go away. With trembling hands, I slowly pulled the blanket below my left eye, and peeked again. My lips quivered. The ghostly pair was still there.

The youngster was playing with some wooden toys, which my uncle had made for me. I assumed that the woman, who wore a long flowery dress, was his mother. She had a pretty face with deep, cherry red eyes; and long, dark hair, which flowed around her shoulders. He was bigger than I was, probably about five or six years of age, with a shock of curly ginger hair. His chubby face, and squinty half smile, helped me relax.

Braces criss-crossed over his shoulders, and held up his short trousers. He was dressed in summer clothes, and I was surprised that he was not shivering. He did not speak, and focused intently on my toys. I'd had nightmares before; and was sure that I would wake up screaming, as on previous occasions. My heart thumped so hard in my chest, I could hear it banging in my ears. Then the lady spoke. She talked to me very quietly, as if she knew that they should not be there.

"This is my son, James; and I hope you don't mind if he plays with your toys."

I nodded, and she invited me to sit with him on the floor. He loved the wooden train, and I showed him how to connect up the various parts. I wasn't scared any more, as he was so nice. Suddenly, the door opened, and my mother shouted. I was startled, and almost fell backwards.

"Stuart, it's 4 o'clock! Who are you talking to?" James and his mother disappeared through the wall behind me. I didn't know what to say. I just shrugged my shoulders. She tucked me into bed so hard, I felt as if I was being strangled.

My job in the family was to remove ashes from the grimy old grate, and twist old newspapers into firelighters. I was always up before 6 a.m., and my parents thought that this was a good way to make use of the early bird. My father was a master at getting a good fire going. He would hold a double page spread of the Daily Mirror over the fire hole, as the embers caught. I loved to hear the whoosh of air being sucked up the chimney, and the recalcitrant red fire bursting into life behind the crackling paper.

He always let the newspaper catch fire. He said that it was the point at which he knew the flames would take hold. He called it 'drawing the fire'. Then he quickly rolled up the burning conflagration in his hands and threw it, venomously, up the chimney; where it disappeared in an instant. I loved it, and couldn't wait until I could do the same thing. He said that it was a skill; but I would have to wait until I was at least fifteen, and my hands had matured and hardened, before I could learn it properly.

When my mother wasn't working at the paper shop at 5 a.m., she slept in until around seven. On these days, she always expected me to have the fire prepared; but this day I was still sleeping. *I must have been dreaming about my early morning visitors,* was my first waking thought.

My mother thought that my midnight marauding was a one-off, because of the closeness of Christmas. She had cried because they had no cash to buy me a football. This seemed odd to me, because I knew that Father Christmas would bring one. It was on his list, so it didn't make sense to me. The house was so cold that we all huddled by the fire, which only threw out heat to about a yard from the grate.

I helped my father to make toast. I admired his genius, as he carefully poked a long two-pronged fork through the crusty bread, and held it over the smoky flames. My mother made tea, and brought it out on an old wooden tray with a tin of leftover pork dripping. Timmy, the old, fat, long-whiskered tabby cat, was still sleeping on a high-backed chair in the corner; and the smell of food woke him from his long, cold-induced sleep. He stretched, purred loudly, and slinked over to join us. Now we had a feast, and started to warm up.

The dripping was spread upon the toast, which was dipped into the tea, turning it into a kind of sloppy soup. The trick was to hold the toast in the tea just before the bread fell apart. It was then a quick movement - out of the tea, and into your mouth. This was always a highlight of family life, and something to look forward to. My mother asked the question again. "Who were you talking to last night, Stuart?"

I just blurted it out. "James. He's my new friend."

"There's something wrong with this boy," said my father offhandedly, as he turned and accidentally dropped the toast off the fork into the hungry fire. "Bugger it!" he screamed. Bread was a scarce commodity, and our ration book was almost empty. I watched, astonished, as he dug the lone piece of blackened bread out of the fire with his bare hands; and then fell back in fear at his sudden outburst. It was the first time that I had heard my father shout like this, and I started to shake. I really only knew my mother.

Although she attended to my every whim, my father was never available for me. He came home from work, at the Rover factory, at about four in the afternoon, had tea, and slept. My mother put her arms around me for reassurance. "Now you listen to me, John. Stuart has a vivid imagination, that's all, so leave him alone!" She raised her voice even higher than he did; and I could see, then, who was the real boss.

My father threw the burnt apology for toast onto the old cracked plate, which was balanced precariously on the worn-out, wooden hearth surround. With a look of thunder in his eyes, he stood up, stormed into the tiny passageway, and grabbed his overcoat from the banister. He dragged open the kitchen door; only to discover that snow had piled so high, that it formed a giant barrier between him and the back garden. He tried the front door, and the same thing confronted him. My mother said that it was the coldest winter she had ever known.

The 'Big Freeze' of 1947 is still considered to be one of the worst in the UK's history, and supplies of coal actually ran out. For me, though, it was the best winter ever, because the snow changed everything. I ran upstairs to view the incredible scene from my bedroom window. Great gusts of wind had blown snow to the height of the eaves of the houses around us, and the street had become completely engulfed. I was now definitely convinced that my new friends were 'snow people'.

"This is bloody terrible!" This, and various other unrepeatable expletives, burst forth from my father, as he desperately tried to tunnel his way through the giant snow hill at the front door with a tiny ash shovel. We had no money, and there was precious little food in the larder. I could hear my mother sighing loudly with dismay, as she tried to turn on the dilapidated old taps in the kitchen. Both had frozen solid.

My mother was a very pretty woman, with long flowing dark hair; but her beauty was retreating in the face of such austerity. My father, too, was a handsome man, with a typical RAF moustache from his time during the war. On the face of it, they had film-star looks; but poverty was ensuring that these qualities meant for nothing, and their relationship was slowly, but surely, eroding away.

A great row erupted between my parents. It was serious; and I hid behind my bedroom door, with one ear to the thinnest part. I trembled, as their voices became louder and more vicious. My mother was tiny - but she was a terrier. She was fearless, and I could hear her punch and slap my father. The thud of her fist hitting him, again and again, almost made me sick. He could have felled her with one crack from his hand, but she didn't care. She beat him until she ran out of steam, and then cried hysterically. I started to cry, too.

I felt as if I was in the wrong body, and did not feel like a part of this family. *Where did I come from? I must be a snow person. That's why I could see my snow friends, and my mother couldn't.* These thoughts made me feel different. I wanted to feel better about my life, but feeling different was the best that I could hope for.

A strange quietness had pervaded the house, and I crept slowly down the stairs to see what was happening. Leaning over the banister, I saw my father stride into the spare room, and slam the door so hard that the noise echoed in my ears. I was too scared to move, and sat on the stairs waiting for something to manifest.

My father had retreated, in the face of a far more powerful enemy, to find solace in his pipe. The aroma of his special blend of tobacco found its way through the ill-fitting door, and hit my nostrils like a leaking sewage system. I hated it.

2. Survival

1947

Our tiny semi in Sheldon, Birmingham was rented. My mother referred to the area as 'Solihull', which had a better ring about it. Solihull was where all the rich people lived, with Birmingham representing the poor. The rent man arrived, every week, for his money; and my father always became depressed after his visit. Although both he and my mother worked hard all week, their combined basic income barely covered this expense, and it became a regular reminder of our perpetual poverty.

Every week or so, all the mothers in the street would walk to the local rubbish tip, pushing old empty prams; with their children marching alongside them. The garbage area had developed on top of an old, disused coal dump; and beneath the rags, and discarded household rubbish, lay a gold mine of low-grade coal that was unsellable to the general public. The women and children would scavenge amongst the debris, plucking out any bits of burnable coal and rubbish with their bare hands.

I loved this excursion, and great camaraderie flowed between the families. The prams were filled to the brim with coal of all descriptions - big bits, tiny bits, slate, scoops of black dust - then neatly covered with a navy blue top, pressed into the sides with shiny studs. The camouflage was vital, due to the illegal nature of the scavenging. The authorities knew about these weekly nefarious excursions to the tip; but turned a blind eye as long as the women did not flaunt their activities, by showing the booty to all and sundry on the way home.

I could hear my mother whimpering in the front room, and slowly opened the door. I had never seen my parents fight like this before, and knew that something bad must have happened. I peered around the door, and mother looked up, staring solemnly at me. She stopped crying, as I walked in. I sat next to her on the scuffed, brown two-seater settee. The cat was also scared witless, and had hidden for the duration of the scuffle. He was moaning, and desperate to go outside. She grabbed him by the scruff of his ample furred neck, strode purposefully to the kitchen door, opened it, scooped some snow away from the great wall in front of him, thrust the cat into the cavity created, and slammed the door. Snow flurries flew into the kitchen, and made their way into the living room. The icy blast instantly turned the whole house into a frozen waste, and I immediately moved within inches of the fire. One side of my body started to burn, while the other side froze.

There were no expectations of anything from my parents. Mother hated the deadness that gripped us, although her spirit was still alive. The fights with my father were manifestations of her frustration to get out and do something, and were a cry from her heart. We sat on the cat hair-encrusted settee, and comforted each other. I had been noticing her ample bosom, and burgeoning belly, for months, and wondered why she was getting so much bigger. *This is the time to find out* I felt the two great mounds; which seemed attached to her chest, and hiding behind an old knitted woollen jumper. "What are these?" I asked innocently. She was obviously shocked, and searched for an answer. An eternity went by.

"They are for your new brother or sister," she explained. This was the oddest thing I had ever heard. Realising the impossibility of explaining such a statement to a three-year-old, she continued. "I thought you would like a new playmate, and I've organised it for you."

Perhaps this was the cause of the terrible tension between her and my father. Perhaps my father did not want me to have a playmate, or could not afford one. "But I have a new playmate." I cried.

"No, I mean a real playmate. A brother or sister," she blurted out. I was hurt and angry, thinking that my snow friends wouldn't like it, and not return.

"I like James. I don't want anyone else." My mother was clearly taken aback, and totally lost for words. She decided to let me have my silly way.

"No, you can still have your friends, but you will have another new friend; one that will belong to you." She had said the right thing.

"Is my brother or sister coming from the snow?" I inquired. She smiled for the first time.

"No, love. A big bird in the sky - a stork - will bring him or her to you. It'll carry your new friend in a white blanket, through the snow, right to the front door." I was confused, but it all sounded rather good. I snuggled up to my mother, and rested my head on her prodigious promontories, wondering what purpose they could possibly serve for a new brother or sister *this is a strange world*. "I don't like you fighting with Daddy," I mumbled, "What's wrong? Are we poor people?"

She contemplated for a while. "No, love, we're rich... and we won't fight anymore. I promise."

Earlier that year, during the summer, things had picked up, bucking up my mother's spirits considerably. Her sister, Pat, was a very special person, without whose support we could not have survived. She'd arranged, and paid for, the three of us to travel to Blackpool for the weekend; ostensibly, for a holiday break, and I was very excited. Walking into a curled-up cottage on the seafront seemed a curious way to begin the holiday. I learned, much later, that the nice lady we were visiting was a clairvoyant, who'd had a vision of me as a millionaire! I knew that my mother and aunt were very pleased, following the visit; and my mother paid a great deal more attention to my incessant questioning about our lives, after we returned.

Christmas came and went. I was surprised that Father Christmas had managed to get through the blizzards, and bring me a football. The snow lasted for weeks, but there was no sign of my snow friends. I watched my father and neighbours from my bedroom window, burrowing their way through the snow like moles, and scuffing the ground. They used everything that they owned, from garden trowels, to their bare hands.

3. A Sister

1948

I woke up with a start. My mother was screaming, and I was so scared, that I was riveted to my bed, unable to move for fear *this is more than just a fight!* I heard the sound of my aunt, uncle, father, and another man; with a lot of rushing about.

"Get plenty of hot water and towels!" was the cry from the other man.

"Yes, doctor," shouted my aunt. I really thought that my mother was dying, and I wanted to run to her; but so many people were dashing up and down the stairs, I decided to stay where I was. Suddenly, the screaming stopped, and there were a few seconds of total silence. I started to shake uncontrollably, as I was sure that she was dead.

Then, the most awful screeching sounds of a baby, letting forth at the top of its lungs, cracked the quiet; like a lightning bolt from the blue. I had no idea what was going on, and was certain that I had been sent here by my 'snow people' to witness how mad people live. I lifted my arms to the sky.

Please take me back! I don't want to stay here any longer! I don't belong here!

My aunt came up to my bedroom. I feigned sleep. I was always feigning sleep. All grownups felt that children of my age should be asleep the moment that their heads hit the pillow. She gently pushed my shoulders.

"Wake up, Stuart... You have a sister." I slowly opened my eyes *should I even be bothered?*

"Come and see!" she exclaimed, excitedly.

"Did the stork come?" was my naive reply.

"Yes, yes. Come on." She grabbed my hand, and yanked me out of bed to see my new baby sister. I already knew how cold it could get outside; and Hilary (that's what they named her) must have felt the same, with only a single blanket to protect her on her journey through the sky *but it's summer now, so why is she screeching?* "Is my mom dead?" I asked.

Her bedroom was full of people, all beaming. Even my father looked happy. Through the melee, I saw my mother in bed, holding a bundle of soft blankets. They covered what looked like a doll, but I could only see its head. The eyes were closed, and its nose was squashed almost flat. It was a wrinkled apparition of a baby. I had never seen a new baby before, and I was not impressed at all. "Give your sister a kiss," beamed mother. That was the last thing I wanted to do, but I complied to make her happy. After a cursory peck on the cheek, I stood back to leave her to all the admiring fans.

"Can I go back to bed now?" I asked, politely. They had not noticed my complete lack of interest in the whole affair. It wasn't because I had no idea of what was going on; but because my parents constantly treated me like a child and, at four years of age, I felt truly grown-up *I'm much more intelligent and aware than they imagine.* I was sure that, if I thought hard enough, the 'snow people' would come to my rescue…

4. Making Money

1949

With the new baby in tow, my mother gave up her early-morning job at the newspaper shop on the main road. She also relinquished her position as barmaid at the Wheatsheaf pub in the evenings. During her time there, I'd discovered that empty beer bottles were stored in the back garden of the pub, and that a small monetary deposit was refunded on every bottle. I could see a way of making money from this knowledge - if I could scale the six feet high wobbly wall that surrounded the pub.

I formed an alliance with a friend of the same age, whom I trusted implicitly; and we produced a plan of attack. I calculated that if I stood on his shoulders, then I could heave myself over. I also knew of a passageway; which led from the back garden, through the pub, and into the off-licence.

So, one dark night, we tested out the plan; during a thirty-minute window of opportunity, when both sets of parents were out. It worked like a dream. I found hundreds of empties lying around in the grass, but decided to return just one as a test; after which we continued our scurrilous activities, making a shilling profit in that week.

I felt that we were well on the way to becoming millionaires; and we were able to purchase two bottles of R. White's lemonade and an ice cream, which we consumed, with great glee, in a local field. We became the envy of the street; but we quickly became over-confident, and stole a further six empties. The bar assistant became suspicious, and questioned my father's ability to afford so much drink. The manager collared me, and I was frogmarched home to face the wrath of my parents; who had to pay back the shilling I had made. I didn't shop my fellow conspirator, but felt bad about getting caught for months afterwards.

The demolished houses had been a topic of conversation between us for months, and we thought that some sort of fight had caused them to fall down. I found it difficult to comprehend a struggle that could have caused so much damage, and the flattened buildings were a no-go area for the kids of the street. However, we had a curiosity that knew no bounds. This was the time. We were tough, we were strong, and we were five years old.

We attacked the debris with a vengeance, and bricks and rubble presented little problem. A dozen or so of us took the first ruined wreck apart until, finally, a cellar appeared; and we stood silently in shock. I was the first to volunteer venturing down the crooked staircase, which was hanging at a crazy angle. A basement area appeared. It was an eerie sight.

"There's money here! I found money!" I shouted excitedly. Within seconds, the rest of the gang had joined me, amid whoops of delight. Farthings, halfpennies and pennies lay scattered on the broken, dust-encrusted concrete floor, which had greened and grimed with age. I had discovered Nirvana, and took charge immediately. "We share it out equally," I announced, with a newly found authority.

We flew out of the dingy, dusty hole, dripping with our ill-gotten gains, and congregated in the back garden for a share-out. It took an age to work out how much money we had made. It was a beautiful moment. We could legitimately go home, and explain our crusading cash adventure. We'd made approximately ten shillings each, which was a small fortune, and I was sure that our parents would be delighted to receive such a massive contribution to their family's funds.

However, this exciting escapade was short-lived. Each one of us was severely told off, and some were strapped for their adventuring. How could we have known that the great explosion, which had destroyed the houses, had killed the inhabitants? That our fathers had buried their remains in the back gardens?

We were ashamed but, after a parents' committee meeting, we were allowed to keep half of the booty; although we never discovered what happened to the other half. Nevertheless, it came with a promise to never repeat such a dastardly act again.

We were running out of options to make money, and my mother felt that I had too much time on my hands. The devil was obviously utilising my spare brain capacity, and she could already see me descending into hell.

"It's primary school for you, my boy, starting tomorrow!" she exclaimed. This seemed the perfect plan for her. She was still smarting from the discovery of my criminal conquests; and so I had to promise to work hard at school, to make up for my villainous activities.

5. Leaving Home

1950

I discussed ways of leaving home with my friend Godfrey, who had his own reasons for leaving The Grove. He'd heard about a place called Australia, and invited me to his house to see his father's globe of the world. "Look, see," said Godfrey, "It's only about a foot from where we live, in England!" He carefully calculated the distance, with the tape measure that his mother used for knitting. "If we dig down, we could be there in a few minutes!"

We had to find a time when all parents were out, and this was the most difficult part of the plan. We needed a spade, so we headed for my father's tin shed at the bottom of our garden. This place was off-limits to me, and I had never dared question this imposition. My father had made it abundantly clear that grave danger lurked there - but the spade took precedence.

The shed was like a fortress, and a big burly lock barred any hope of entering through the old, rusting, tin door. We sat on the grubby grass area, pondering a possible forced entry. Leaving for Australia was magnificent motivation, and embarking on another adventurous activity seemed worth the risk. We would soon be in another country, and our parents would never find us. We crept around the perimeter of the tin shed, like two professional robbers. Then we found it - a weak spot. Part of the tin wall was not attached to the ground.

"This is it," I cried excitedly. "You keep a lookout, and I'll pull the tin up," I whispered to Godfrey; and with all my might and strength, I managed to lift it by about six inches. "We can crawl in, now. Come on," I whispered. We wiggled our way in, like slimy worms disappearing into the earth. A great, dark shadow filled the interior. My father spent a great deal of time locked in here.

I'd often heard crashing and banging noises from this area. A weasel-wafting beam of dusty light curled in from our break-in point and, slowly, the shiny rear bumper bar of a car came into stark view. We stood in shocked amazement and, as our eyes adjusted to the semi-dark, we could see that it was, indeed, a complete car. I screwed up my eyes, and could not believe it.

The emblem atop the radiator grille announced its name, 'Jowett'. Now, it was clear what my father had been doing in this shed, for as long as I could remember. He was building his own car. The spade was forgotten, as we explored and caressed every part of this incredible machine.

"Let's sit inside," I suggested, with gleeful anticipation. I had never been in a car before. My mother said that only people in Solihull had cars *we must really be as rich as them!* She had been telling me the truth all along; and we <u>were</u> rich. The smell of the leather seats felt good, as it permeated the air; and I was soon in the front seat, turning the steering wheel side to side. It was enormous fun.

In an instant, the shed was ablaze with light; and my eyes blinked in horror. The side door of the shed had opened; and the silhouette of my father engulfed the space, like a giant about to stamp on a hapless victim. Flames of frustration billowed from his entire being, and incoherent oaths spouted forth from his mouth. He yanked us both out of the car, and belted me all the way to my bedroom *if my mother had been in, she'd have belted <u>him</u>*. My backside was sore for days. Initially, it didn't hurt; for somehow, my body had known it was in for a thrashing, and had prepared itself for the worst. I did not understand, as it made no sense for my father to keep such a magnificent secret from us.

Godfrey had run for his life. We had no choice now. We had to get to Australia as quickly as possible. I looked out of my bedroom window, and saw my father at Godfrey's front door talking to his father. My heart sank as, within seconds, screams of another thrashing rang out loudly enough for the whole street to hear. All my exotic escapades had ended in disaster, and I became even more depressed. This time, I had caused my friend to receive the beating of his life. I did not tell my mother about my own.

"I'll come with you to Australia," said Alan, another street friend. He was a happy-go-lucky character; with a ready smile, and almost white hair. I was, apparently, a bad influence on poor Godfrey, who was now barred from any further involvement with me. Such a burden infuriated him and, when he finally heard that Alan was my new partner for the exodus to Australia, he broke his enforced embargo to pay me a visit.

I heard my mother pleading with him, "Go home, Godfrey, or you'll be in even more trouble!" Then, I heard the smash of breaking glass. The frustrated five year old had lost both his temper, and his mind. He had nipped around to the back garden and, with the force of a karate champion, put his clenched fist right through the window. I ran down, and witnessed my mother in total shock, frozen to the spot in disbelief. Godfrey's badly gashed hand was still protruding through the shattered pane, and blood dripped from his fist.

"I want to play with Stuart," was his plaintive cry. Unconcerned about his wounds, he had vented his feelings in the most dramatic way at his disposal. He would definitely need stitches, and his father would be apoplectic with rage. My mother tended to him as best she could, before leading him home; but I feared a further excruciating encounter for Godfrey with his father later on.

Alan had a smaller version of the globe of the world, and thought that we could get to Australia in five minutes. My mother's trip to the local greengrocer was the perfect time, and Alan hopped over the broken-down fence that separated our back gardens, wielding a handy-looking spade. Great expectations filled the air as, soon, we would be out of this morass of negative parental upbringing. We took it in turns, and I attacked the earth in my father's tiny allotment, between two sprouting rows of potatoes; since the ground seemed much softer there.

"Can't be much further down," I yelled.

"You've already dug down a foot. Let me have a go!" cried Alan. He worked furiously, and was soon down another foot. Sweat dripped off our foreheads, as we sat around the cavernous hole we had worked so hard to create. Something was wrong. We looked at the globe again. "Look, it's directly underneath us," stated a puzzled Alan, pointing at the spot where Australia lay.

"Let's keep going. We have to get there before mother gets back," I replied, with a heavy heart; and began the onslaught once more. The more earth I removed, the more slid back into the hole *this can't be happening!* Alan took over as I became exhausted, and the same thing occurred to him. We were getting nowhere, fast, and our disappointment was palpable. We had failed miserably in our mission.

"It's further than a foot. It must be," I commented.

"Maybe it's four feet, or even five!" responded Alan, desperately. We'd been digging for over an hour; and the two feet deep hole, that we had so industrially created, had become one foot deep of its own accord. It was an impossible job. "Perhaps that's why people sail there," was Alan's final quizzical submission.

"I didn't know that people sailed there," I replied.

"They must have tried digging, like us, and found it too difficult," was Alan's pathetic and breathless response. We filled the hole in, tidied it up, and sat underneath the old apple tree, pondering our next plan to leave home.

The summer was filled with street cricket and car spotting. We puffed our cheeks out with boredom, and tried a new game called 'First to spot a lady driver.' After sitting by the side of the Coventry Road all afternoon, we had noted just one each. Godfrey had been very quiet all summer long. He longed to get back with the gang, as we seemed to be having all the fun. Then, one day, we spoke face to face. He had been utilising his time of constraint very well.

"I knew you wouldn't get to Australia," he muttered. "It's thousands of miles down - not a few feet. I've been reading about it." I was astonished at his prodigious knowledge.

"What have you been doing, then?" I asked politely.

"Working on a better plan than yours," was his smug response. "Come and have a look," he continued. His parents were out, and we strolled round a side entrance, through a neatly manicured back garden, and into his garage. "What do you think of that?" he announced, with peacock-like pride.

I could not believe it. He had built himself a four-wheeled cart; although he did admit that his dad had helped him, for being a good boy for so long. It consisted of a plank, with a set of pram wheels on the back and front. The front wheels were steerable by two ropes. At the back of the plank was a well-constructed wooden box to sit in. "Want to have a go?" he suggested. "I'll push, and you steer," he added.

We flew up and down The Grove. Godfrey ran like the wind, and the cart went so fast that I got scared; but it was the most fun I'd had in years. The suddenness of the thought struck us both at the same time. Godfrey rushed into his house, and returned with a biscuit. I found a slice of bread and a stale cake. We were off, never to return. With our speedy chariot, no one would catch us.

"Where shall we go?" I propounded, steering the cart as Godfrey pushed.

"Don't know. Let's just keep going." We found our way onto the main Birmingham highway and, keeping to the pavements, headed somewhere...

We had left in bright summer sunshine, and now it was dark. We had pushed and steered alternately for hours, and were now getting tired and very hungry. Cobbled streets, and a large market place, appeared before us. We had evaded our parents, and they would never find us again. We were independent, and it was a wonderful feeling. No prior thought had been given to survival techniques, but we had made it *if they haven't captured us by now, they never will.* We figured that, after an hour or so, they would simply give up looking; and forget us. That was our fervent hope. We sat underneath the light of an old gas street lamp, the moon's glistening glow giving it a special aura. Tiredness was overtaking us rapidly, when two giants loomed over us.

"Okay, lads, the game's up," came a booming rendition from one of the policemen.

"I can't believe you've got so far," said the other, "You must have travelled over ten miles!"

Well, that was that. Every great escape episode had ended in tears and, although I feared another bellicose barney brewing, between Godfrey and his father; my mother ensured that such repercussions never manifested for me. However, just like our cart, my paternal relationship was going downhill fast.

6. Christmas Past

1951

I heard my mother crying again - something about not having money to buy me football boots, and other toys, for Christmas. By now, I was really beginning to think that Father Christmas did not exist. Her sister Pat had married Bob, an aircraft engineer, and had set up home not far from Birmingham Airport. They had miraculously managed to reach us, like Scott trudging through the Antarctic. She was consoling my mother, and I could vaguely hear a conversation about a loan of cash. They were whispering in the living room, but my ears were as sharp as a pin.

I tried to stay awake as long as I could, in the hope of seeing James and his mother again. It must have been about 2 a.m. when I heard my bedroom door being slowly opened. Out of one squinty eye, I saw an amazing sight. My father gingerly placed a sack at the end of my bed, and then pushed a tiny, bright red, three-wheeled bike alongside. I shut my eyes tightly, and waited for what seemed an interminable interlude. One low - one high, was the sign that I could make my move. I scrambled out of bed, and almost tore the sack apart with excitement. There, sitting gloriously at the top, was a complete football kit, a pair of 'Stanley Matthews' boots, and a 'Stanley Matthews' football book. I was in heaven. Now I could play the game properly *as soon as it's light, I'll be out in the snow kicking my football!*

I looked at the bicycle in amazement. It was not new, but seemed to have been made from many spare parts; some of which didn't look as if they matched the bike; but I didn't care, so long as it worked, and I could ride for the first time. The rest of the sack was full of homemade toys.

The dawning of truth finally spliced the mainbrace of my brain. There was no Father Christmas after all. My aunt's husband was a genius at making things from scrap and spares. He was even building his own car from scratch. The penny dropped. My mother had borrowed money from my aunt and her husband to finance the football gear, and my uncle had made the bike and toys. It all made sense now, and I felt quite grown-up to uncover the Christmas conundrum.

It was still dark when my mother blustered into my bedroom. I must have been making quite a din, in my excitement to open all the gifts.

"I sent a letter to Father Christmas, to tell him he'd forgotten to deliver your sack of gifts. That's why I've been so upset" She bent down, and gave me a hug, perpetuating the lie of all lies; but I kept up the pretence, and hugged her in response.

I wanted to share my gifts with my 'snow people', but each night brought disappointment. I lay awake, staring at ghostly flickering images that the street gaslight shone onto my ceiling; and trying to imagine shapes that corresponded with the outlines of my new friends. Inexorably, however, my eyes became heavy with the effort, closed, and another sad morning came around.

I was the only soul in the vastness of Elmdon Park. It was dark, and I could only just make out the goal posts; encrusted with ice, and puffed out with snow. I had woken early again, and could not resist the temptation. The house was quiet, apart from the tuneful vibrato of parental snores. I looked out of my bedroom window, and the area was still. Nothing moved at all.

Within seconds, I had my kit on, the football was in my hand, and I found myself walking the desolate, snow-laden streets of Sheldon. I had been to the local park with my mother before, and only hoped that I could find it again. The Birmingham City football team trained there, and my mother was a fanatic *if I work hard, I could be another Stanley Matthews! This would make her happy.* It didn't seem at all odd that I would be embarking on an adventure to the park, at seven in the morning.

There they were - the goal posts. I was ecstatic. The adrenalin flowing through my veins had ensured that the sub-zero temperature had not yet registered in my brain. The snow was at least a foot thick, and it was impossible to kick the ball. However, I was in my element, pushing the ball on and on through the snow; and in my mind, I was playing right wing in the final at Wembley.

Then it hit. Terrible pains in my hands now made me cry. It had taken me nearly an hour to walk to the park; and I suddenly realised that I was in serious trouble, and must reach home as fast as my little legs would carry me. I had not noticed the low temperature when I left, as there was no ice-cold wind to alert me. Pain crept up from my hands to my elbows, as I ran faster and faster; whimpering like an injured dog.

I arrived home, gasping for breath. My heart felt like bursting, as the pains increased. The house was in darkness, and I'd left without taking the key. I kicked the door furiously, and shouted for my parents. Their deep sleep ensured no response. With the last crumb of energy and feeling that I had left, I grabbed a small stone lying under the hedge; and with a despairing heave, threw it at their bedroom window. It was a direct hit, and cracked the pane. In an instant, my mother was looking down, shocked, at her crestfallen son, standing like a shivering snowman in the back garden.

I screamed and cried for hours as my father, who knew something about frostbite, held my hands forcibly in a bowl of lukewarm water. It was an excruciating lesson that I would never forget.

7. The Holiday

1951

Whilst I had been looking forward to attending primary school, or 'big school' as my mother preferred to call it; my experience, so far, had been two years of sheer boredom. The summer holidays were the worst. I spent hours sitting alone on the pavement, watching people come and go; since most of the families in The Grove, and everyone in my gang, were on their annual excursions to Cornwall. All my money-making schemes had led to naught, and I longed for the day when I could leave school and start work.

Since my father's little secret had been blown, I would occasionally watch him tinkering with the Jowett. A handle protruded from the front of the engine and, with grimy hands, he started to wind it round and round with furious intent. Suddenly, with black smoke gushing from the exhaust pipe, it burst into life; and he almost fell over backwards in shock. For the first time in my short life, I saw him smile. It was truly his greatest achievement, as the car had been a 'non-starter', only fit for the scrap yard, when he'd acquired it; and he'd been repairing it with spare parts that he had begged, borrowed or bartered.

"Now we can go!" he blurted out into the air. I was breathless with excitement. The thought of going on my first holiday, like the rest of the kids in The Grove, was overwhelming. At last, we had joined the ranks of rich people!

The highways and byways of the countryside went by, with flashing speed and, at one point, we touched 50mph. I had never seen such beauty before. Greens, browns, and indescribable colours bathed my eyes, touching my soul. My sister, just three years of age, blissfully slept through it all. The 280 mile journey to Lynmouth, in Cornwall, should not have taken us much more than six hours in all. However, it was a full ten hours later that we reached our destination.

Although it had a four-cylinder engine, the Jowett was only currently capable of running on three of them. Aware of this, my father had chosen the 'scenic route', for fear of breaking down on one of the main arterial roads. Now, up ahead, a great hill loomed. It looked like the vertical face of a mountain; and a stream of traffic rapidly built up behind us, as my father wrestled with the clutch, and the lowest of the three gears in the car's transmission.

"No!" my mother screamed.

"Bloody hell!" soon followed, from my father. The car was exhausted. With one cylinder not firing, and the other three dragging it along behind them, the car could not make the climb; and we juddered to a halt. It was a narrow country road, impossible for other cars to overtake; and we caused a terrible traffic problem. Steam gushed from the engine like a geyser, and it seemed that our rich vein of luck had plummeted into poverty once more.

My mother, sister and I were all frightened, and got out of the car. With incensed indignation, my mother grabbed our hands and, acutely embarrassed, strode back down the hill, hiding her face from mystified motorists. The sanctuary of a corner café saved our lives, and my mother's addiction to Woodbine cigarettes saved my father's life. It took three hours for all the cars to become disentangled, and my father to freewheel ours, back down the hill, into a lay-by.

It was an enormous effort for my mother to 'button her tongue', since she was already teetering on the brink of calling it a day with my father. He walked right past us into the café, as if we did not exist; then did the same on the way out, carrying a container of water. We watched him empty the contents into the radiator, my mother chain-smoked, and my sister and I coughed and spluttered all the way to Budleigh Salterton.

Our B&B was a simple semi-detached house; owned by a middle-aged couple who made cash on the side by renting out their spare rooms for the summer. Our holiday home hosts were about to retire, thinking that we had let them down; when our bedraggled family unit finally arrived at their door. We settled in for what little was left of the day, and the 'three cylinder' Jowett was put to bed for the duration of our holiday.

Nothing else mattered to me now, because the sea beckoned. Ever since my mother had thrown me into the deep end of the Solihull Lido, during an exasperated swimming lesson, I had become a 'flying fish' in water. Her philosophy of life was sink or swim; and she had taught me a valuable lesson.

The new day started well, as we strolled down to the bay; but we were greeted by the shock and horror of miles upon miles of pebbles lying before us, with not a single grain of sand in sight. I had dreamed of sand for as long as I could remember. My heart sank, my sister and

I sulked, and arguments broke out. However, with ice creams in hand, to placate two tiny souls, we made camp on the stones.

Great rollers roiled and broiled, smashing onto the shoreline. I was the first to tempt the wallowing waves. One roared towards me and, with perfect timing, I dived straight through its heart, emerging on the other side unscathed. The next wave carried me back to the shore again. This was a good game, and I yelled for my mother to join me. "Come on in, it's great!"

It was soon after she did, that we were hit by a tsunami of a wave, which had come out of the blue. One minute we were holding hands; and the next, my mother had disappeared beneath a giant roller. As I surfaced, I saw my mother's tiny frame repeatedly being lifted and pummelled into the pebbles. She rose, fell down, and rose up again. She was holding her hand to her mouth. Something was wrong, and she was crying. We crawled back to our camping spot.

"What's wrong?" I asked.

Hilary thought the scene was rather amusing, but mother's cries continued. "It's my teeth," she exclaimed. "My teeth have gone." I thought that they had all been knocked out, and was shocked.

My father and Hilary instantly rallied round. I had no idea that my mother wore false teeth, and I had never even heard of such things *another secret!* In a second, my mother's pretty face had transformed into that of a toothless old woman, and her mouth had completely sunk in. The day had ended before it had properly begun, and mother wanted to return to Birmingham immediately, there being no possibility that she would spend the next two weeks on holiday without teeth. Dejection followed, and arrangements were reluctantly made to drive back the following day.

This was my first holiday, and it had lasted just one day. I felt guilt galloping through every part of my body, and I was desperate to stay. I loved the pounding sea, as it challenged my wayward spirit. I was pitted against the full force of nature, and I could beat it. I needed more, and returning home meant the usual depression. For a few days, we had been going to experience what it was like to be rich. Now, Hilary and I were forced into bed early, in readiness for the long haul home the next day. From my bed, I watched the light over the bay dim, and heard the gentle lapping of the tamed sea in the distance. The roaring lion was sleeping. The stars twitched and twinkled. This was the place to be and, for me, it was heaven. The household became quiet and still, and everyone slept, except for me. I closed my eyes.

I remembered the moment when the 'snow people' had arrived, three years earlier. They came when the zenith of nature merged with the nadir of my soul *now, I must connect again.* My feelings were the same, and I really needed to see James again *I must go to the window and wait, just as I did before.* I grabbed the top blanket, pulled it around my shoulders, sat on the small stool by the window, and stared aimlessly into the half-light.

I imagined the winter snow whispering by the open window, and the scene outside transform into a wash of white. Every so often, I turned. The vision of James and his mother, waiting by the door, became clear in my mind. The hairs on the back of my neck rose, and goose bumps sprang up all over my body. I covered my head with the blanket, and turned my head slowly. Peeking out of one eye, I started to tremble with anticipation.

James and his mother had appeared, in a wisp of whiteness, although I was certain that my mind was playing tricks. Both of them wore the same clothes as they had three years ago. Her dress was long, with wispy patterns of finely fluted flowers. Her dark hair ran down her shoulders, and hung halfway down her back.

James beckoned me to sit with him. "We were with you on the beach today," his mother offered, politely. "We saw what happened." I tested myself, and started walking, right through James, to my bed *what am I doing to myself?*

"Don't you believe my mother?" James interjected. "We can prove it, can't we, mum?" he continued. His mother sat on the bed next to James, and looked directly into my eyes. Hers were faded and black, and they scared me. However, her kind demeanour assured me of their good intentions. They both appeared to be a curious concoction of white, and various shades of black and grey.

Why I am so scared? I had so wished for them to return and, now that they had, I was a quivering wreck.

"We know where your mother's teeth are located in the sea. They're safe, and we'll show you where they are. See you tomorrow." They began to melt away through the wall.

"Don't go," I shouted loudly, forgetting where I was, or what I was doing. In an instant, my father was in my bedroom.

"Who the hell are you talking to?" he blasted away.

"No one," I responded meekly. "It was a nightmare."

"Don't start this nonsense again! I've got enough problems with your mother!" he ranted, before turning away and leaving again.

Breakfast was a tortuous time. Poor mother had been dealt a terrible blow, and totally refused to eat. She covered her sunken cavity with her hands, and would not talk. Ostensibly serving the cornflakes, it was obvious that our landlady was also greatly disappointed.

From nowhere, James and his mother appeared, standing behind her, smiling. "Come on, Stuart," shouted James. "Let's go and collect your mum's teeth."

"Okay, great," I answered, before realising my stupidity. An already silent table suddenly became even more quiescent, all eyes riveted on my sudden and peculiar outburst. "The cornflakes are great," I mumbled quickly. Our suitcases were packed, and the Jowett had been fired up. My brain was working overtime, to come up with a ruse to go down to the beach before we left. I began to plead with my parents for one more walk by the sea, before we left. "Please! Please!" I wrung my hands, and used every emotion and expression that I could muster, pleading as if my life depended on it.

My father turned, and looked at my mother for a decision. An eternity went by. She sighed deeply; turned her head towards the front door, where James and his mother stood, waiting for me to make a move, and acquiesced. I was still unsure that I had not created this wonderful world of 'snow people' in my mind; but I knew that this was an excellent opportunity to prove it…

A powerful onshore gust had awoken the sleeping lion; and the sound of waves, careering onto the shore's billions of pebbles, rang out in my ears. My heart was pounding. Maybe they wanted me to join them *maybe the 'snow people' will lead me to my death today.*

It would not have been humanly possible to find mother's teeth, in the morass of ocean that stretched for miles along the coastline; and I shook with trepidation. We walked silently to the beachfront pathway; keeping well away from the maelstrom of sea that was bearing down on the pebble shoreline which stretched for many miles; like a great giant, trampling over an unsuspecting cornfield. James' mother held my hand; and James held Hilary's hand, although she was not aware of it.

"In a minute, James will lead you to your mother's teeth," said his mother. Now was the moment to tell my mother. I yanked on her hand, and she bent down to listen, amid the raucous reverie of the sea's continuous cadence.

"I'm going to find your teeth." I shouted. Such was the surrounding furore of noise; I knew my father could not hear, and seemed uninterested anyway. "My friend James is here, and he's going to show me." I knew, by the change in her expression, that she was intrigued; but had no idea of what would transpire. Frankly, nor did I.

James suddenly took off towards the firestorm of an ocean. "Come on. Come on!" he shouted at me. I now knew that there was no turning back. I ran like the wind, away from my parents, and caught up with James. I was instantly pursued by my father, and mother screamed. My shorts, shirt and pullover were off in a second, and I stood before the wall of ocean with James. My father was within a few feet of sweeping me into his arms, back to safety; but it was too late. Although the sea seemed monstrous, and ready to pound me into the pebbles, James was through it in an instant, and I followed; once again, timing it perfectly. With a dolphin-like dive, through the eye of the ocean wave, I joined James on the other side.

There was one more roller to ride, before reaching the calmer waters further out. I allowed it to sweep over me, and was immediately sucked down by the swirling tide of the apoplectic Atlantic. I opened my eyes, and millions of pebbles swished and swirled across the ocean floor. I was amazed, as everything was crystal clear under the surface. Then, I was back up again, gasping for breath. My father was a distant dot on the shore, and I could see him shouting, and pointing at me; but my mother knew of my intention *if I die, I will have done so for her* and this made me feel good.

James and I floated side by side. "I'm going to take you to the spot where your mother's teeth lie. When we get there, swim directly down, and look for a large cone-shaped white stone, with brown rings circling around it. Lift it up, and you'll find them," he said, with a steadfast certainty.

"Okay, let's go," I spluttered, "I hope it's not going to take too long."

The shoreline was disappearing fast, and I was concerned that I would not make it back, even if this miracle was going to happen. Five minutes of swimming later, I became exhausted.

"Go down now!" he shouted, excitedly.

I took three deep breaths, whipped my body over, and flippered my way down to the ocean floor *if I don't find the stone the first time, I'll die for sure.* The silence and beauty of the view below belied the dark danger I was really in. I was galvanised from head to foot. The stone, which James had so delicately described, came into view. I had a few seconds of breath left *it's now or never,* completed the distance, and pushed the stone aside. The most beautiful vision suddenly appeared. A complete set of perfectly polished false teeth lay smiling up at me; and I wanted to scream "Yes!"

James and his mother <u>were</u> real, after all. It wasn't my imagination. But the operation wasn't over yet. I knew that it would now be a major challenge to return to the shore. I grabbed the set of teeth, and held them so tightly that no force on earth could prize them from my palm. I seemed to have been underwater for hours. Time stood still, and I surfaced with barely a second of breath left. I gasped and gasped, taking in great gulps of air; elated beyond any feeling I had ever experienced before.

James was there to greet me. Dark clouds were rolling in from the open ocean, and rain started to pour down, making the impossible scene complete.

"This way," pointed James, "This is the only way back." We both made a parallel swim to the shore, in a crab-like movement. James had proved that he was my closest friend, and I followed him like a younger brother. The sea took me in its arms, so I did not have to do much in the way of hard swimming. I floated on my back, keeping an eye out for the shoreline, and let the tide do the job for me until, gradually, the beach came into stark relief. We were almost there. I looked around, and James had disappeared.

"James!" I screamed, "Where are you! Come back!" I was distraught, and started to cry from my heart. I landed on the beach with a bump, sobbing. I sat up, clenching my prized possession, amidst the soapy sea lapping at my feet. I turned, and saw that I had travelled at least half a mile from where I had so madly joined nature's most powerful force. I realised that, in those few minutes, my poor family must have been going through hell. However, I was going to save my mother's pride, and our holiday; but most of all, I was finally going to prove to my mother that I had friends who were not of this world. I ran faster than I had ever done before; and my little legs were a blur, even to myself.

Hard, relentless rain unleashed itself from the heavens, pelting my exposed body; but I was oblivious to its fury. Fuelled by adrenaline, I laughed loudly all the way, as three miniscule people came into view, becoming larger as I got closer to them. Tiny shards of broken pebbles cut into my feet on the pathway to my parents. I felt the pain, but didn't care. I couldn't wait to see my mother's face, when I proudly presented her with my prize. Their cries started to reach my ears, gradually becoming louder and louder.

"Oh, my God!" screamed my mother. Hilary hid behind her skirt, scared of what would happen to me next. Apparently, my father had searched for a lifeguard, unsuccessfully. His countenance announced rage, and a forthcoming punishment that I would never forget; until I unclenched my hand in front of mother's face.

The brightness of the pearly white false teeth cut the strangest scene imaginable. They seemed to have acquired a life of their own. They smiled, and beamed forth such happiness to be reunited with their owner. My mother immediately grabbed them from my quivering hand, and popped them into her mouth. They had been cleaned to perfection by the tide's swaying action on the sea bottom; and had been kept safe, against the crushing capability of the rapacious rollers, by the stone on top.

A lone family, soaked to the skin, on an equally lonely seashore pathway; had waited for, and expected, an outcome infested with disaster. My mother went wild with delight. "It's a miracle!" she exclaimed, "It's a miracle!" Simultaneously, I had thrust a dagger through my father's heart, and any vestiges of our relationship had ended here, on this spot. His mind was too small to open up to possibilities such as he had just witnessed; and I had proved, beyond any doubt, that my synchronicity with the 'snow people' was real.

"I don't know how you did it, but it must have been pure luck," he grudgingly offered, turning his head away from me *what? I've just swum out to sea; found mother's teeth on the ocean floor, amongst billions upon billions of stones; and he thinks it was a coincidence!* Looking back at me, his eyes had become dark, and I saw a quiet fury building up inside his soul.

The supper provided by our hosts was the best ever. They were equally astonished and bewildered by my exploits, and our landlady had prepared a raspberry tart which was fit for royalty. My father sulked, and sat outside, smoking his interminably insufferable pipe. My sister and I had a joyous feast with mother, who hugged me constantly.

"Don't thank me, mom," I suggested. "Thank James and his mother. They're here somewhere." I had no idea why they arrived at the oddest of moments. I realised that I must have needed them so much, I had actually created their intervention *maybe they were busy helping other people all over the world.*

"Thank you, James and his mother," beamed my mother, looking all around her, "Keep up the good work." I thought that my sister was far too young to understand what was happening.

"If you had a wish, mother," I suggested. "What would it be?"

She thought hard, and long. "When you're a millionaire, take me around the world," adding "And take me on safari in Africa!"

Wow, that is the challenge of all challenges! Her teenage years working in the circus had fired her imagination and, after all, the clairvoyant in Blackpool had confirmed that I would make all her dreams come true. But I was only seven, and miracles such as this could be easily forgotten. My 'snow people' had taken three years to visit me again, and James had simply disappeared into thin air. I had to think that he was watching over me at all times. That was a happy thought.

8. The Flowerpot Men

1952

After observing the fear in my sister's face, as she witnessed the extraordinary events on the seashore, I saw her in a different light. I connected with her. I even offered to play with her. I saw, for the first time, a truly lovely little soul. I was like that, at one time; but now I had friends, and could see things that my parents could not. I could see the future, with the help of the 'snow people', and wondered how long it would be before they would visit me again. It had become obvious that they would not simply arrive. To summon their help, I had to first reach down to the deepest depths of my soul, before focussing incredibly hard, to win their trust of companionship; and I vowed to practise these techniques.

My mother indulged me for the rest of the holiday, with the spending money that her sister had provided. Lemonade, mixed with small blocks of ice cream, was my 'Achilles heel'. Shopkeepers did not have the capacity to keep their lemonade cold; and so the ice cream, when slowly mixed with the lemonade, cooled the drink while causing the mix to become luscious and smooth. I was hooked on the taste of my new ice cream formula, but the cost of it depressed me greatly. *This is a one-off treat, that I'll never experience again,* I thought, with sad resignation. However, just like a modern-day junkie, I knew I had to have it. This became a great motivator for me, and whipped up my taste for making money.

Hilary lived her life in my shadow. I was constantly bursting with energy, and felt like Superman. Over the next few months, however, it became obvious that I was only as good as my last 'trick'. Although I excelled at sport, which got me noticed, primary school was also beginning to get academically tough. I wanted to tell all my friends about my alien allies, but couldn't; as they would simply vilify my character, and shun me as crazy. I fended off my mother's constant 'snow people' questions and; as summer ground to an end, and the golden autumn leaves spread their curled up crispy patterns on the pavements, I decided to focus once more.

I talked to the 'snow people' every night, even though they were not visible, and I thanked them. I felt that they could hear me, and know that I was still their grateful friend. My father knew what I was doing, but no longer interfered. We became like ships in the night, which suited me fine. Our rows had since subsided, even though it always felt like the calm before a storm. My mother must have been some sort of saint, to live with him under such conditions.

On reflection, my father was not a bad man. In fact, he was quite normal and, in many respects, a very kind individual; but he must have wondered what he had done, to sire a son whose spirit was twisted and torn by devils. Perhaps he had decided to make his own plan, because he became passive and compliant; spending a lot of time in the shed, and tinkering with the car that had stubbornly remained out of action after its tortuous trip, travelling halfway around England.

If my father had a plan, then my mother had hers, too. She kept up the charade of being rich and, as this juxtaposition continued to confuse me, it was time to confront her. I'd been playing at a friend's house, and was astonished to hear voices emanating from a brown wooden box in the corner. I'd stood in front of it, in silent awe. We didn't have one of those. "Why not?" I shouted at my mother, later. "If we were rich, we'd have one!" She started to cry, covered her face, and wept from her soul. I was ashamed. I had hurt her deeply. I put my arms around her, to comfort her. "Don't worry," I said, " I'll make some money, and buy one for us,"

Thank God for my aunt and uncle, who were always there when Hilary and I needed something special. I arrived home from school one day, and a great deal of activity had hijacked the house. My uncle was a wonderful man, who hated any form of religion, and was an unadulterated atheist. He was, however, so full of love, compassion, honesty and kindness; that he truly embodied the spirit of Christianity. He knew that 'Bill and Ben - The Flowerpot Men' had excited and inspired children all around the country with their first appearance on television, and that I craved to see them. Not so much to see them, but to see how they fitted into a brown wooden box with a tiny grey screen, and were able to walk and talk inside it.

I sat watching my uncle finishing the installation. He'd bought it just for me, as a pre-Christmas present. "It should work," he announced confidently, while twiddling interminably with the two black dials, "It's the finest nine inch television you can get." I was enthralled, especially when, after much crackling, it burst into life. "Lobalub, flobberpop, and bapap ickle weeed," were the first words I heard on television, and I was immediately addicted. Bill and Ben, and Little Weed, became my saviours. I loved Little Weed; and I left school early, without permission, to see them. They saved me from talking to, or even acknowledging, my father.

One day, the headmaster of the school turned up at our house; and informed my mother that I had, on several occasions, walked out of school without permission, missing my last lesson. He wanted an explanation, since I had refused to supply one. My mother tried her best to support me, but was given a severe ticking off, and an ultimatum. I found it quite amusing, and chuckled. My new 'oddle pop' world, of flowerpot men and a little weed, was far more important than school; but a chink had opened up in my mother's perception of my genius, and her heart sank once more. She seemed so sad, I promised not to play truant again.

Desperate for me to provide an instant exit from our poverty, she prayed that my 'snow friends' would conjure up another miracle, and convert me into a child prodigy of some description. Her ever-enduring mantra, propounding our affluence, was wearing thin. I was now old enough to know the difference, and she never mentioned it again. With money, she'd be able to wave goodbye to my father; and I think that this was her greatest wish, because each dull day of drudgery carved another notch out of her soul. Poverty was the only thing that held my parents together.

"Stuart, I've got a new job," she blurted out, as silent tears rolled down her cheeks. It was during our Saturday morning routine in the back garden. I was pulling hand-washed clothes through an old wooden mangle, while she turned the handle. My heart reached out to her *life really is awful*. The shirts and sheets came out of the mangle as stiff as cardboard.

"I can't keep up with the bills, now that Hilary is growing," she continued, brushing tears from her face with a forearm. "I'm going back to work as a barmaid at the Wheatsheaf in the evenings." I suddenly realised the insidious implications of this decision, and the reason for her tears. My father would now be responsible for Hilary and me in the evenings.

Oh my God, this means that I'll have to talk to him. My mother would not be around to protect me from his hatred of my bedroom chats with far off friends. It was a daunting prospect. Nevertheless, I vowed to focus harder in my attempt to make contact with my 'snow friends' again. They were my only hope, and I had to risk it.

It turned out to be as bad as I'd thought. "Go to sleep. I don't want to hear a peep out of you!" were the most endearing words that he could muster as a goodnight salute. I was thus reduced to whispering; pleading, begging and praying for my 'snow friends' to return.

I sobbed silently for our appalling predicament, and worried constantly for my mother. I wanted to wave a magic wand and transform her life, but the cold light of day always destroyed these hopes.

My mother never informed us what time she'd return, and it was always well past midnight before I heard her tiptoeing up the stairs. She always checked in on me, and I always feigned sleep. As soon as I heard the signature snores, I became alive; continuing my appeals to the heavens. I called to the 'snow people' with every emotion that I possessed; standing, bowing, praying, crying and searching the darkness for the slightest sign of a white apparition. Sleep only came when exhaustion took over.

9. Journey Into Space

1953 - 1954

Our street wasn't strictly a street. It was a grove - almost a cul-de-sac, but not quite. The children in The Grove seemed much brighter than I was, and able to study hard; whereas my favourite activity was sport. Their parents were of the white-collar type, while mine were uninterested in the details of academia.

I often wondered about my mother's upbringing, and sixty years would pass before I was able to ascertain the truth. She had been forced to join the circus, at thirteen years of age, by her mother; who worked on the railway, cleaning carriages. With ten other siblings, and a father who had died of heart disease, the Depression of the early twenties was a very bad place for penniless people.

I found it difficult to imagine my mother being an acrobat with 'The Five Figaro's'. They were a well-known troupe, and travelled the country in a horse-drawn, covered wagon. The shilling a week that she earned was sent home to her mother. From my point of view, the forties did not fare much better, and this pattern of poverty continued. However, the coronation of Queen Elizabeth II brought new hope, joy, and national pride to the entire country. Street parties were held across the land and, at one such event, I got to show off my love of boxing; dressed as Randolph Turpin, my hero.

Things moved forward a pace with us, too. One day, I saw my father soldering bits of wire, and screwing what looked like tiny glass light bulbs into a conglomeration of spurious parts. The kitchen table was alive with scientific activity. I was intrigued, and watched patiently as the myriad of components slowly came together, and became a Bakelite box with an external dial.

"It's a crystal set," announced my father, finally, with great pride. "We just need an aerial now." I was still in the dark, and I am sure that he intended keeping me in that state, until the great surprise had been sprung. He read from a crumpled sheet of paper. "Place a copper wire into the aerial socket, and attach to a high point on the wall until a signal is received. In the event of copper wire not being available, use a cat's whisker." He rubbed his chin, and I was no wiser; until the penny dropped, and I suddenly felt fear creeping over my whole body, as he reached for his scissors and cruelly called, "Here kitty, kitty."

My father was an upholsterer. He fitted roofing felt, by hand, into the ceilings of the new cars that rolled off the production line. He cut great rolls of curtaining material into shape, and tacked them perfectly into the roof space. He had taken me to the factory one day, to show me what he did. I had never seen scissors like those before - they were huge. He did not actually cut the material; but skilfully slid the scissors around pencilled markings, like a knife through butter and, in seconds, a beautifully-shaped piece of material was ready to adorn a new Rover 25.

It was truly unbelievable how he attached it to the roof of the car. He scooped a great heap of tiny tacks from a large can and, with one movement, slapped them into his mouth. The hammer was a magnetically charged instrument; delicate, and specially moulded to allow free and efficient movement for hand, eye and mouth coordination. It was an amazing sight to watch him work. He placed the magnetic part of the hammer into his mouth, and a tack became instantly attached. With one strike, the tack impaled the first piece of material into the wooden strip surrounding the roof of the car. In minutes, the ugly roof space had been transformed into a thing of beauty. Each tack was spaced perfectly, and in complete symmetry. He didn't miss once, and I was astonished; but also sad. He seemed to enjoy it, though, which struck me as odd *I'd go out of my mind doing such a job!* At that moment, I vowed that I would never be like my father.

He stealthily crept around the settee, giant scissors in his hand. Timmy was sleeping. Suddenly the realisation hit me. "NO!!!" I screamed. The cat woke up in an instant, and saw my father leering at him. From the cat's viewpoint, it must have looked horrifying. For some reason, Timmy was scared of my father anyway, and always hid behind the settee when he was around. I ran, and opened the kitchen door. "Run! Run! Quick!" I screamed. The cat was very old, but this was about survival. He shot through my father's legs, and through the kitchen door, with the speed of a mature cheetah.

The chase was on, and it could have been construed as a classic comedy moment. My father chased the cat through the weed-strewn back garden, and I careered after my father. Timmy shot up the first available tree, and looked down, terrified. He cried as only a cat can, when in total fear. They were sad meows. I started to cry, and pulled on my father's trousers. "Please don't," I implored pathetically.

"It's only one whisker. He won't miss it, son. Don't be a baby," he responded. He climbed the tree slowly, and Timmy crept higher and higher until he could go no further, swaying precariously on the thinnest of branches. I could see in his eyes that he wanted to jump, as my father got ever closer. But he was too old, the game was up, and I couldn't watch as the dirty deed was done. Timmy had been hurt and humiliated; and for this, I never forgave my father, and refused to call him Dad ever again.

Later, that evening, we all sat around the kitchen table for the unveiling of the special box. Hilary was asleep, and my mother and I looked on. I could see Timmy's whisker protruding from the crystal set, and I had a mental image of sticking it back on the cat. My father switched on the magic box, which sprang into life as he moved the dial. It crackled, and made weird screeching noises. Then, out of the blue, a commentary burst forth - 'Journey into Space.' It was an incredible moment, and we all sat entranced. All thanks to Timmy's whisker. However, it didn't last long, as one of the valves blew, and the set was rendered useless. But I'd witnessed the future.

Timmy died not long after; and I was mortified, blaming my father for his death. I dug a shallow grave in the back garden, and buried him myself. A small cross was created out of twigs from the hedgerow, and I cried for weeks. Life seemed of little use to me. I saw my friends in the street going on regular summer holidays to the seaside, but we could not afford such luxuries.

Although Hilary, at five, desperately looked to me for attention; I kept her at a distance as much as possible. She was too young to play with, so there was little point in developing a relationship with her. I only wanted to be with my 'snow friends'…

I found a certain solace in the early hours. I could search my mind, and send messages rapidly to James and his mother (I'd learned that her name was Sally), and they showed me how to visualise anything.

"I want my own orchestra, Sally," I pleaded one night. I had started to hear music in my head. It just arrived out of nowhere, and I asked for her advice. No one that I knew played an instrument, and this made such a possibility impossible.

"Look into the depths, and you will see how to make the music." She did not manifest, but her words echoed expansively in my head.

I focussed, with a stillness that surprised me. Slowly, a screen appeared in my mind, and I could see the orchestra and the instruments. My members would include my friends Celia Shepherd, Alan Gregory and Hilary (now much more grown up, at six…).

I searched among the reeds and weeds by a grassy bank in the local field. "Yes," I exclaimed, as I found my flute. I snapped off several tall stalks from weed-like flowers, their barrel-like interiors tapering off towards the end *perfect!* I then worked hard, over the next few days, examining methods of extricating sounds from my 'reed flute'.

It was exciting to gather together the members of my orchestra, and allot their instruments to them. Hilary would play the R. White's lemonade bottle, after I had carried out experiments to create the correct sound. By filling it one third full of cold water, it provided the perfect sound and pitch. I hummed the orchestral piece to Celia, until I felt that she understood this great musical score. It was her job to conduct, and keep the band in time. Alan would play the kettle.

We gathered on a sunny Saturday afternoon, in our rubbish-strewn back garden, with our instruments at the ready.

"Okay. Everyone follow me," I proclaimed.

I puffed out my cheeks, and blew air through the stalk-like flute. Percussion and bottle followed brilliantly. Celia made a cracking conductor, and the orchestral sounds permeated to The Grove's perimeter, jaunting joyously beyond. Alan's father was mightily impressed, and took a photograph for the local paper. We were going to be famous…

10. A Touch of Genius

1955

It wasn't that I didn't understand the schoolwork. I was just too tired to take anything in. My report was in a sealed envelope, which I handed to my parents. My mother's eyes grew wide, and tears flowed. She tore the summary into shreds and looked into my eyes. "Why, Stuart, why?" I was in a no-win situation. My future, and that of my mother and sister, lay in my contacting the 'snow people'. However, they only came in the early hours, and it had been a long time since I had seen them. Not for the first time, I wondered if my mind had been playing games with me, but I knew that my imagination could not have found my mother's teeth in such a vast expanse of ocean. It was a distressing dilemma.

The headmaster held discussions with my mother, about my lack of academic ability. She told him, in her usual spirited style, that I was far more intelligent than most of the children in The Grove; but this cut no ice with him, and I was placed in the slow learners' row of the classroom. Somehow, I always came alive when any sporting activity was organised; and in addition to my boxing skills, I was number one at throwing a cricket ball, the highest jumper, and the top footballer in the class. My brainpower, however, was being fully utilised in my valorous night vigils.

"Right, Sharp," my English teacher proclaimed. "I want this essay back tomorrow - not in a week. Do you understand, young man?"

I hated essays the most. I never finished them, and what I wrote was usually marked as rubbish. The theme was 'Going on a Journey', and it was a 'one page minimum' test. I sighed with dismay. Most of the children had parents who could offer help and advice; but my poor mother had been a circus acrobat at thirteen years of age, and my father was a sleep freak. Neither was remotely academic, and felt that school was the only place for a child to learn.

The street gaslight shone its interminable streaky yellow light through the crack in my bedroom curtains. It was midnight again, and I had given no thought whatsoever to the essay. I leaned over from my bed, grabbed my satchel, and lifted out my English homework book. The blank page simply stared at me, so I took a deep breath and, with a sharpened pencil in hand, stared back at it. I shook my head twice, not bearing to imagine failure. All of a sudden, a white translucent hand covered mine, before disappearing; and James' voice came into my head. "Write."

"James, is that you?" I whispered cautiously.

"Just write, Stuart," he answered.

"But I want to see you and your mother. Where have you been?" I asked earnestly.

"We never leave you. We're always here. Now write," he responded. I tried to keep myself together, and was hurt and upset that I could not see them. I couldn't understand why they didn't just appear *what's the problem? And what does he mean, 'just write'?* I didn't know what to write. "Listen to what's in your head, and write it down," James continued. I was panicking, because I had a total mental block, and didn't know what was in my head. I closed my eyes for inspiration and, suddenly, a great castle appeared on the windswept edge of a mist-maligned, moonlit bay. My hand began to move before my eyes, and words started to flow out onto the page. It was like reading a book, as it became an adventurous and entertaining story. I was both shocked and excited as the last word appeared on the page.

"Thanks, James, thank you," I murmured. There was no reply.

The English teacher looked up. She had finished marking the essays and was making various flippant remarks about each one.

"I have left your essay, young Sharp, until the last." She paused, and my heart began to race. She showed no emotion. "I was tempted to mark your essay 10 out of 10. The only reason, that stopped me from so doing, is that there is no such thing as perfection. I also cannot believe it is by your hand alone." She paused again, and the class fell silent. "Did you have any help in constructing this truly wonderful story?"

Oh my God, now what do I say? Fortunately for me, she was aware of my parents' limited capability, so she continued, without waiting for a reply. "It is a work of genius, and I could not have written to this standard myself," she continued. "I'm going to keep your essay, and hand it to the headmaster. It is remarkable, and I expect you, young man, to continue with the exceptional progress you have made."

It was the worst day of my life. My essay was held up to the whole school as an example of excellence, and the English teacher was lavished with praise for her unique teaching skills, for having turned a slow learner into a genius overnight. She was now the master of motivation, but she still scared me with withering looks that could slice a heart in two. Now that a spine-tingling spotlight shone upon me, I was expected to produce similar work at all times.

My classmates, and the rest of the school, had their own opinions; and planned devious deeds for me. They were out to show me that new notoriety always came with a demoralising downside. She had put me on a pedestal so high, that pot-shots of all descriptions could not fail to hit; and they did not take long in coming.

"So what's the genius gonna do now?" screamed the ringleaders.

The roughest children had me surrounded in the playground, and taunted me until I sat down on the floor and cried. I was a pariah.

Although an on-duty master rescued me, I was still shaking with anticipation of the next tortures to terrorise me. My fears were soon realised. I often took a shortcut home, across a field straddled by a meandering brook.

"Get 'im!" The viciousness of the callous call caused me to shift instantaneously into reverse. I was about to cross the stream with a quick hop, but quickly diverted momentum, and flew in the opposite direction. My athletic ability, and fleetness of foot, saved me from a terrible beating. The same roughnecks, who had surrounded me in the playground, had planned the attack with cunning and guile. They knew my route home, and had lain in wait for me. The chase was on, and I reached The Grove without looking back. I was truly trapped.

My mother was preening herself with pride, in the knowledge that her son was, at last, the genius that she had thought he'd become; and was happy that the 'snow people' had finally come to my rescue. Now, she could look forward to the situation being converted into a financially rewarding future. I was the talk of The Grove.

"James, it's a nightmare. I don't know what to do," I offered up to the heavens. I sat on my bed, extolling my woes to the 'snow people'. If I was to get through school in one piece, I needed to become the slowcoach again. I knew that I could rely on James and his mother when I needed them most; so a new plan of action was required, and I soon realised that I needed to adopt the middle road. 'Keep the power in, and don't use it until the right time,' was the lesson I had learned.

From that moment on, I kept a low profile; and almost sent my mother into an asylum after the genius appeared to leave me. This time, though, I did not react in any way to her cries. My survival was more important. I now knew how to keep the 'snow people' in my head, and communicate silently *one day, I will use the power to its full effect.*

I stared at the exam papers, which rapidly became a blur. I didn't understand the questions, and they might as well have been written in Chinese; so I filled in all the answers with guesses, a strategy absolutely guaranteed to scupper my chances of a grammar school education

"No! No! Stuart, this is terrible!" was my mother's woeful conclusion to my pathetic attempts at the '11-plus' examinations. Her little genius had become a total failure. Her hopes and dreams of a fabulous future, through her son, had dried up like the great Zambezi river in a summer draught.

My father had removed himself from anything to do with my life. He made no comment, but simply emanated vibes of doubt and disdain. He had already abdicated his responsibility for my wellbeing; handing it over to my mother, years before. For me to pass, or not pass, the '11-plus' meant nothing to him. He lived in his own world, and I could tell that he was simply waiting for his opportunity. Hilary was a little gem, and behaved quite normally; but she was beginning to acquire a sense of the madness in our household. It would seem that all of us were biding our time.

11. Murder in Mind

1955 - 1957

I was living in a world inside my mind, and confined to a small area around my street. It had become dangerous for me to venture further than a fast sprint from home, since prowling predators could always be spotted close by. Taking a severe beating, or worse, prevailed as a prominent thought. They were rough, they meant business and, should I cross their boundaries, they were ready to pounce upon me. I could easily have won, one on one, in a fair fight; but against a gang out for blood, I wouldn't have stood a chance.

My mother had been scouring 'The Morning Advertiser', which advertised pub tenancies and jobs all over the country. She sighed heavily when possibility after possibility had to go begging, because of the lack of funds for a town tenancy. She had the experience, but the breweries required the husband's name over the door; hence the softening of her relationship with my father over the past year.

Country tenancies, because of their low deposit (and correspondingly low income), were a viable option; and she desperately wanted to leave Birmingham. The thought of sending me off to a Secondary Modern School was anathema to her, as most other mothers tried to send their children through Grammar Education. Secondary school began to loom large in my mind, and I wondered if the local scab-laden scallywags would also attend. It was only a few days away, and I was already becoming nervous.

My mother left me at the gates, sobbing and sniffling, disturbed by the dregs that might drag me down. It was my second day. On the first, I did my best to hide from anyone I knew to be an enemy, but this did not stop me from being forcibly pushed from behind, headlong down a stairway. Everyone around me had laughed nervously, feigning amusement because they, too, were afraid of the perpetrator.

Feeling totally desolate and isolated, the school seemed to go on endlessly. Countless corridors. Innumerable children. I felt miniscule, in a sea of deadbeat dropouts *do the scum of society end up here?* I knew that this thought could not be true, but I was now conditioned to spot the slightest sign of aggression. Searching through the mass of children for the playground 'predators', I infiltrated the mayhem of miscreants, hoping to find a buddy *anyone of my size and general appearance will do,* acutely aware that the melee of sweaty souls confronting me now appeared even more menacing, and only needing a spark. The scene before me suddenly slipped into slow motion; as the crescendo of noise, created by thousands of children, abated.

"Look out!" one of them screamed. I knew, instantly, that I was in serious trouble. The eyes were black and soulless; the face twisted and contorted with rage. He was a foot taller than I was *he looks like a man, not a boy,* his arm was raised, and I saw the knife *this doesn't make sense* descending in slow motion *I haven't done anything to provoke him* to within an inch of my exposed neck. He was a bigger and stronger version of my previous attacker, but this time, fully intent on killing me. There was no doubt in my mind about it, and I instinctively brought up my cupped hand to cover my neck. The knife went in deeply, slicing through the webbing between my thumb and first finger. It was a surreal sensation, as I felt no pain. I could see inside my hand *how weird,* which was spurting blood from the wound. Part of the playground turned bright red.

My brand new school uniform soaked up the rest of the river, which was cascading copiously from my hand. Real time returned rapidly, as screaming children surrounded me. The playground teacher in charge was steaming a path through the crowds, totally shocked at what he saw.

I felt calm *perhaps this isn't really happening,* although I didn't know why *perhaps it's because I should have been killed.* The knife would have plunged into my neck, and the consequences of that would have been worse than dying, had I survived. I was now in the human jungle *this is why my mom was so distressed,* and every mother's worst fear had come true.

The attacker had fled the scene, running away through the school gates. He had failed in his intention, but left me seriously injured. Without a first aid kit in the vicinity, the burly teacher shouted loudly for a handkerchief; and several clean ones appeared from the pockets of nearby children. An attempted murder in the playground, at the start of a new term, had set a new low in the history of the school.

All around me was panic. I was manhandled into the washroom by the teacher, who pushed my hand under a tap. Hot water gushed into the wound *Ow!!!* and, mixed with blood, created a pretty, pink fountain of fluid that filled the bowl. Other teachers were now in attendance, and a bandage was applied to my appendage. I was the only one appreciably unconcerned. Within minutes, we were wending our way towards Solihull Hospital.

I was impressed by the teacher's car. He had pimped and polished an ancient Austin 7 to look like new, and was concerned that none of my blood made its way onto the well-kept luxurious leather seats. To this end, he had wrapped a towel around my bandage. However, I noticed that even this additional safeguard was beginning to turn pink.

"Mmm, you may be lucky," said the on-duty German doctor. "We were fighting you in ze war, and," he continued, "Now I am here to help you." He gave me an ironic smile. He had been well briefed on the incident. "Now you are fighting yourselves. If you young people had experienced ze war, you would not be doing such zings!" he exclaimed, as he fiddled with my hand. "I have to stitch you farst, so zere will be no anaeszetic. I'm sorry, but zis is going to hurt, so please feel free to scream as much as you vant!"

I braced myself, as he poked through a drawer of large semi-circular needles. An imposing-looking nurse arrived with thread that, to me, looked like baler twine. He whistled a tune while threading the needle and, if he thought that this would put me at my ease, he was wrong. The nurse held my hand down on the table with the ease, and grip, of a sumo-wrestler.

"No, it's okay!" I shouted *this hurts more than the wound!* She looked puzzled, and relaxed her vice-like fingers. The doctor turned, holding the huge needle and thread behind his back *I've already seen this instrument of torture, so what's the point in creating a deception?*

"Turn your head away," he commanded sternly.

This is it! He forced the oversized needle into my flesh, and I nearly fainted with pain. I counted each of the eight times that he pushed and pulled the thread through my hand *this is far worse than the knife!*

"Okay, zat's it," he announced, "you are ze very brave boy. A fraction furzer over with ze knife, and you vould have lost ze use of your hand."

There was much wailing and self-recrimination awaiting me at home. The police had arrived, and requested that a charge of grievous bodily harm should be made against the young assailant. However, James advised against it, suggesting that the attack had been a life-changing moment for me. In the end, he'd said, I would see it as a unique moment of good.

"No sir, leave him alone, I'm okay." Silence greeted my remarks.

"I'm asking your parents to think about it. At the moment, we have the young man under arrest," the officer continued.

"Let him go," I offered. "I don't mind, I'm fine."

I trusted James, and saw it as an opportunity to move forward. At the very least, I would never be attacked again.

Attending school with my arm in a sling, to witness his punishment at the school assembly, was the only reason that I went. Although the headmaster had been stunned by my forgiveness, he had decided on his own form of retribution for the incredible, unprovoked violence that had been wrought upon me. It would be 'six of the worst', on the stage during assembly, thus causing total humiliation. His parents had written a sincere letter of apology, and expressed thanks for my 'overwhelming act of kindness'.

The head brought down the cane, on his trouser-covered backside, with such venom never before seen in the school. Other such beatings had been merely window dressing, for the sake of dishonour only. This time, however, the head had the backing of his parents to 'really go for it'. Each swipe of the cane was inflicted with a complete and utter lack of restraint, and the victim's head jerked backwards sharply, with a deep intake of breath, as each blow was delivered. He left the stage in palpable pain, crying like a baby; and his humiliation continued as the school erupted with pleasure and condemnation. He was booed off the stage, and became a future figure of fun and hatred. I simply walked out of the assembly, and never set foot in the school again.

My aunt knew about my mother's zeal for a new life in a country pub and, unexpectedly, my murderous attacker had helped in bringing her vision a step closer to reality. Aunty Pat would make every effort to persuade her husband to join forces with her, my mother, and my father for a joint business venture. As a team, they could muster the money necessary to complete a contract with a brewery. Both of my parents had experience serving behind the bar, but none of running a business. Children in The Grove rallied around, and expressed great concern and compassion for my ordeal. My young body must have been tough, as the wound healed without the help of anti-infection lotions, pills or potions; but the hospital's supply of such items was non-existent anyway. The National Health Service was still in its infancy, so that's how it was, post World War II, for poor people.

It couldn't go on for ever; and sitting around licking my wounds was no longer an option. Months of missing any form of education always caused concern with the authorities, and sympathy for my situation was wearing thin. The thought of attending the school, where I had missed being murdered by a split second, filled me with horror, and I became morose and depressed. James and Sally had not dropped by. Winter was setting in, and I prayed that the snow would bring them back into my life.

Massive action was needed, and so my mother had galvanised her troops. Excitement abounded, as my parents arrived back from somewhere east of Birmingham, to announce that we were moving to a fantastic country pub. So many secrets surrounded this move, and everything was on a need-to-know basis.

It transpired that my father's elderly Scottish parents had been living in a laconic Leicestershire village with the odd name of Shepshed. Keeping their ears firmly glued to the ground, they had all the inside information regarding the upcoming pub vacancy.

Our relatives on my mother's side of the family were a very close-knit, happy-go-lucky lot; and I always enjoyed their company when they visited. My father's family, on the other hand, had always been a murky mystery. They had never been mentioned, and I had never asked about them. I had never met my grandparents on my father's side, but all would be revealed in due course. There was no rush, since his world was of no interest to me.

It was decided that my father would take the post of landlord, and my mother would run the bar, with her sister Pat assisting her. Uncle Bob would become a sleeping partner, and find work in his own profession as an aircraft engineer. My misfortune at school seemed to have done the trick, and brought everyone together for a great cause. "We'll come and visit you when you've settled in," was the cry from all our friends and neighbours in The Grove.

The old Jowett, smoking and rattling away on all three cylinders, waited patiently in the street on that cold November morning, and all the possessions that we needed for the move were packed into the car. My sister and I were squashed, and almost crushed, between the medley of motley bags and the oddest of items. My poor sister seemed a lost soul, as she had fared the worst. It had taken her all her seven years of life to accumulate a close-knit group of friends, and now they were no more. We may as well have been going to the moon, since Shepshed was at least 50 miles away from home.

"Why is the pub called 'The Gobbins'?" I asked, with a naivety that pulled my mother up short. I had been in so many ruffian-induced scrapes, it was thought that I had nothing to learn about the dark side of life from my parents. She was, at last, feeling proud to be sitting in the front passenger seat, as we trundled out of Birmingham for the last time. So she ignored my question, and replaced it with "Good riddance! Let's go and enjoy the country."

I have no idea why I didn't share her excitement. I just didn't. Hilary looked tiny and downcast and, as the truth dawned upon her, she began to weep silently. Suddenly, I felt responsible for her grief, and held her hand for the first time in my life.

"It's going to be horrible, Stu," she whispered, with rivulets of tears coursing down her sallow face.

James said that it would be a change for good, and I hoped that he was right. Something was different about my inner mind. I had always felt the presence of the 'snow people', even if they didn't communicate. Maybe it was the trauma, and now the travel to the new life; but whatever it was, their presence had disappeared. I had learned silent communication skills, but I now felt nothing, and panicked. I squirmed and sighed, as the car eventually pulled into a narrow tunnel, adjacent to the pub, which led to a tiny car park.

"It says 'The Lifeguardsman Inn', not 'The Gobbins'," I observed *Hilary was right. This is an intimidating scenario, if ever I saw one.* The façade was of a decaying three-storey ancient monolith, whose rightful place was back in the sixteenth century. My aunt and uncle had followed, some way behind us, in their Austin A30. Hilary squeezed my hand in fear, as we alighted into our new life. At eleven years of age, I was truly her big brother. She did not feel safe, nor happy; and from a tiny, town, slimline 'semi', to a rambling countryside monstrosity, was a bridge too far for her. I lived in the hope that it would be a stepping-stone to greater things, if James was to be believed.

We were to meet the outgoing tenants, for a short changeover period. My father's first job was to nail a plaque, displaying his name, above the front door. Hilary and I were allowed to explore the cavernous building. The long passageways upstairs creaked, unnerving us. The door leading to the second and third storeys was padlocked; and ancient, spiderless cobwebs made kaleidoscopic patterns on its exterior.

"Don't go up there!" My father had caught up with us and, having learned how disused, dilapidated and dangerous the upper floor was; made it clear that this area was out of bounds.

"Where are we going to sleep?" I exclaimed, and received no response. I couldn't count the bedrooms; there seemed so many. Hilary was to sleep at one end of the corridor, and I at the other.

"I'm not sleeping on my own," Hilary blurted out, and began to cry again. My father's efforts to placate her only made things worse, so a compromise was struck. If she didn't like it, she could sleep in my bedroom.

I thought that this was a good idea, and would be glad of the company. My bedroom was huge, and our voices actually echoed as we talked. Everything seemed so old, and musty smells emanated from every nook and cranny. The beds were made of great iron struts; but broken springs jutted out from all angles, so my father used brute strength to force them back into place.

The upstairs area was an oddball of a configuration. A customer's side entrance led to the only door to that part of the building. With security in mind, the previous tenants had installed a mortice lock on the door; ensuring that it could only be opened, with a key, from the outside. This meant that anyone upstairs wanting to get out, couldn't; and my parents thought that this was the perfect security for Hilary and me.

Once we were safely upstairs in bed, nobody but family members could have access to us; and the only form of communication was when they made occasional checks on us during our evenings of incarceration. They could serve to their hearts content, knowing that we were safe *this is a baptism of fire*. The only family toilet was disgusting, decrepit, and wedged behind the rust-ridden bath, in the family area downstairs.

The tectonic plates of my mind crashed against each other, causing great confusion. Thoughts of a new school, in this alien area, almost brought me to my knees. Where would Hilary find new friends? Everywhere I looked struck fear into my heart. My mother proudly introduced us to the bar area, but even this seemed odd *it's stuck in a time warp*. Birmingham had bristled and bustled with fast-action people, fast-moving cars and fast-service enterprises. Now, we had travelled back in time, to an era of the horse and cart. I had noticed only horses in the village *where are all the cars?*

Hilary and I brightened up, as Aunty Pat and Uncle Bob arrived. It was the first time they had set eyes upon their new home, as they had left all the arrangements to my parents, and trusted their judgement entirely. They visibly winced as they joined us in the bar, and a jaw-dropping silence fell over the whole scene.

The smelly bar top, the beer-encrusted rickety table, and the sand-streaked sawdust, which covered half of the bar floor, was a sickening sight. Typically, Uncle Bob broke the icy atmosphere that pervaded all around us. A bright metal bowl, adorned atop an equally bright metal plinth, stood proudly at centre stage. Bob was intrigued, and inspected the item. "Not bad workmanship," he offered "for a spittoon."

I was to learn, later on, that customers were allowed to spit into this strange vessel; or 'gob into it', as the locals preferred; during an evening of debauched drunkenness. It became forever then 'The Gobbins'.

The living quarters consisted of one pokey family room, a tiny kitchen with exposed wires hanging from a box on the wall, and an apology for a bathroom. Now, we were a family of six, with a living area much smaller than our old semi in Birmingham.

I found it beyond comprehension that Pat and Bob could have jumped over such a cliff. They were intelligent people, who had their lives together; but this venture was obviously mired in decisions of desperation, and I was overwhelmed with guilt. Looking at the miasma before me, I should have taken the police officer's advice, given evidence, and stayed in the Midlands. With all the demons of the jungle, Birmingham was a million times better than this hell-hole; but they had taken this chance because of me, and I knew, from their vibes, that the exodus had not ended well.

By default, my father had unexpectedly found himself elevated to king of the castle; and his name was now proudly displayed over the front door as Landlord. Thanks to Pat and Bob; he had become something, from nothing. He stood behind the bar, pipe in hand, looking every part the main man. He had slicked back his thick black hair with Brylcream, trimmed his moustache, cravatted his neck, and looked more imposing than his five feet ten inches. Bob exchanged an untrusting glance with him. He had never been too impressed with my father. He paid for most of my toys, and our trips to the coast; and this venture was the ultimate sacrifice for him.

Bob was a well-respected employee at Elmdon (now Birmingham International) Airport, with a great future; and had given it all up on a whim. I learned that they couldn't have children, so Hilary and I were their chosen substitute. I noticed that, on arrival at the pub, he did not shake hands with my father, but kept a respectful distance. He would have to find work, as the pitiful pub takings could not sustain all six of us; although as it turned out, it would not need to.

The whole place had an eerie, dead feel about it. It had not received a lick of paint for decades, and the dust seemed to have fossilised everywhere. It was immovable. I ran my hands over its sheen, behind the bar shelf, and it was rock solid. Aunty Pat forced a smile of such strangeness, that I felt scared. She was, like my mother, a very pretty lady, with long golden hair. Bob was a tall good-looking man whom I loved and respected. I did not respect my father, nor did I love him. I did not understand why I felt like this, I only knew that I did.

The cold light of day had dawned with a formidable freezing frost, and it mirrored the plummeting temperature in the pub. One stinking paraffin heater stood menacingly in front of the blocked-off chimney in the bar area, and this would constitute the entire heating plan for the whole building. We were already feeling the chilliness, and the winter had not yet geared itself up to flash-freeze us into eternity.

The previous publicans were supposed to spend part of the first night with my folks; and introduce them to the customers, but that never happened. After a quick check on the inventory, they were off. Odder still, was no appearance, nor even mention, of my father's relatives.

It was decided that we would all sleep in bedrooms adjacent to each other on the first floor. Hilary and I inspected my bedroom. The high ceiling was uneven, and cracked in many places. A lamp shade, which had never been cleaned, hung from a short wire, and sylph-like cobwebs cascaded halfway to the floor. I swished at them, and as my face became entrapped in a sticky snare of spider floss, I fought furiously to rid myself of this nauseating noxious net.

I tried the wobbly brown light switch on the wall. It sparked and crackled, made me jump, and I released it quickly, my heart continuing to race for several moments afterwards. The light didn't work anyway, and I insisted on having a torch before I would enter the room at night. The two single beds looked forlorn and forgotten; and stood shakily on a wizened wooden floor, which creaked with our every footstep.

"I'm not sleeping in my room," Hilary piped up. "I want to sleep here with you." We were both fearful of the night, and I willingly agreed. We checked underneath the beds simultaneously and, in perfect unison, pulled out two great porcelain pots. "What are these for?" Hilary inquired.

"I don't know," I responded. "Maybe to put flowers in."

"Oh yes, of course, we can put them on the dressing table," she offered, and then tried opening the two drawers. They were stuck solid, and had warped so badly that they'd been rendered useless. We peered out of the window and, to the left, the old pub sign swayed and groaned in the ever-increasingly cold wind. A faded painting of a ship, tossed about in a stormy sea, sat uneasily on its facile façade *pretty fitting for us*.

Two rusting iron bars, protruding from the building, held it in its precarious position *this whole building is falling apart*. Priorities were put in place; and tasks were assigned to everyone to prepare for the evening's trade. Bob worked on heating the bar area, but nothing was arranged to keep Hilary and I warm upstairs. Extra thick, rough, army-style blankets were always the preferred option.

We were used to below-freezing point temperatures, and our bodies had adapted accordingly over the years. My mother and aunt unpacked, and made a stupendous effort to clean the bar. My father, who knew nothing about beer cellars, was given the responsibility of 'putting a barrel on'.

I was intrigued; and followed him to the cellar which, it turned out, was not a cellar at all. Hilary followed the procession, and we arrived at a shambles of a shed abeam the car park. He unpicked the lock with a giant-sized, wrought iron key, then wrestled with the door for a while; before wringing his hands in despair at ever reaching the holy grail inside. The huge lock actually belied any illusion of security since, with one kick, any part of the shed could be broken down, and its most secure section was the unopenable door!

Finally, it opened and, through the gloom, four wooden barrels of beer sat triumphantly, each on its own wooden plinth. He scratched his head in wonderment and whimsy. He was about to tap into his first barrel of beer and, with his children looking on, he must make a good fist of it. "Now we need the tap," he mumbled to himself, and looking, every inch, the consummate landlord. He grabbed a cone-shaped, elongated brass tap and a wooden mallet from the 'tap shelf' above the barrels.

Hilary nudged my arm, and pointed to the floor. Leaking beer had formed an oxbow lake, as it meandered its way to the drain hole in the centre of the recently concreted floor. There, lying happily perplexed in the beery brine, was the mother of all spiders. To say it had had 'one over the eight' was an understatement. This was an alcoholic arachnid that obviously loved its liquid litmus test. It was a gigantic red blob, its 'legless' legs so uncoordinated that it simply arched round in permanent circles. Partly staggering, partly swimming, it cut the funniest of visions. Hilary and I giggled.

"Oh no!" I shouted.

My father, focussing on lining up the tap with the barrel, had missed the spindly comedy being played out by his foot. He leaned back, with his hammer arm raised to whack the tap into the barrel; moved his foot for better leverage, and repositioned it smack on top of the unsuspecting creature.

"Ooh!" Hilary and I moaned in harmony. The splat, and ensuing squishy spider squelch, coincided with my father's first blow to the tap. There was obviously an art to 'tapping' a barrel, because it bounced right off the solid wood front. From below, I could see that he was not lining up the tap in the correct place, and I silently pointed to the softer cork lower down. It was the right area, but his over-zealous attacking swing produced the wrong result. The tap flew straight through the corked area, disappeared into the barrel and, within a second, the entire contents of the pressurised container erupted from the newly created hole, like a geyser in Yellowstone National Park. Nothing, and no one, was spared. The cellar flooded within seconds, and all of us were soaked, covered in beery bubbles.

Hilary and I backed out into the yard, to watch this farce develop from a safe distance *this is a punishment for killing the spider*. My father's panic-stricken efforts, to plug the hole with his finger, were futile; and he gave up, joining us in the yard, dripping from head to foot.

Mother was furious, Bob was fighting back anarchic anger, and Pat lapsed into some sort of litigious laughter. We had just lost the beer supply for the weekend, and our profit for the entire week. Every penny counted, and the till had just suffered a major blow.

Bob hadn't yet worked out how to produce hot water from the tiny, complicated, electric water heater; so Hilary and I stood half-naked, in freezing conditions, washing the beer from ourselves with numbingly cold water. We shook and shivered, and felt sure that we would die. We were hillbillies in reverse. There was no forgiveness for my father, and the rumblings of discontent continued right up to the moment of opening time.

Hilary fell asleep instantly. I was wide-awake, bored; and my mind settled down to important matters. My mother had made a good job of tucking us in. Several layers of blankets weighed me down heavily, making it difficult to move. The bedroom was in half-light, and harsh shadows appeared from nowhere. Situated at the foot of Hilary's bed was the dressing table, a very old piece of furniture, with an almost frosted-over swinging mirror. I wondered if a day would come, when some form of heating would be invented for bedrooms.

The ancient Jowett and, for that matter, even Bob's brand new Austin 30 had no heating; and in winter months, they often drove while peering through frosted or frozen windscreens. Pressing their hand onto the windscreen, until some form of defrosting took place, created the only clear vision. If that didn't do the trick; it meant that the hand had frozen, and the other hand needed to be brought into action.

The bedroom window was beginning to freeze over with alarming speed, and I suddenly felt claustrophobic. My 'snow friends' had deserted me, and I felt alienated and alone *they must be punishing me for something I've done*. My mind raced back and forth over every detail of my life since our last communication. This frustration always fragmented my belief in them. "Maybe this is why" I whispered to myself, "Maybe they can recognise when I wobble." I was talking myself into a plan.

I decided that it was okay for them to connect with me whenever it suited them. My job was just to believe and trust in them *I must never waver again*. Without them, my life was miserable. I felt my heart thumping deliriously, as the window became totally opaque. The closed-in feeling, in this frozen waste, chilled my soul as well as my body *there's no choice, I have to open the window!* I looked over at Hilary, who had since disappeared under the blankets. I hopped out quickly, to check if she was still breathing, and then rushed to open the window. The low drum of customers, getting to know their new landlords, seethed down in the bar below. I wondered how my mother was making herself known. She would be the one most able to win them over.

The extreme cold quickly had a natural effect on my waterworks, and I needed the bathroom badly. I jumped out of bed, drew the billowing brown curtains, and made my way downstairs. Banging on the bottom door, to make myself heard, was an act of futility; and the idiocy of this self-styled imprisonment became clear. By the time that they decided to check on us, we could be dead. If we needed them at any time, we could not make contact. I had to go to the bathroom somewhere, and I remembered the porcelain pot.

"Oh, is it you, Sally?" I yelped. I glimpsed a tall ghost-like lady, in a long laced dress, looking down at me from the top of the stairs. It was a fleeting glance, and she moved off. I ran back up the stairs to the first floor landing, and looked to the right. I could hardly breathe with excitement and fear, and began to shake. The cold was acute, and my breath formed white clouds in front of my face. She had reached the end of the corridor, and was turning right. "My God, she has two children with her," I garbled. They all turned, and projected strange and unwelcoming looks at me. They turned again, and filtered into the second storey.

My mind was ablaze with thoughts *could my 'snow friends' have invited other 'snow people' to visit me? That was not a friendly glance from the ghosts, though.* I was now scared half to death. I was shivering, in only my pyjamas, outside my bedroom door, and literally frozen to the spot with fear. My eyes were transfixed on the area into which the ghosts had merged; and it was then that I felt inexorably drawn, as if by a merciless magnet, to the end of the corridor. I didn't want to go, but my feet decided otherwise. It was as if I'd been hypnotised, with no power to resist, regardless of the terror I was experiencing.

As I neared the forbidden door to the second storey, I heard the faint sounds of many people chattering, and machines whirring away inside. I flattened my ear to the door, and it was as if the volume had turned itself up *there are definitely people working up there.* My father had marked this part of the pub as 'no go' area, and I wondered if he had a separate business venture operating; but I dismissed this thought as madness, because no light emanated through any of the cracks around the door.

Suddenly, I heard the downstairs door opening. The spell broke, and I ran back along the corridor, nearly bumping into my father as he reached the landing outside my bedroom door.

"What the hell are you doing?"

I was out of breath, and in an obvious state of distress. I knew he would take a dim view of my new visions of ghosts. "I needed the toilet and I was banging on the downstairs door and you couldn't hear me," was my rushed and plaintive explanation.

He grabbed my hand, dragged me into my bedroom, and picked up the porcelain potty. "Now pee in here, and leave it under the bed. Bring it down in the morning, and empty it in the customers' toilet in the yard!"

After a cursory check on Hilary, and folding the blankets down to expose her face, he turned to leave; momentarily glancing at the wind-strewn curtains. I thought that my time was up. However, he turned again, marched down the stairs, and slammed the security door. Hilary was still in a deep sleep, but her unconscious mind operated her arm, pulling the blankets back over her head. I did the necessary, whipped open the musty old curtains, and launched myself back into bed *what's wrong with me?* Ghosts, of all descriptions, were running riot around me, and I did not like it one little bit. James and Sally were kind and friendly, but I'd linked up with a group that did not like the look of me. It took a good hour for me to warm up in bed *how come my father can't hear what I'd just heard upstairs?*

It was all hands on deck at the Gobbins, during the first year, as we tried desperately to improve our lot. My mother and aunt had to work long hours behind the bar, and learn the in's and out's of running a business; whilst also trying to maintain a home. The men were now working in various jobs; in Uncle Bob's case, travelling many miles a day to work and back, and arriving home far too tired to make a dent in the never-ending list of tasks. Even Hilary and I had designated chores, which meant that the first year flew by in a daze, and it was not until February, 1957, that anything of note was to happen in our lives.

I always hated Mondays at school. It was after lunch, and my mind was full of imagining a way out of the hell our family had dropped itself into. I did not want to be where I was, and began daydreaming. I looked out of the window; and the teacher's voluminous voice became a blur of incoherent resonance, growing into a rumbling sound that filled my mind. It grew in volume, and then came the screams.

Reality struck instantly. The desks and chairs, with children hanging on, slid slowly towards the outside wall. The room was no longer straight. I glanced at the blackboard, which was now at a strange angle. No one knew what was happening, and even the teacher hung on to her own desk which bobbed and bounced towards the wall, like a listing ship in a swelling sea. The school began shaking, and I could hear the crashing of tiles and chimney pots smashing to the ground.

I was transfixed, as my eyes took in the school football ground through the window. I watched in amazement as the goal posts fell to the ground, as if an invisible hand had pushed them over. I was more aware, and upset, that my football match would be cancelled, than of the school falling down. As the sub-sonic sound and shaking subsided, and the children's screams turned into whimpering cries, the teacher took control, "Right. Now children. Don't panic. It's alright. Just follow me."

We clambered over the forlorn furniture. Most of the class, frightened out of their wits, fearfully and tearfully scrambled behind their teacher *it's an earthquake!* The rest of the school was herded into the corridors, which looked like scenes from the Mad Hatter's tea party. Panic hit us all, as we became aware that another tremor could cause the school to collapse.

Our class was on the second floor, which meant traversing two flights of stairs; an expedition that would now make even a mountain climber think twice. We all hung on to each other, and a bedraggled and bemused bunch of schoolchildren finally extricated itself into the schoolyard below.

The Gobbins escaped the worst of the quake's primeval pummelling of the village. Just one chimney pot from the pub's rickety roof, amongst hundreds of others in the area, lay smashed and scattered into a thousand pieces in the street. Mother and Aunty Pat were visibly shaken and traumatised by the tremor's effort to destroy the pub.

As we all gathered in the bar, small aftershocks continued to cause concern; and rolling vibrations made the floor churn under our feet. They would stop, and we would wait, with heart thumping anticipation, for the next wave to hit. Although the air was full of our fear, locals started to drift in, seeing the pub as a communal sanctuary and information exchange; and filled the place well before opening time. As the tremors subsided, the worst seemed to be over. Hilary and I were assured that all would be well, and that bed was the best place for us.

The following morning, it was work as usual; at the dairy by 5 a.m., filling milk bottles, and delivering them locally in a cart; followed by a paper round at 7 a.m. Then, instead of leaving for school at 8:45 a.m., it was all hands on deck for the rest of the day to sort out the mess.

I lay in bed that night, reliving the events of the last forty eight hours, and wondering if we would ever go back to school. I'd have been very happy not to. It was another cold night and I could not sleep, feeling more closed in than ever. I ventured out of bed to open the window, but the wrought iron latch was jammed in its socket, and refused to move *oh God, this is a nightmare!*

I looked around, and spied Hilary's tiny leather shoes lying neatly next to her bed. With one of them, I tried to tap the latch quietly, but it didn't work - it would need a big hit. I garnered up a final uplifting swing, smacked it with all my might, and the latch lifted. Seeing that Hilary remained undisturbed, I breathed a sigh of relief.

The next major hurdle presented itself in the form of frozen moisture, which had secured the window to its frame, and Hilary's shoe would not be up to this stage of the challenge. I needed something solid, and the old dressing table chair provided the answer. I guided one of its four bandy legs at the exact angle to the window and frame and, *here we go* with a sharp thrusting movement, hit the spot dead on. The window flew open and, to my dismay, so did the entire windowpane. I closed my eyes, tensed, and waited for the crash and splintering of glass on the pavement below.

This would have been a catastrophe too far for Bob, who had already made it clear that he did not suffer fools gladly. In some ways, he was beginning to scare me, too. I had known him as an uncle, and he obviously cared for me from a distance; but now that we were locked in this bullring of hell together, he might lose all patience with his adopted adolescent. He might even think that I would follow a pattern of deleterious paternal habits; and I was keen to prove that I was the absolute antithesis of my father.

There was no sound from below *how long does it take for a pane of glass to fall fifteen or twenty feet?* I leaned far out of the window and peered down. The pub sign creaked loudly on its rust-riddled hinges, and the light above it shone onto the pavement below. There was no sign of the glass pane, or any shattered pieces. It seemed to have just vanished *did James and Sally come to my rescue?* I peered down again, in incredulous amazement. There, in the old hanging basket, bedraggled and untended since its summer glory, lay the pane of glass *Wow! Tomorrow I must rescue it. Then come up with a wonderful explanation of its amazing ability to jump out of the window frame into my hands...*

"Thanks, James. Thanks, Sally," I uttered. "You've saved me from a fate worse than death." It was my intent to keep on thanking them for whatever saving scenarios came my way in future, regardless of their involvement. I would do this, whether or not I felt that they could hear me. This would be my new plan.

I could smell the snow arriving. Those nagging northerly winds breathed heavily through the open window, giving me hope, and I prayed that my 'snow friends' would ride in on them. The salubrious sounds of customers, leaving the bar, filtered up from the street below. The crusty old light over the pub sign was switched off, and the moon's occasional glow, as it nipped in and out of snow clouds, created additional, intermittent, sinister shadows.

"Look out!" I had slipped into a dream state, and shot bold upright in bed. My eyes flashed wide open, with Sally's easily recognisable voice echoing in my head. I had a sudden flashback to the playground attack and, in a split second, was ready. The bedroom shook, and roof tiles cascaded past the window, smashing to pieces on the pavement. The whole building was vibrating and, standing at the end of my bed was the ghostly apparition of a hoary old wraith with long, straggly, black hair; her eyes ablaze with anger. She was holding aloft the old dressing table chair above her head. *"GET OUT! GET OUT! YOU DON'T BELONG HERE! THIS IS OUR HOME!"* Before she could bring the chair smashing down upon me, I was already halfway down the stairs. The security door opened in a flash.

"It's okay, it's okay." My father's trembling voice meant that it wasn't okay. I saw beer glasses and bar stools lying prostrate on the floor. This was not my imagination. The ghost had shaken the building to its roots with her power, I was certain of it.

Within seconds, we were all standing in the middle of the road, along with many other residents. Hilary was cradled in my mother's arms, covered in blankets, and still sleeping. The ground beneath our feet continued to undulate until, suddenly, as if by magic, it stopped.

"It's another earthquake," people shouted. Smashed roof tiles adorned the whole area. A few doors down, a chimney had collapsed.

Bob's eagle eye noticed the pane of glass sitting comfortably on the hanging basket, still swinging from the buffeting.

"Can you believe it?" he retorted, and reached up to rescue it. "That'll save a few pennies. I can fix that."

An aftershock had got me off the hook. My family had experienced years of German doodlebugs destroying many parts of Birmingham. They had lived in an area directly under Hitler's flying assault dogs, and hidden under beds when the sirens sounded another attack. By comparison, this was a minor event; but it had still unnerved them. Nature had made its feelings known, but I knew better.

Hilary was put back into bed without ever waking up, but I refused to enter that bedroom under any circumstances. Sally had alerted me to a major problem within the pub, and I blurted it out.

"There are no such things as ghosts! It was an earthquake, and you were dreaming!" My father was exhausted and exasperated. I hated him for not believing me, and he had simply had it with me, I could tell. "Right, I'm taking you to your grandparents tomorrow. You can stay there for a while."

I had never met them before, but anything had to be better than living in this place, I reflected; and insisted on sleeping between my parents for the rest of the night *when that horrible old witch returns, <u>they</u> can deal with her.*

One low - one high; I was now in the middle of the harmonic gurgling sounds I had only previously heard from a distance. The nauseating noises must have cancelled each other out, in order for both parents to sleep. I sat up, and tuned in. I whispered my thanks to Sally. "Please come back soon. Please," I implored.

12. Full Circle

2002

The M6 was an impossible mess. The satnav advised going via the M1, but this meant nothing to my mother, whose only concern was visiting the Lake District. I had taken her all over the world, but now it was time for the rest of the UK to enjoy mother's mellifluous Brummie humour. She had humbled a president, poked fun at a pop star, and squashed a world champion squash player. My mother had no social graces whatsoever. However, her heart and humour won everyone over. It was a great gift, and nobody left her company without a smile.

The motorway traffic had ground to a halt. The great three-lane snake was tired, and had decided to take a nap. I was grateful for a top of the range Peugeot 607 automatic with climate control. I'd bought the beast to ensure that my mother would enjoy comfortable countrywide travel, and it rivalled the first class flights around the globe that I'd provided for her. I had focused on making her dreams come true for over thirty years and, climate control or no climate control, we had to get off this broken concrete conveyor belt.

"Look at that," she piped up. She had spotted a sign indicating that Shepshed was one mile to the left. "Let's go there, and see if the old pub's still standing." I was surprised and startled to see the name again, under such circumstances. Had we not been advancing at ten miles an hour, I would have missed the turn; and having taken forty-five minutes to reach the turnoff, it was a detour that was obviously meant to be.

The village was unrecognisable. It was now a modern bustling town. The pub lay on the road to Quorn, and I headed in that direction. Charles Dickens would have been in his element at 'The Gobbins', during the time I'd been exchanging glances with the ghosts.

Thirty years is a gulf I'd not expected the old place to bridge The old road had acquired modern, architecturally aesthetic buildings from stem to stern; but there it was, looking pathetically out of place and time, sandwiched between two office blocks. It had not changed one jot. Even the creaking sign was as I remembered it. *This can't be happening.* The shining silver surfer slithered smoothly to a stop, directly outside the front door of the pub. I looked at my mother.

"Can you believe this?" I exclaimed.

"Come on, let's go in," she exclaimed, as we were systematically scrutinised by the locals. It got even odder. The bar had not changed. The old customer table, although on its last legs, remained in the same position; and the spittoon and sawdust were ready for the next hundred years *this is a true time warp...* Once our livelihood, and grateful for it, it was now even more of an eyesore than it had ever been. Laser-like looks burned holes in our backs. Old, wrinkled, unshaven locals, playing dominoes, were dumbfounded. It was clear that people like ourselves never ventured into this pub. The chattering buzz of the bar was replaced with Sargasso-like silence.

The flashback was instantaneous. *I was the pub's pint-sized son. I saw myself standing by the security door, in fear of my life, staring across the vast expanse of the bar area.* It was the same bar, but now a quarter of the size. For some bizarre reason, an afferent force had attracted us here, and the Dickensian drama continued to unfold. The landlord stood behind the bar, proudly sporting one leg and a crutch *he seems a friendly, affable sort of fellow.*

"What can I do for you fine people?" he boomed. A martini on the rocks, with a twist of lemon, caused the intrigued open-mouthed locals to burst forth into raucous laughter.

"You won't get fancy drinks like that here," shouted one, with a voice gravelled from a lifetime of smoking.

"I know that man," my mother whispered, and made a beeline for him. "George!" she bawled, and planted a kiss on his crispy white face. This caused him and his cohorts to turn into temporary pillars of stone. They had not missed the affluent silver saloon that was filling the window space. They had noted a wealthy looking lady, and what they assumed must have been her driver, ordering sophisticated drinks at their bar. It must have been the strangest sight they had ever witnessed here. The silence was broken. "Is it Phyllis?" barked the spokesman, his eyes and mouth now wide, and happily, open.

The celebrations went on and on. I had never seen my mother serving our customers in those long forgotten days, and now I realised just what an incredible impact she must have had on them. There was a genuine love emanating from the roughest of these men. It was drinks all round, on us; and the bar stayed open for the rest of the afternoon, and well after closing time.

I was standing quietly by the bar *there has to be a reason for this intuitive introduction to the past.* Mother reminisced with the clients, as I desperately searched my mind for the reason for this mystifying, roundabout route to the Lakes.

Our one-legged landlord was also thinking. "When did your mother vacate the pub, lad?" he inquired.

"1958," I replied, without hesitation.

He was quick, and had a memory as sharp as my surname.

"Is your name Sharp?" he responded. I nodded and smiled.

"We took over from your parents. Hang on a minute, I'll get the missus." He half walked, half hopped, towards the living quarters, banged on the door with his crutch, and yelled excitedly for his wife; who joined the unexpected merrymaking.

"The ghosts. Ask about the ghosts." James had joined me for this retrospective reconciliation.

"I'll put it another way," I inadvertently interrupted.

The landlady had ears that could pick up a dog whistle, and responded. "Put what way?"

"Erm, I just wondered if any, er, strange things had happened here; after we left." The flock around us chuckled. I had hit a nerve.

"Nothing good," she propounded, in a broad northern accent. "My husband lost his leg to cancer, and has to have the other one off shortly."

I raised my eyebrows in concern and respect *he's mightily cheerful about it, and she's so matter of fact.*

"Yep, that's right - the other one's going," he piped up.

Okay, it's getting stranger and stranger... That seemed about it, and she continued her thoughts while downing another double gin and tonic.

"Apart from the ghosts, that is. Drove us barmy, they did - banging the doors, movin' furniture about, an' all. We had to get the exorcist in. Got the local vicar to work out what was goin' on. They frightened my poor daughter to death."

My mother was instantly taken aback. She had accepted my 'snow people', but ghosts were a spiritual bridge too far. Now, she was getting confirmation of the past in the most powerful way possible.

"They lived up in the top rooms. Had a milliner's business there in the 1700's. It was a family affair, and they all died here. The bedroom at the top of the stairs used to be an important workplace for them, and my daughter decided to sleep there. They didn't like it. She came face to face wi' one of them; an old lady who kept screaming at her. She had to sleep with us in the end, and it went on for months. If we could have found somewhere else to go, we'd have left ages ago."

She paused, frowning, then continued, "The vicar 'ad an idea. He said we should clear the room out completely; and he'd go in with holy water, and explain to them that we'd never use the room again, and it would be locked."

My mother and I waited with baited breath.

"And?" I queried.

"And they never bothered us again," she nodded at me, "from that day to this."

13. Joey and the Grandparents

1957

The placating present was a budgie. It was a dream come true, but it came at a cost. It was my payoff for agreeing to move in with my grandparents. I had become a protesting pain for my parents. Having to take care of me by day, and refusing to sleep in my bedroom with 'ghosts' at night, was the final straw for them. I was truly petrified, but they could not understand.

The budgie was the ultimate sacrifice for them. They were losing money, and Bob was watching every penny. Financing frivolities, such as a budgie for a petulant ghost-buster, seemed absolutely insane to him.

"In my day, you'd have got a clip round the ear. Bloody ghosts!" he mumbled, as he tried to balance the books. Finding an unmarked cheque stub, he roared, "We're missing fifteen pounds!" Bob had displayed alta voce anger for the first time ever. We all took a step back, and I started shaking. My father had no choice, but to admit it. The Jowett had needed a part; and he figured that, as the landlord, he had the right to utilise the chequebook. This single act was the beginning of a major rift in the family.

I had never met his parents before, and had refused to visit them. However, with budgie in hand, and witnessing a serious breakdown in my family's affairs, I was ready to go *it's the better of two evils*. Killing myself was an option I'd seriously considered. Provisional placement, with my father's parents, was for a couple of weeks only. However, the deception was double-dyed. "Dinna worry, John. We'll need nothing but a bit of auld fashioned discipline to cure him." They sounded like Scottish terriers, with their harsh Glaswegian opening salvo. "Reet, we'll have the budgie over here, and it'll stay here," his mother screeched.

My father was flustered, confused, and his troubles at the pub meant that I was now effectively banished from his life. I was to be taken in hand by his elderly parents, to be returned a reformed character. My mother made it clear that it was for only a week or so, and that she would visit me twice a day. I was clearly destroying their ability to build up the business. "Reet you are, mather," my father replied, and left. My father's instant switch into a Scottish accent shocked me, and I was baffled. He had never shown this ability before, and I found it a rather curious part of his character.

It was a ragged, terraced cottage; with a thatched roof, and a 'ready to collapse' outside toilet with a rotting wooden door. The cottage overlooked my school, and my bedroom window opened up onto the playground. The goalposts still lay in disarray.

"Now ye'll stay in here 'til tea time," she commanded, intent on breaking this wild young stallion.

"I want Joey up here with me," I bleated.

"Ye're an insolent young pig, and I'll have none of ye cheek. So, ye ne're wanted to visit us, eh? Well, now ye ha' nay choice." She slammed the slatted wooden door, and the latch skipped in and out of its seat.

I needed the 'snow people' more than ever, and made a plan to make use of my forced imprisonment. I believed that I could stick the two weeks, which my folks needed to sort themselves out, and to recover from my nocturnal nagging. However, garrulous ghosts now seemed a better option, having been replaced with live relatives who were far scarier.

Now I knew why I hadn't wanted to visit them. I must have been born with an inner sense of the future. I never knew why I didn't like my father; I only knew that I did not like him. There was no rhyme nor reason for it; and it was an incontrovertible irony that I was now his family's prisoner.

The local newspaper reported that the epicentre of the recent tremor had emanated from an extinct volcano, a few miles away in Charnwood Forest; and it was one of the most powerful earth tremors ever recorded in the British Isles, causing damage as far away as Bristol and Blackpool. The first tremor had caused scenes of panic in the local cinemas. As the floor, seats and screen began to vibrate, there was a mass stampede of people trying to reach the emergency exits. Hundreds of chimney stacks across the region were shaken to the ground. The school suffered serious damage, and would remain closed *maybe they'll chain me to the bed…*

My grandmother was, by far, the more fearsome of the two. She was sharp of tongue, nose, eye, and attitude - but not of wit. If I needed the toilet, I must make a polite request. A key would be provided, which unlocked the malignant shed with the odorous hole, exposing a stinking wooden latrine cover. I felt sure that, at thirteen years of age, and given the chance, I could make a much better fist of life than my whole family combined.

The early hours were my time. "Shhh," I whispered, as Joey's eyes flashed open. I peeked under the smelly kitchen cloth which covered his cage. He understood immediately that a nefarious night-time activity was in progress. He was obviously pleased to see me, and held forth on a major squawk. I placed his cage on a space next to my pillow. "Now, Joey." A serious conversation was about to be struck up. "What are we going to do?" He looked me in the eye, wanting to chatter, but instinctively knowing that something was wrong; and so quietly muttered to himself. "You're right," I answered. "We will escape. I have friends, you know." Joey continued gurgling. "My snow people. They always know what to do. They said that only good things would come out of all this, and I believe them."

I opened the cage door and scratched Joey's speckled yellow head. He closed his eyes, and felt the love I had for him. Even Joey knew more about love than my family members did. I wondered about Hilary. She was only nine years of age, and already a pillar to post pawn in the desperate dalliances of my parents.

"If ye take that bird to bed with ye again, we'll sell it!" shrieked my grandmother. "Ye won't git another warning." She was reading the part time employment ads in the local paper. "School's off for the time being; and ye need to contribute to ye keep."

It's fine by me. Anything to get out of this dismal den I would never be scared of a ghost again, I reflected; and prayed that my mother would take me back very soon.

"No! You can't!" I yelled. People had arrived to check out Joey.

"We'll be back in the morning to pick him up," they confirmed, and handed over the cash to my grandmother.

"Git upstairs, before ah bring oot the belt to ye," snarled my grandfather. I had defied the curfew, and had stealthily removed Joey's cage every night from its stand. I needed his company through the night, and he was my friend and companion throughout the early hours. The moon shone a glittering glow. It was bright as day outside. The cottage was still.

"Right Joey, I'm risking a beating by bringing you up here, you know that?" He garbled his usual reply, bent his head over, and waited to be scratched. "I know you love me, and I love you, but we have a problem." More gurgles, as his eyes closed when my finger gently caressed his nape. "What do you suggest?" I whispered, insanely. He opened his eyes and gurgled again. "Yes, you're right. We have to escape," I replied.

It was impossible to leave with a birdcage under my arm and, anyway, the back door key was well hidden. I gazed at the silvery light outside, and opened the window. Craters on the moon's surface were easily visible, and ominous black clouds gathered in the distance. That rasping chill cut through to the bone, and I breathed in deeply *soon, very soon, the snow will arrive. I can smell it.*

My ears tingled, my back shivered, and my hair stood on end. The moonlight lit up James as I'd never seen him before. Sally stood behind him. Joey perched patiently on James's hand. I was overjoyed, and bursting with emotion. I tried to put my hand on James' shoulder, but it went straight through. He moved to the window, and held Joey out into the winter wind. There was the flutter of wings, and Joey was gone; as were my friends.

"So what have ye done wi' the budgie?" screamed my grandmother. I had replaced the cage on its stand, and returned to bed. The rickety old black-stained stairs to my bedroom led to the kitchen. They leaned almost at a ninety-degree angle, and it was a dizzying drop to the ground.

I peered wearily down, at the large mouth extending the width of a head, and exuding venom. I had spent the night in tears. Although my best friend had gone, I thanked James and Sally over and over again, for they had ensured that Joey would enjoy freedom. He belonged to me, but he was being sold like a slave. It was better that he take his chances in the wild. James and Sally had read my mind, as I could not have taken the final step. They had done what I could not, and I pleaded with them to visit me again soon.

Suddenly, my grandfather appeared next to his wife, slowly unstrapping his brass buckled belt. "Na git doon here." He was spitting blood, and intended that I shed some too. His silver hair and shrunken, old, wiry stature belied his strength and speed; and I complied, with apparent contrition, with his command to bend over the settee - but an instant before the first blow struck, I was off like a hare.

The chase was on - round the living room bric-a-brac, under the dining table, out through the door, and into the kitchen. The belt lashed down, repeatedly, missing by inches. "Wicked child!" and many other indiscernible rants about my unruly bad behaviour, were vented into the atmosphere. I cowered under the kitchen table, and was finally ensnared. My view of old, criss-crossed spindly legs meant that there was no escape. James had expressed that a move to the country would be good for me; but it didn't feel so at this moment, trapped like a fox awaiting a terrible fate. Then a loud knock on the back door, followed by sharp raps on the kitchen window, suddenly became the sweetest sounds I'd ever heard.

"Reet, git oot from under the table. Your mather's here. Come on, laddie, move yeself."My mother was confused.

"He's a wicked little liar. Why would we sell the budgie?" they hollered. "If he doesn't git the discipline now, he'll end up in prison."

Prison, I pondered. Now I was sure that all grown-ups were mad.

"Come on, Stuart. We're going," she announced, grabbing my hand. The door was slammed behind us, and we would never see them again.

14. Back at 'The Gobbins'

1957

My bed began to levitate slowly; then dropped, with a sharp bang, onto the floor. I could not breathe, nor could I believe it. My breath glistened in palls of white clouds. It had already been desperately cold, but the temperature now dropped even further. I had never seen my breath silhouetted like this before. I was in shock, and unable to scream.

I couldn't move, as a powerful force held me down. My breathing became laboured and, such was the fear running through my body, I was sure that I'd pass out. In an instant, James and Sally appeared. They looked tenderly at Hilary sleeping, walked over to my bed, and stared at me. James put his hand through the flowing stream of white, that was my breath, and a great roar issued from my mouth. The bed rattled, and began to levitate once more. The sinister spectre reappeared, screaming oaths; but was confronted by Sally, who stood between the wobbling bed and the manic manifestation. Howling, wolf-like sounds continued unabated from my throat. I was powerless. Oh, please, God; stop this noise coming from me!

Sally raised both hands, and the demon disappeared in a flash. The bed slowly settled down; and the evil, exuding from my mouth, subsided as I returned to normal. My eyes flickered, and James and Sally had gone.

I looked over at Hilary, whose contented sleep made nonsense of my horrific experience. In some ways, her inability to wake, during any catastrophic cataclysm, helped me to calm down. I reasoned that it was all a nightmare, and my intimidating imagination was to blame; but as my torment subsided, Pat's began.

Doors rattling, and heavy footsteps stomping along the creaking corridors, became regular occurrences at the Lifeguardsman. Everyone slept through them, except Aunty Pat and I. Pat's screams echoed along the landing, piercing the night like an injured animal *they're not human, surely*? They died down into a desperate cry, as Bob's reassuring tones calmed her down. The hoary wraith, previously intent on dashing my head in with a chair, but now thwarted by Sally, had picked on my aunt instead.

Even Hilary was awakened, along with the rest of the family, by Aunty Pat's nocturnal nightmares. They occurred at 3 a.m. regularly, and Bob was driven almost insane by his wife's defenceless torments.

He was always within a few inches of Pat whenever she described, hysterically, that "They creep out of the cupboard, with their hands out, ready to pounce on me."

"Pat, Pat!" he bawled, his voice echoing along the passageway, and curling its way into our bedroom.

Hilary and I sat bolt upright, and listened intently.

"They're coming to get me," she whimpered, sobbing helplessly.

"For God's sake, there's no one here. Go back to sleep," Bob moaned. Pat's mewling diminished, and faded completely within a few minutes. It became her habitual night-time horror story; although Bob was convinced that both Pat and I were weak-minded, and unable to control our vivid imaginations.

Our final Christmas approached. Snow had already settled, and my heart raced. I envied Hilary's ability to sleep instantly, once in bed; while I was preoccupied with thoughts of every titanic trauma that was wrought upon us each night.

Many small gifts had been donated for the 'poor children upstairs'. I laid them all out on the cold, sparse bedroom floor, and waited. I closed my eyes, and descended deeply into thought. *Was there a connection between the earthquake and the ghosts appearing? What is it that mysteriously manifests James and Sally?* They always appeared at a time of greatest need. It was a polarising puzzle, which permanently perplexed me.

15. The Move to the Red Lion Inn

1958

'Portacabins' were being erected as temporary classrooms, but this took some time. During the interim period, I called on local shopkeepers to find more work. A butcher gave me the job of cutting a small patch of grass in a back area, for a shilling. I was delighted, and thought it would take me just a few minutes with his lawn mower. However, he gave me a pair of scissors!

The job took me many hours, and I felt that I was just one step removed from those boys who crawled up chimneys to clean them, in an earlier era. The butcher brought his customers round the back, to watch me; several of whom laughed uproariously *what kind of sad creature is he?* I thought of the shilling, which was more important than my feelings, and I remembered to be very thankful and to smile. Looking back at my formative years, this incident helped me in later life, in dealing with other such people.

Back at the pub, things had changed significantly. My father had been banished from the bar, as his presence caused tension between the customers and my mother. Bob had insisted that he find work, as he had done, and leave the running of the pub to my mother and aunt.

"You'll have to find alternative work as well, Stuart," my mother whispered lovingly, "I've applied for another tenancy on the other side of the county, in Sibbertoft." Hilary was beaming.

"Are we leaving?" I yelped.

"Yes, as soon as we get confirmation."

Bob had found work close to this area, and had seen the pub vacancy advertised. In order to conserve money, he had purchased a 150cc BSA Bantam motorcycle, and travelled over a hundred miles a day to and from work. He showed me, by example, that such a work ethic was vital, in order to succeed. He was my hero. He rose at five every morning, and always maintained a high level of overtime. He managed his own world, and subsidised the loss-making pub venture. In the meantime, my father tried his luck at the Vauxhall factory in Coventry.

The creaking 'Lifeguardsman Inn' sign was replaced by a slightly less creaky 'Red Lion Inn' sign. We had arrived. I had learned quickly of the great divide between town and country folk; and that their trust had to be earned. My mother, a charismatic character, knew how to break down the bigotry. She jested her way to the jugular, and her reputation for fun and laughter spread far and wide. However, the meagre takings of fifty pounds per week, for seven days hard labour, would not sustain the family.

My father relocated to Vauxhall's in Luton, and came home every weekend; while in Baginton, Coventry, Bob worked every hour that God sent. This left my mother and my aunt, or the 'terrible twins', as they became known, to run riot in the pub; since the men were a hindrance to building the business.

16. Fresh Spirits

1958

A month had passed at the Red Lion, with no ghosts, and no screaming. This was proof-positive to me. The relentless, rogue-like nature of the spiritual beings at 'The Gobbins' meant that they really existed; and I now understood what my family could not. We had invaded their territory, and they did not like it *how could a scornful spirit make itself known any clearer?*

Hilary and I found integration with country folk very difficult, as they viewed us with great suspicion. The scrawny, soporific elders hated change; and town people entering their domain signalled the end of life as they knew it. For them, it was the thin end of the wedge.

"Yer'll see," moaned the locals, "they be tekkin' over shortly."

However, Hilary and I saw everything in relative terms. Things seemed calm, and the countryside was all-embracing in its beauty. My father was now seldom seen. His once-weekly home visits had reduced in frequency, after he had convinced my mother that the expense of travelling from Luton, in the old Jowett, could be utilised elsewhere. Bob's long working hours meant that he came home, ate, and went straight to sleep. Bed had finally become his sanctuary, a world apart from his previous nightmarish experiences at The Gobbins.

I quickly recognised that the common denominator, existing between the local lads and myself, was football. It was their Achilles' heel, and the village team was always on the lookout for new talent. I felt that it was prudent not to push myself into the fray of local life right away; but football was my love, too. Every Saturday I would watch from the sidelines, and marvel at the skills of the Lee brothers, who made up 90% of the team.

George Lee was short in stature, but massive in ability and heart. At centre-half, he thwarted most opposition attacks; and converted almost certain defeat into winning positions. I loved watching him play. I also knew that I could bring something special to the table, for their team. They were weak on their right wing, and this was my football-playing forte; but I decided, for now, to become a quiet supporter, and make myself known from a distance.

"Do you play, then?" I turned, almost in disbelief. One of the players was actually addressing this youthful anathema from another planet. If I couldn't make the grade as a soccer player, then my future relationship with the country folk would be in jeopardy.

"Oh, hello. Yes, I love it," I replied, turning to face the chisel-jawed youngster *I need to imitate his Leicestershire accent. Otherwise, they'll think me too posh to enter into their world.* Joe Lee was a great player and, along with his brothers, turned out for the team with metronomic regularity.

"Fancy a kick around?" he continued. The village green was rough, and molehill mounds abounded; so we used two of them as goal posts. I was excited, as a breakthrough was on the cards. The week was full of nervous anticipation of my soccer trial with Joe, and enrolling into the forbidding Clipston Old Grammar School.

It really was as old as its name. Built in the 1600's, it didn't look as if it had changed in the meantime. The headmaster also taught all lessons.

"You'll have to go up to the secondary modern next year," boomed Mr Cartmell. Each of the five rows of desks, in the one-roomed school, denoted a particular lesson. He started with maths in row one, and moved along to English in row five! "Right, Sharp," he announced, to the rest of the schoolchildren. "We have a townie amongst us. Can't be all bad, as I think he plays a mean game of football!" He laughed at his own uproariously unfunny litany, and handed out a maths question on scrap paper. "As soon as you think you know the answer, put your hand up."

I was worried that I might not be as bright as my country counterparts but, after a quick look at the question, worked out the answer immediately.

'If a boy was 6 feet tall at 15 years of age, how tall would he be on reaching 30?' My hand was up in a flash.

"Yes, Sharp."

"12 feet, sir." This was the worst and best of answers, as the trick question had been set to test me out. I found out, in the break, that the same question had been posed before. My innocent, unintelligent answer caused great hilarity.

"So, we know now that townies are not as smart as they are made out to be. Eh, Sharp?" Cartmell's gruff voice unnerved me, and I wanted the undulating concrete floor to swallowed me up. "Did you read the question to the end?" he continued.

"Er, yes, sir." My dignity was to take another dive.

"Right then, Sharp; or should I call you 'Not so Sharp'?" (more sniggering from the class) "Quiet!" he boomed, "Let Sharp read the question out loud." The last line of the question read: 'Do not answer this question' *I'm doomed.*

I blasted the ball past Joe, who had taken the first turn as goalkeeper. It was my first shot, and I'd hit it with power and precision. He was impressed, and I scored eight out of ten. We played dribble the ball, and finished off with heading practice. I'd made a new friend, and was jumping for joy.

"I think you could play right wing in the senior team," he suggested. "You're really fast, and have a great shot."

The seniors looked like a professional outfit, and defenders on the opposing side were built like tanks. I was half the size of their left back, and my short legs whizzed around him. I cut inside, let fly, and the ball hit the back of the net. I was surrounded, and almost crushed, by my jubilant teammates. I'd scored all five goals in our thrashing of the opposition, Joe was congratulated on spotting this new townie talent, and I was in.

I merged into the country lifestyle, as had the Romans before me. I smoked their 'Woodies' until I became violently sick; and joined them in their pursuit of poachers, on behalf of their farmer bosses.

Hilary however, became isolated and depressed. She attended the local primary school, and became friendless. I didn't know what to do for her, and she took the brunt of the acerbic arguments between my mother and Aunty Pat, who had changed a great deal.

Pat had been the life and soul of both families in Birmingham, but since then she had become downcast and depressed. Her sparkling personality had been decimated by her garrulity with the ghosts, the ignominious moves had taken their toll on her, and her confidence had been crushed. Pat and Phyl (or Phyllis, as the customers preferred to call my mother) became the great unloved, and various horny farmers tried to take advantage of such a valuable vulnerability. I wasn't stupid, and could see what was happening, but I never knew if any dalliances took place.

The new school was daunting, and a flashback to the secondary modern in Birmingham filled me with fear. The sheer size of the teenagers was intimidating, being, on average, six inches taller than I was. I'd promised my mother that I would make up for the '11-plus' debacle, and it was time to fulfil that commitment. I was now older and wiser, things had improved, and I had not seen James or Sally for months *maybe they're just happy to let me go.*

17. The New Joey

1958

I arrived home from school, and jumped for joy. The squawks of a budgie echoed from my bedroom. I ran upstairs and rushed through the door. "Joey!" I yelled.

Mother was soon at my side. "It's a new Joey, love," she explained. He looked like a clone of the old Joey, a reward for the progress I had made over the past school year *now, my life is complete!*

Taking up music, in the next grade, was a cool consideration that had been running through my mind *perhaps if I could understand the fundamentals, I might make some progress*. I was worried about Aunty Pat, though. Her eyes seemed distant, and disconnected from the world about her. She and her husband had risked everything for me; and only trauma and twilight zones, filled with screaming ghosts, had been her reward *if I could make something of myself, and lead the family into a fantastic future, I could change everything*.

Hilary was intellectualising, and staying out of all the problems. Her plan was germinating, but she was too quiet; mentally marking off the years, months and days to the time when she could fly from this dysfunctional dance.

18. Christmas Again

1958

"How can you say that, Joey? It's completely mad. I'll never make the grade..." He stood, almost motionless, on my fingers; looked me straight in the eye, and chuntered continually. "What do you mean, you agree with the 'snow people'. Have a fly around, and clear your head." I was not looking forward to my new appointment, and listlessly made my way up to the farm.

I chased the chickens from one end of the endless hen pen, and old farmer Cooper sat on a stool, halfway along, with his sheep's crook held out in front of him. This was death row, and these poor creatures knew it. They squawked and screamed, as they watched their kith and kindred fall, one by one. It was a desperate struggle, and I hated it, but Cooper showed no mercy. Brushing off fag ash, from the birds' flailing feathers, was the only compassion he displayed. *At least I've secured a few weeks work,* I thought, watching another long stalk of ash fall from the Capstan Full Strength companion that was glutinously glued to his bottom lip.

Eventually, all the terrified chickens fell prey to Cooper; as they fled past him at full speed, then hooked by the neck with his death stick. In a second, they were flat on their backs, their necks stretched by his experienced executioner's hand; and hung up on the rail ready for plucking. Speed was of the essence, as hundreds of chickens required plucking while their lifeless bodies still retained heat.

That's how Christmas came and went; up to our waists in feathers and red mite; while roaming rats, lurking on rafters, casually watched our pantomime. They were clever creatures, and I was amazed, when I once saw a pair work as a team to steal eggs. One member clutched an egg, then dropped onto its back with all four grimy claws grasping onto it for dear life. The other clasped its partner's tail in his mouth, and dragged him back through a hole under a chicken box.

I must have won Old Cooper over, I considered, since he paid me regularly. Christmas without the 'snow people' saddened me. I talked to them every night, and wondered if they were simply keeping an invisible watching brief on me. Mother was becoming depressed again; as freezing temperatures in January meant that few people ventured out, and passing trade was non-existent.

19. A Right Shower

1959

The reverie in the shower room was more haughty, and spiced with hilarity, than usual *why is everyone looking at me?* Fingers pointed at my naked body, and I was confused. My eye caught a reflection in the aluminium sidewalls. Big Jim, as he as was known, ran the playground's extra-curricular activities. He was a true gangster in the making, and had his own protection racket well established. All the smaller kids handed over their tuck, and bits of change, to the monster in their midst.

I'd already survived one murderous attack, and I felt tougher than the rest; so I'd eyeballed him *he's nothing* when he asked for his dues. He was now urinating on my back. As I turned, he continued his animal act over my chest. His giant frame towered above me; but I stood my ground, and let him finish. His growling laughs continued after all others stopped. As the shower died to its last dribble, once again we were eyeball to eyeball. He couldn't back down now, and had to crush this little critter before him. I was ready for the attack.

He roared like a lion, and lunged. I knew that he could flatten me, and I rolled with the passado. The timing was perfect. A split second later, and I would have been dead meat; but my small frame came to save me. With legs bent, and hooked nicely into the flabby fold in his belly, I thrust forward using his momentum. He flew over my shoulders, and hit the solid, tiled wall like a shell from a cannon. The crack was sickening, and he crashed to the ground like a felled hippopotamus. A hideous heap of overhung humanity lay unconscious, a gaping wound on his head spurting blood.

"Is he dead?" asked one of the stunned onlookers.

"Hope so," said another.

Now I'll be arrested for attempted murder. To my surprise, I became the talk of the school. 'The Karate King' was my new title. The belligerent beast had been bested, and battered into oblivion *if they only knew it was pure luck and timing*. Teachers congratulated me. Everyone in the shower room had testified to my self-defence statement. More than his skull had been fractured - his prestige and honour were in tatters. With my self-esteem established, I was inspired to work hard, and sailed through study surprisingly easily.

20. Peter Walker, and the Guitar

1959

I became a good student, and reports of a conscientious child, who could go far, reached the ears of my mother; and she began to have some hope for me. A new set of townies had arrived in the village to brighten things up. Although in his early twenties, and sporting a 'musketeerian' moustache and bristly beard, Peter Walker seemed like an old man to me. As a musician, he had formed a skiffle group, and required a rehearsal room. My mother took a shine to his engaging personality, and offered him the empty bottle shed.

I sat in the corner in awe, transfixed by the band. 'Ghost Riders in the Sky', 'Rock Island Line', and many other popular songs rang out late into the night. I watched Pete's fingers flash across the guitar strings. Dave Chiltern played rhythm guitar, and Mike Hearly slammed out a solid drumbeat *I want to play like this, but it all looks impossible.*

"Do you want to join our band?" Peter blurted out nonchalantly, "We're looking for a bass player." He knew that I did not play an instrument, but added that he was willing to teach me the basic chords on a guitar. One evening, several weeks later, the lesson ended with an abrupt conclusion; as I realised that it would take me years of total commitment to acquire even basic guitar skills, before considering joining his, or any other, band. What had looked impossible now proved to be impossible.

"Okay," he said, "don't get down. Take this guitar with you, as a gift, and practice what I've shown you." I had no ear for tuning it, and could not even discern when two notes matched. The cat-strangled noise emanating from it, during my practice sessions, was hurtful and depressing. I could not train my sausage-like fingers to make the chord stretches, and had no rhythmic sense whatsoever.

"Okay, try this." Peter had acquired an electric bass guitar; which sat alone, plugged in, and waiting for a bassist. I thought that he was either mad, or could magic some special musical knowledge into my head. I didn't get a choice, as he quickly slipped the guitar strap around my shoulder. "Now, when we start playing, pluck away at any part of the guitar strings you feel like. You don't need to know any chords for the moment, just hit anything!" What Peter and the rest of the band heard did not bear any relationship to the assault on my ears. It was too terrible to describe. "There, you see, that was incredible, you're a natural. You're in. We've got a paid gig in Market Harborough on Saturday afternoon. This is your big chance..."

21. My First Gig

1959

I looked out at the large audience, and stood right next to the huge speaker at stage right. I wanted to be as inconspicuous as possible.

"Come closer to me," Peter indicated, and I nudged into the limelight as the crowd quietened with expectation. "1-2-3-4..." Peter stomped in, leading the vocal. The band followed, and my incomprehensible unmusical plucking, at any old notes on my bass guitar, boomed through the massive speakers. The crowd was listening in stunned silence.

"Get off!"

Such cries, intermingled with loud boos and, even worse, expletives, arrived within thirty seconds. I didn't need a second warning. I unplugged, and exited immediately; followed by Dave and Mike. This left Pete playing alone, blissfully unaware that the rest of the band had gone AWOL.

"What's the matter with him?" I shouted out over the din. Dave smiled, unconcerned about the debacle going on around us.

"He's quite deaf. And short-sighted," he replied ruefully. It all began to make sense.

"Get off, for God's sake!" screamed the event manager.

Pete continued to play in his usual style - eyes closed, and blasting out a vocal into the microphone. To great applause and laughter from the audience, the manager stomped across the stage, grabbed Pete by the lapels, and hauled him off. I caught a glimpse of Pete's belittled bemusement. It was a classical comedy moment, and marked the end of my musical involvement with an otherwise competent band. However, it had ignited my interest to discover more about this alien activity.

22. The Music Class

1959

Click-clack, click-clack... the familiar sound of chalk on a blackboard flashed fear into my heart. My second music class had begun, and the teacher's hand flew across the blackboard at incredible speed, forming an endless series of musical notes on a stave. Mr Walker, affectionately known as 'Wally', reached the end of the board and looped around, continuing writing from right to left. He was razor-thin, with narrow deep-set eyes and, when he turned to us, there was no doubt that he was ruler of this domain.

"Therefore, the notes on the spaces between the lines of the stave are easily remembered by... what? Anyone?" He spotted me. "Master Sharp, enlighten the class, please." I felt like a deer in headlights, since I had absolutely no idea what was being represented on the blackboard. He continued, "Do you remember our discussion on Monday?" All eyes were upon me, and I squirmed unceremoniously. "F-A-C-E. FACE, Sharp!" he screamed. "You are obviously flat today, Sharp," he sniggered at his sarcastic tirade, and the class responded in a similar vein. "And what is the name given to this type of memory aid, Sharp?"

"Uh... it's... well..." I blustered frantically. "...that word."

"What word?" he replied sharply.

"That word. The... the one that helps you remember," I offered embarrassingly. The inane conversation continued.

"Obviously, it didn't work for you then, did it?" The class sniggered. "What kind of word?"

"I'm not sure."

"Or, you don't know at all. Which is it?"

"I... know what it does... I just... can't remember what it is."

"All right. Tell this celebrated class what 'it' does."

I felt the sweat begin to drip laboriously down my forehead. It was more like an inquisition, than a music class. "Helps you remember things," I muttered. The class broke out in muffled laughter, and 'Wally' was not amused.

"Move over, William Shakespeare. The distinguished man of letters, Sharp, is redefining the English language. 'Things!'"

"I mean, it reminds you of the letters."

"Sit down!" he belted out. His eyes bore into me and, if looks could kill, I'd have been fried alive. "Can someone else give the class 'that word' to remember 'things'? Miss Pettingale?"

Laura was smug, bright, and happy to show off. "The word is 'mnemonic', sir. In this case, a pattern of words which help you to remember a group of letters"

"Precisely," he sighed, and glowered at me. "Now that you know the word, Sharp; what is the mnemonic for the notes on the lines of the treble clef?" I agonised, and went blank. "You have no idea, boy, do you?" I shook my head in disgust with myself. "Don't you ever get tired of just taking up space in this world?"

"No, sir." The crassness of my comment was not lost on the class. They could not contain their amusement, and more gales of laughter filled the air. Wally was furious.

"You're a dunderhead!" he screamed, and I sank lower behind my desk. "What are you?" He was determined not to terminate my torture.

"A dunderhead, sir." The girls giggled, and boys flashed ungallant gestures behind him. I felt pressurised to the point of exploding until, suddenly, all sound disappeared. His lips continued to exude a vial full of vitriol, but there was simply no sound. I could feel myself imploding into my own body *soon, I will not be here.*

"Don't worry." It was the voice of James. I looked up. James and Sally stood next to Wally Walker. I'd been rescued in the nick of time. I broke into a smile, and instantly relaxed. "Your day will come. He is nothing, and you will be something in music," James continued.

"Thank you." The words slipped out, and I was back in the physical world as the classroom chatter boomed loudly in my ears. Wally's rant continued unabated.

"Thank you…? Thank you? You are not only stupid, but insolent! Put your hand out!" He reached behind his desk. James and Sally looked on in horror. He flexed the cane between his hands, and moved menacingly down my aisle. A surreal silence fell over the room. The 'snow people' slid silently through the desks, and stood between the master and myself. The blow was sudden and devastating, cutting through James's transparent body, and slicing into my naked knuckles. It was instant. Blood spattered over a child in a nearby desk, and his bright white shirt became speckled with it. He stormed off to the front of the class, flung open a cupboard door, and removed something from inside. "Get in that corner; Boy! Put this on, and stay there until the end of the lesson!"

A fellow student offered a handkerchief to stem the flow of blood, as I followed the teacher nervously, expecting another blow. I could not understand why I did not feel pain, but I was determined to be brave in front of my fellow students. He thrust a dunce's hat on my head and, with a hurtful shove, sent me into the corner. James and Sally joined me.

"He's not worthy of you, Stuart," offered Sally kindly, "he has done you a great favour, and this is a good thing." I was getting used to 'good things' manifesting as 'bad things', resulting from their advice; and wondered what other 'good things' were waiting in store for me.

"Oh, good," I whispered without thinking.
"GET OUT! NOW!" He dragged me across the room, and I found myself in the head's study within seconds. I learned to write with five pencils in one hand, and a hundred lines were achieved in minutes. 'I must not answer back in class, and only speak when spoken to'. This penance was played out after school, every day for a week.

23. The Summer of 1959

The summer was sizzling; and farmer Cooper was a Red Lion regular, a top skittle player, and water diviner to boot. He was deaf when he wanted to be, and this became apparent when it was his turn to pay for a round of beer; but I needed a job for the summer holiday period. This fastidious farmer always turned up his hearing aid when the possibility of slave labour became available.

I agreed to work for two and sixpence a week, starting at the crack of dawn, and through to whenever he felt like finishing. A week, for the cantankerous old countryside codger, meant seven days of hard labour. Haymaking was hellishly hot and heavy work, and throwing large, bulky bales onto the cart required a technique. Grabbing the baler twine in the right place, leaning back and, with the speed of a weight lifter, whipping the cumbersome bale onto your knees, was the first stage. Continuing the momentum until it was shoulder high, pushing upwards in the right direction, and hoping for the best; was the second.

The catcher castigated you if you got it wrong, and there was no time for poor performance in the haymaking field. By the third day, I could not move. My skin was torn to shreds by the rough hay; which created deep scratches in my legs, arms and shoulders. I marvelled at the Lees, who moved like automatons. No scratches for them, as each part of their body had been annealed by daily farm life.

The brutal blast of the alarm bell sounded at 5 a.m., and the bright summer sunshine raced through the bedroom window, making it impossible to give up on the job. I wanted Bob to think of me as a net contributor to the family coffers; and his inspirational ability, to keep soldiering on with relentless regularity, was a powerful motivating force for me.

Country folk liked people who worked hard. I wanted to be appreciated, and this was another way to prove my worth. Farmer Cooper berated me, on many occasions, for not keeping up, and resting when I was exhausted. During the haymaking period, he removed his hearing aid; which had the dual purpose of ensuring that he shouted the loudest, and had no chance of hearing a recipient's response. As such, he revelled in his despotic darkness. It was useful in some respects, though, as I was able to rend forth some unspeakable oaths back at him, with insolent impunity.

His wife and her sister were also slaves; working as thistle cutters, and general dogsbodies, for a pittance. I saw them busying away in a twenty acre field nearby. A break for ten minutes at lunch, under the shade of an old dying oak, saw the sisters rushing, at full march, with the tea urn and lunch caddies. I suppose that we were lucky to be fed. Cheese sandwiches without butter, and warm sweet tea, were the order of every day. Old Cooper's mantra was that 'Someone as inexperienced as myself should not be paid, until fully fledged'. He was somewhat surprised, then, that my mother had browbeaten him into agreeing the two and sixpence payment.

Alice and Grace sat beside me, and Cooper stood over us menacingly, timing the break to the second; his ever-present cigarette end dangling from his mouth. He didn't actually smoke the cigarettes - he coughed them; this time loudly, as he sucked in the last vestiges of the butt-end smoke. Wasting this would have been a crime to him. A further waste would have been to use a match to light up another; so he used the dying embers of his fag end to begin another burn-up.

Grace was obviously upset, and I could see tears beginning to trickle down the deep lines in her careworn face. She was at pains to ensure that Cooper could not see her distress. "I've lost my ring in the field," she confided quietly. She was an old lady, and I was boiling with anger that she should be labouring like this.

"Don't worry," I replied. "I'll help you look for it."

"No, no, the master would get mad if you stopped to look for it and, in any case, I don't know where I lost it. It could be anywhere in that field, or the other one over there." She pointed to another adjacent twenty-acre pasture. I breathed in deeply, and sighed. It was do or die. I left the laconic lunch party, and marched purposefully toward the grassland in question.

"Where are you goin', you little whippersnapper?" came the expected exaltation from farmer Cooper. He hadn't paid me in five weeks, even after much badgering from my mother. These were the times in which he came in for his drink without his hearing aid; staring wildly, and coughing smoke into mother's face.

So now, I didn't care; and trudged on. I hopped over the fence, and listened to the fading tones of the old man. If I wasn't back in one minute, my job was in jeopardy. I was in another world again, swimming out to sea, searching for mother's lost teeth. I sat down in the long grass, and disappeared from view. Streams of actinic light sliced through greenery; creating a fountain of speckled spirits, which danced curiously across my eyes. A frightened field mouse darted out from the grass beneath me, and scurried into the undergrowth *I could stay here forever*. Salty beads of sweat poured from my forehead, and dripped down onto my lacerated legs, causing a burning sensation. I grabbed a handful of grass, and dabbed it quickly onto the affected areas. There was no air, and breathing became difficult. I had to think quickly *where should I start looking for the ring?* My heart had reached out to poor Grace.

"Over here…"

Oh my God, it's James! Am I hallucinating? I shook my head, and a swelter of sweat cascaded in kaleidoscopic colours all around me *everything is so beautiful here*. My heart raced, as only it could when I felt the presence of James and Sally, and my hot sweat turned to cold goosebumps. I rose, and the sight of my 'snow friends' took my breath away. Happiness abounded in my soul, as I followed them through the flailing field of grass, across a dried up brook, and into the second ponderous plot of thistles and hedgerows. They stopped, and offered their hands. I held them tenderly. With James and his mother at my side, I felt that I had a real family. Walking with the 'snow people' felt cool in the midday sun. My heart rate slowed until I could no longer hear it. I was in my element, and totally relaxed. They stopped abruptly. James knelt down, having released my hand; and pointed at the tiny object, which was sprinkling sparkling light particles in the air.

I looked closer, and the prickly light danced fancifully around me. Suddenly, it was there, wedged upright between two tiny stones, held in by dried-up dirt. One diamond stood proudly atop the ring, which seemed happy to have been found. Picking up the ring, from the grime and dirt-encrusted narrow track that ran alongside the field, felt amazing; and my eyes blazed with excitement. I turned to thank James and Sally, but they had disappeared. I was happy and sad at the same time. I just wanted them to be with me at all times.

I had been missing for an hour, and found the two ladies stoking hay in the bottom field.

"I car'not believe it!" yelled Grace, crying tears of joy. Hugs were quickly replaced with questions, and the impossible had happened again. I was really happy and excited for her. It had made her day and, possibly, her life. It meant so much to her, and I 'cocked a snook' at Old Cooper on my way home. I would not give up, and I was going to make him pay something for my five weeks and four days of hard labour. My mother and aunt relied heavily upon the local farmers for trade, and could not kick up any kind of fuss. He was well aware that the local buying power lay with him and his cronies.

Eventually, after a skittle night, in which his efforts helped the team win the match, he dropped an envelope onto the counter. It contained five half-crown pieces. I just stared at the glistening coins *I'm going to be rich!* It was a great lesson for me, and the loss of Grace's ring brought James and Sally so much closer to me. My mother was thrilled at my find, and we finally seemed to be moving, very slowly, out of the darkness.

24. The Disappearance

1959

My father had not returned from Vauxhall's, in Luton, for a very long time. He had also ceased to communicate during the week, and we assumed that he must have opted for a lot of overtime. Finally, sensing something odd; my mother called the car plant, and discovered that he had left the company several months earlier; providing no forwarding address.

I knew immediately that I was to blame. My strangeness had made his life hell, and I had disgraced myself with his parents. Now he had made a statement, by wiping his previous life, with us, off the planet.

Mother had complained for years that the pittance left over from his earnings, even taking into account his digs in Luton, made no sense but, on balance, she was happy to be left alone. His visits put a downer on the happy-go-lucky atmosphere that she was creating in the bar; but his name was above the door and, legally, he remained the landlord. Suddenly, the possibility of losing the licence loomed large.

"We have to find him," mother bemoaned dejectedly. Her life, and that of the rest of us, now hung in the balance. Bob was incensed, but refused to take any part in the upcoming problems. A call to police in Luton yielded nothing and when, after initial enquiries, they put his disappearance on the back burner, we were in a real bind.

However, my mother considered that what the brewery didn't know wouldn't hurt them; and decided to continue on, as if nothing had happened, while hoping for the best. The customers were already used to his irregular appearance behind the bar, and he always put mother on edge, constraining her bubbly personality. Pat did not like him at all, and made this very clear with her dismissive attitude. Locals had more fun when he was not around, and only made the occasional reference to his departure.

25. Moving On

1959

Trying to produce a tuneful sound on the guitar was an impossible task, as my fingers would not move in any sort of collaborative combination. Frustration filled my brain, and I hurled the guitar at the bedroom wall; almost immediately ashamed of my action, and regretting it. The neck broke instantly, and Joey's peaceful nodding sleep was shattered. He squawked his disgust vociferously.

"Sorry, Joey." I opened his cage, and gently placed my hand inside. He hopped onto my fingers, knowing his treat was coming. He whizzed round the ceiling, screeching with excitement. His ability to miss the odd-shaped objects dotted around the room amazed me; and I lay on the bed, fascinated by his flying feat. Eventually, exhausted, he alighted onto my shoulder, and tenderly pecked my ear. He was my true friend.

The 'snow people' know everything I could not imagine what 'good things' would result from the obvious disasters, except for more disasters. Starting the woodwork class had meant the end of music for me. It also depressed my ability to study anything, and I went into an academic tailspin. Wally Walker's beating had branded me as educationally ignorant.

Failing my basic GCE's had made my mother cry, and she'd sobbed from her heart. Another visit from James and Sally assured me that this was also a useful experience, and that my mother needed me to fail *it's so difficult being an ordinary mortal, not being able to see the big picture. One day, I'll ask them where this will all end*. It seemed as if I was only getting information on a need-to-know basis. Maybe, they didn't quite trust me, or maybe they felt that I wouldn't be able to cope with the truth of future experiences. All in all, though, I'd started to associate 'good things' being 'bad things' from my point of view.

I wondered when good things (for me) would start to happen but, whenever I broached the subject with the 'snow people', they disappeared for months *their advice is crucial to me*. If I made my own decisions, I knew that I'd be wrong, but I had to do something with my life.

The following months were interminable. Washing beer glasses every night, and being an unpaid cleaner in the day, was no way to exist. I tried to make myself useful by getting up every morning at 5 a.m., and cleaning the whole pub before mother and Pat arose. However, they simply cleaned it all again. "You've missed this, or that, or not polished the brasses," were their continual chastisements.

I made a list of all the things that I enjoyed. It was a very short list – 'Labouring'. I liked working on the farm; lifting bales of hay; cutting thistles with a scythe bigger than myself; ploughing a field with a Fordson Major tractor so big, that I had to stand, rather than sit, for twelve hours a day. This life suited me.

"Right, Stuart," My mother was reading ads for vacancies in the local paper, "call this number, and get yourself an interview" *this has to be a joke!* The position of junior reporter for The Harborough Mail required five GCE O-levels and an A-level; and I refused to call them and embarrass myself. Then came the incentive. Uncle Bob promised to buy me a moped on my sixteenth birthday if I acquired the job. I heard my mother's phone conversation with the editor.

"He's got five GCE's," she lied *Oh, my God! What's she doing?* "Right. Thank you. Tomorrow, at nine."

"How can I tell him I've got five GCE's? He'll need to see the certificates. It's ridiculous. He'll just throw me out." I shouted.

"Just get on the bus at eight thirty and be there, or there'll be big trouble."

I sighed with exasperation. "What do you think of that, Joey?" He chattered away, as I related the whole story to him. Midnight conversations with my budgie helped me to unwind from the day's frustrations. "So, you think I should go, then? What makes you think that, Joey?"

26. The Job Interview

1959

The editor was a scary man. He was tall, pale-faced, and bespectacled. He smoked, and could obviously multi-task. He addressed me while typing with one finger, at a speed that I found frightening. "Excuse me, I have to get this story finished for a deadline; so we can chat at the same time. So, you're from the secondary modern, eh? I have six other applicants, all from the grammar school, who have more than 5 O-levels and a number of A-levels; so why should I employ you, eh?" If the floor could have opened up, and swallowed me alive and whole, I would have been grateful.

"Tell him your mother lied." James stood next to the editor, reading his article. "You can do this, Stuart. It's easy." I visibly shook, astonished that James would appear at such a moment. I nodded my approval.

"My mother lied, sir; I don't have any O-levels" *now he'll throw me out, and that'll be that*. He stopped typing immediately, finding this scenario much more interesting. He rubbed his chin, and lit another cigarette.

"Well, that's a new one," he contemplated. "No GCE's, eh? So, what have you got to offer?" he continued, gazing directly at me with black eyes that penetrated my brain. He gave the impression of understanding all about life, from his thirty years as a journalist and editor.

"Honesty. Tell him honesty," James piped up; while still reading the editor's article, which stuck out from his brand new Royal typewriter.

"Honesty, eh? So who is the chairman of the Market Harborough Urban District Council?"

"I have no idea sir, I'm sorry," I answered immediately.

"Can you make a good cup of tea?" He carried on with the oddest of questions, with babysitting being included in the job description. I said yes to everything, and left.

He said he would let me know in due course, and was looking for a start date in February. However, I was just happy to get out having told the truth, and not squirming through an interview that would have been a testimony of lies and deceit.

An explanation of openness with the editor would not have gone down well with my mother at this point, so I avoided it for now. However, I thought it best to have a few days of peace during the wait, so I started to plan for another job. I looked forward to working in a labouring capacity during the day, and serving behind the bar at night.

It was November, and a number of farmers had chickens to kill, pluck, and prepare for the markets. After a chat with the old scoundrel, Cooper; he employed me as a 'chicken killer's assistant' for the Christmas period.

The inevitable call from the editor came. The phone had announced its proud new position in the off-licence area, and mother leapt on it like a panther pouncing on a kill. "He's on his way over!" she exclaimed to me, with obvious excitement. "Well done, Stuart, you've got the job!" I could not understand what she was saying; as there was no way that I could possibly have secured such a position, which I didn't want anyway. I was sure that my mother had misinterpreted his words.

"Did he actually say that I've got the job?" I asked.

"No, but why would he come over? He wants to have a chat with me," she replied positively *probably because you lied, and he wants to give you a good telling off.*

We sat around the newly polished oak table in the barroom, and he glanced around at the miscellany of brass adornments. Bob had a knack of finding ancient objects, and used his engineering skills to turn them into works of art. Ken Hankins was an editor who wasted no time, and spat it out. "He's on the short list."

He smiled disarmingly at my mother, and I nearly fell off the wobbly old stool *there's no rhyme, nor reason, for this turn of events.* I held my breath waiting for a reference to my lack of education. "I liked your honesty, young fella. I believe I can train you, if you're willing to learn." I was not willing to learn, but I was being squeezed like a lemon into a gin and tonic.

"He is so looking forward to it, sir." My mother humbled herself magnificently, "He's available right now."

"I have a bit more considering, yet; and you do live way out in the wilderness. The work would mean long hours, and having no transport would put you at a great disadvantage," was his considered response.

"We're buying him a moped for his sixteenth birthday." Mother's keenness was spilling over into desperation.

"Okay, we'll talk again after Christmas." He stubbed out his cigarette in the copper ashtray, and left.

27. The Junior Reporter

1960

"You're sixteen in a few weeks, and you can't go on like this," mother cried. Work had dried up on the farm, and she insisted on calling the editor. Mother's mood changed in an instant.

"Stuart's got the job, but it's a six month trial period; followed by a five year indenture programme. He will start on a salary of five guineas per week." There was much joyous celebration, as I was now joining the world as an upstanding member of the community. My mother could announce, to her curious customers, that her son would soon be a famous journalist.

I quickly discovered that tea-making, and babysitting for the editor, were vital pre-requisites for the job. I was handed over to pipe-smoking senior reporter Bob Hemmingway who, with his northern accent and ready smile, put me at my ease.

"Two things you've got to learn, laddie. Typing, and making tea for everyone. We've all had to do it, and it always falls upon the most junior member of staff. As you rise through the ranks, other juniors will do it for you." He dusted down a cranky old Royal typewriter, and placed a copy of last year's paper on my desk. "Now, pick any article, and re-type it."

I felt as if I had stepped into a moment of singularity at an event horizon, and was about to be sucked into a black hole. The slow and painful tick-tack of the typewriter keys, as I searched forever to find the letters, contrasted with the flashing speed of Bob Hemmingway. His fingers became a blur across the keys; and I knew, in my heart, that it would take me a lifetime of drudgery and boredom to achieve such professionalism. But at least I could now pay my way at home, and the gift of a dual seat NSU 50cc moped was a stunning reward.

The editor made me the correspondent for the county. He expected me to use my knowledge of the locals, to sniff out stories like hounds chasing a fox. However, I wasn't used to sitting over a desk, for several hours a day, trying to learn one-finger typing.

"Your job is really easy," Bob pointed out. "You simply read up all the back-stories, see how they are formatted, and use them as a template. You'll only be doing births, marriages and deaths for the first six months; plus anything you can bring from the pub." He laughed at his last comment.

Serving endless cups of tea, every time my name was called, sent me into a silent swearing mode, whilst smiling sarcastically. I did not enjoy being a slave, and the six months trial period at the paper was to discover if I'd become a willing one. It seemed patently obvious to me now, why I had been given the job. They'd assumed that my ability to serve would spill over into pandering to this newspaper hierarchy.

The rebel in me went unnoticed *but they'll find out for sure one day*. I enjoyed working in the pub at weekends; and acquiring a taste, for the beer that I'd previously detested, was a surprise to me. Customers recognising my mother's disapproval, of my newly acquired alcoholic activity, spirited the odd beer through the living room window.

"Don't you go spilling the beans on me, Joey," I whispered to my budgie. "What do you mean, you will?" I raised my voice, and stared into his cage. "If you give the game away, I'll cover you up." I threw an old tea towel over the cage, and he screeched like hell. "Okay, okay, that's just to show you what will happen if you do. Now, behave," I cautioned, removing the cover. Joey was becoming naughty and argumentative, and we often had big rows. My mother felt that my personality was changing; and charged me with neglecting the budgie, which was visibly greying. I lay in bed, later on, feeling bad; as it was the first night that I had not taken Joey up to my room, for our usual chats.

"Yer goin' to the Committee Dance tonight?" My footballing friend, Joe Lee, was keen that I should attend. It was another Saturday night, and my explanation of excuses did not sit well. "Would yer mom let y'off early?" he pleaded.

"Saturday's busy in the bar," I replied. I had little interest in the local village hall hop.

"Aw, come on, dun't be a spoilsport. It dun't get gooin' til ten-thirty, an you'll be finished be then." One way or the other, he was going to ensure that I attended. "Just ask yer mom, okay. Dave an' me'll be by 'bart ten-thirty and see."

By nine, the pub was heaving. We always knew if we were making any money by the amount of blue haze that pervaded the bar areas. If thick smoky fog coursed its way into all areas, then we were doing well. It was over two years since we'd last seen my father, and it was no coincidence that business had bucked up. People came from all over to see our crazy antics. We 'cocked a snook' at closing time laws, and continued until customers had parted with most of their cash. Mother was busy, trying to keep up with the beer orders, as I furiously washed the glasses.

It was about ten-thirty when Joe and Dave appeared at the off-licence. They looked like a pair of thugs, with their noses pressed hard against the steamed up windowpane.

"What the hell do they want?" growled mother, before being dragged back to the bar. I opened the window.

"Did ya...?" Joe inquired.

"I forgot to ask," I replied, disinterestedly. He was crestfallen, and it made no sense to me that my attendance would affect him like this. "I was too busy. Sorry, Joe."

"No! Y'ave t'ask," he pressed. However, I refused to get into such a ruse without an explanation.

"Uh, well..." Dave smirked. "It's 'bart this bird. Joe wants t' meet 'er, but 'e ain't got t'balls t'ask." Joe was a tough character, and did not take kindly to Dave's effort to coerce me. He received a sharp blow to his arm as a reward. *This is all very odd.* Then Joe finally came straight out with it.

"Yer can explain to 'er 'bart me. Yer can tell 'er in the proper way, 'bart a date an' all that."

"You're joking?" I replied stiffly. "My mother would skin me alive if I left now, so there's no point in even asking." I continued.

"Five minutes! Yer'll be back 'afore she knows yer even gawn."

Mother was enthusiastically engaged with a multitude of bar regulars. "Who is this girl?" I asked him, intrigued.

"'E don't know 'er name," blurted out Dave, for which he received another, much stronger, blow to his arm; and winced visibly.

"I tol' yer to keep it shut, Dave," Joe responded, as he delivered the punch. I sighed, and decided to give them five minutes.

We flew round to the village hall in under a minute. All the teenagers from the village, and other areas, gathered there; and an ancient gramophone cranked along, playing scratchy 78's. Most of the couples dancing were girls, and the boys lined the perimeter like elephants in must. Joe searched through the melee of bodies, which shuffled around the crowded floor. I was acutely conscious of the time. "I dun't see 'er," Joe piped up.

"What does she look like?" I replied urgently. Suddenly, Joe spotted her and, with great excitement, pointed to a young woman with long golden flowing hair, and wearing spectacles.

"Good lookin', ain't she?" Joe grinned. "Now, can yer goo an' git me a date?"

28. First Love

1960

"Sorry, I've got to go now. Someone's picking me up at midnight." My head went into a tailspin. The organiser was clearing everyone out, and we were the only couple left on the dance floor. I looked around for Joe and Dave, but they were nowhere to be seen. *Now I have a big problem*, I realised, as five minutes had stretched to over an hour.

She was on her own, and had accepted my invitation to dance. Finding the words, to link her for a date with Joe, did not come easily. In fact, they did not come at all. I became lost in her beauty and personality, and could not continue in my matchmaking role.

"What's your name?" I pursued her, as she rushed to the door.

"Jo. Jo Dunmore," she replied, before jumping into a neat black saloon, which immediately sped off. I was in serious trouble, and I knew it. The few streetlights that the village possessed had been extinguished, and it was as black as pitch as I ran at full speed back to the pub. I did not see it coming, as the screams came out of nowhere.

"She wa' mine, an' ya stole 'er! Thought ya' wa' me mate!"

"Joe, you don't understand. I was trying to figure out what to say and anyway she has a boyfriend with a car," was my garbled response. It was a desperate and defensive exchange, and I felt bad about it. Joe had watched me dance deliriously with his potential date, and saw it as the ultimate deception. He had waited in the dark alley, a furious anger building up inside his skinny frame. I was livid with myself, and could not understand why I'd been so dim-witted.

"So!" shouted my mother, "I know what you've been up to. Let me tell you to keep away from girls!" One of her customers had turned spy.

"It's not what you think," I responded, highly embarrassed.

"Girls will get you into trouble. Don't do it, for God's sake."

It took a long time, but it wasn't until Joe found the love of his own life that we became friends again.

29. The Rebel

1960

Another week of re-typing old and irrelevant articles, from past editions, drove me to distraction. It was now obvious that the outdoor life was for me. I took a deep breath, and missed the smell of the farm. Haymaking, ploughing fields, cutting thistles, and working with animals, was the kind of life I imagined. Writing any kind of an article was beyond me.

"You'll have to learn shorthand, me boy," Bob piped up. He could type, smoke his pipe, and talk at the same time. I was in awe of his power, having risen to the pinnacle as chief reporter. But I just didn't get it, and my frustration was beginning to show.

"SHARP!" His voice now had a cutting edge, and it was now taking Ken Hankins three attempts, with increasing amplitude and inflection, before I complied, with slave-like speed, rushing to the kitchen to make tea. Had it reached four, I'm certain that he would have exploded.

It was now Month Four of purgatory. "What do you mean, you won't babysit on Saturday?" He gave me a penetrating look - the kind that said 'I own you, and you are defying your master'. My explanation, of helping my mother at the pub, did not go down well.

I must admit that he was totally open and honest when first employing me; stating that babysitting and tea-making were part of my trial period. For him, it was a means to an end. For me, although I recognised that he was God in this organisation, I was not a follower. "Okay. Go." He waved me away, turning back to his typewriter.

Bob was astonished that I had defied the deity. "Hell! I'll have to babysit now," he blustered. "Don't forget; in a few months you'll be signing up for five years, so don't upset the apple cart now."

Do a story on Frank Woodhouse. Ken

This was the cryptic message on my desk, when I arrived at eight thirty on Monday morning. Frank Woodhouse lived in my village. He had a willing smile, was a favourite customer and, at eighty-one years of age, an inspirational character. I was being asked to write my first story, and I was shocked. "Well, go on, boy. What are you waiting for?" boomed Bob.

The old man, whom I served every Friday night, had a story of epic proportions; and I empathised with his life. He had broken in Golden Miller, the country's most famous steeplechaser. Ken knew this, and trusted me to create a story about Frank's life. It was my first test of editorial manhood.

"SHARP!" I was becoming truly exasperated, hearing my name blasted forth around the office with metronomic regularity. I knew that it must concern the article I had written, and the tone of his voice did not augur well for my hard work.

I had sat in the bar with Frank until two in the morning, listening to his incredible stories. He had worked for Earl Spencer; known as the Red Earl, because of his ginger hair. Frank was a great jockey, and had ridden in many Grand Nationals. Eventually, he had caught the eye of Dorothy Paget, who owned Golden Miller. After the interview, I covered up Joey, who screeched his discontent; and retired to bed, knowing that I had a beautiful story to write. Frank's life could fill far more than the few paragraphs requested *a few lines in the paper can't possibly do this justice*. With pencil in hand, and sitting on the edge of my bed, I waited for the words. At 5 a.m. the notepad was still blank *this is impossible!*

"Now, write." I heard Sally's voice in my head. I was shocked, but happiness abounded in my heart *thank God, my snow friends are back!*

From the corner of my bedroom, James and Sally manifested, as if by magic. They walked towards me, and looked intently. "Write," Sally repeated. They seemed different. James walked around the bedroom, and Sally was full of sadness.

"What's the matter?" I asked.

"You are not on the right path, and you have to learn a lesson; but for now, write." My heart beat faster, and felt hurt. I did not understand her, and she pointed at my notepad.

"SHARP! GET IN HERE!" the editor continued his raucous request. "You're supposed to be a reporter. Haven't you learned anything in the last four months? If I'd wanted a book, I'd have employed an author! There are thirty pages here. You know how much I wanted? Eh? Eh?"

"No, sir, I wasn't sure," I replied meekly. Sally had given me a colourful cornucopia of wonderful words, and they'd been dismissed with a derisory flick of his pen.

"Well, you jolly well should. I wanted a maximum of five paragraphs!" He attacked my work with a red marker, reducing it to almost nothing within seconds. "Take this to Bob, and bring it back with something sensible."

That's it! Enough is enough. There is no way that I will sign up for five years of purgatory when this trial period is over I was amazed with the story that I'd created, with the help of my 'snow friends'. The potential for a powerful book was there, if he had only looked deeper. Sally's exciting and eloquent exercise had fallen on deaf ears. I pondered, once more, over her words, and finally slapped my forehead in exasperation.

30. The Punishment

1960

"JOEY!" I screamed.

It was in the early hours of Sunday morning. I felt bad. I was lying in bed, unable to sleep, and thinking about Joey. I had treated him very badly, recently. I had absolute power and control over his life, but had left him in the kitchen overnight, and had not talked to him as a friend for ages. The realisation suddenly hit me, that he was always right in his observations *I'll apologise, and bring him up to my bedroom in the morning.*

I dashed downstairs, and my mother was already in the bar, polishing brasses. The kitchen window was open, the door of Joey's cage was ajar, and ghostly filigree fingers faded into the ether as Joey flapped his feathers and flew to freedom.

Oh, my God! James has already handed out justice! I knew instantly why. I ran out of the pub like a person possessed, followed by my mother. Joey landed on the highest branch of a tall tree close by, and heard my desperate pleas as I held out my hand. "Come on, Joey," I shouted. He looked directly down; and thought for a while, ruminating on his recent trials. "I won't leave you in the kitchen again. I promise." Despite my exhortations, however, he simply chortled, and flew off again.

"Serves you right," mother commented, "leaving the cage door <u>and</u> the kitchen window open. What did you expect?" I looked at her mournfully, shook my head, and started to give chase, running across fields full of ruts, and stumbling over styles.

He alighted on the uppermost branches of trees far and wide, and waited for me to catch up. I was breathless. He squawked continually. "I agree, Joey. I was bad, but I <u>will</u> look after you. I'll get you a new cage, I promise. Now come on, come down. I love you."

He heard my pleas, looked directly at me again and, cocking his beautiful little yellow-flecked head, took off again to fly over the valley that dipped down towards the horizon.

I visited that hillside, hidden behind the great oaks, every week for months. Ritually, I called out for him, praying that he would hear my call. It was a sultry summer's day, and farmers tended their fields in the valley below. The smell of newly cut grass wafted on the warm gentle breeze *this is the scent of God*. I was sure that I could hear Joey, whistling away in the weather-beaten trees on the hillside *he must be enjoying his freedom, but he doesn't know about winter storms and freezing temperatures*. I decided to keep all hope alive, until the cold northern winds signalled the approach of winter.

"You'll see him again."

James and Sally appeared next to an old oak nearby, and walked wistfully towards me. "These are lessons you'll have to learn. Remember them. Always remember them," Sally continued, as they slipped away, once more, into infinity. My head throbbed with the power of their words *what am I doing with my life, and where am I going?*

31. Sacked

1960

The editor was furious, and flung his marker across the desk. "What do you mean, you're not signing the indentures?" screamed Ken Hankins. "Explain!"

"You didn't read my story," I offered.

He was bemused. "What story?"

"The Golden Miller man. You put red ink through it all without reading it," I explained, simply.

"And you are putting your whole career in jeopardy, because I was doing my job in making a reporter out of you!" *I'm confronting the king.* All of his anger seemed to seep into a purple vein which dilated, visibly, on his forehead, before erupting into a triumphant tirade as he pointed dramatically to the door, and emphasised each word with a gesture, "RIGHT! NOW! GO! YOU'RE FINISHED!"

I walked out without a word, nor looking back; and as I entered the brilliant sunlight of the high street, I felt just as Joey must have done, flying to freedom. I'd written a great story, and it had been consigned to the editor's rubbish bin. Sally and James assured me that only good would come of this, I told myself, as I walked into the unknown.

The next week, as if in spite, my article headlined in the newspaper:

Sibbertoft man broke in Golden Miller, the famous steeplechaser
by Stuart Sharp

32. Looking for More Work

1960

"How old are you, son?" he asked. The manager of the local brewery delivery company was surprised by my sudden appearance at his office. I did not intend to return home, without another job offer in my pocket, so I wandered around Market Harborough, looking for some vibrant signs of activity where I could fit in. I yearned to be labouring, because being desk-bound destroyed my spirit of adventure.

He was intrigued by my life at the Red Lion; and offered to visit the pub, to confirm my story. "I'm looking for a warehouse assistant, who can double up as delivery man's assistant on the lorries."

My eyes lit up, and I yelled my delighted reply, "I'll start right now! Do you need some help now?" My enthusiasm was palpable, and he was a good man. He smiled, lit a cigarette, and inhaled deeply.

"You're a bit young; but if your parents agree, then you can start next Monday."

She's going to be livid, I thought, as I purred along back home on my moped; but I was happy. I stopped off at the hillside to feel the freedom and, as I looked out over the undulating dales and hills, I understood Joey's decision. A few moments of autonomy are worth a lifetime of restrictions, it was now clear to me. Joey had understood more about life than I did. He had shown me the way, and James had made sure that I did not forget it.

Mother didn't speak to me for a week, Pat was incensed, and Bob was disgusted. I had let my family down badly. They had all pulled together, to see me launched into the world of professional work, in a powerful way. A sought after job, for which I was totally unqualified, had been handed to me on a plate; but something in my spirit had snapped under duress.

With my mother (right) and Auntie Pat, on the way to the clairvoyant in Blackpool (Summer 1947)

Seeing snow for the first time (age 3)

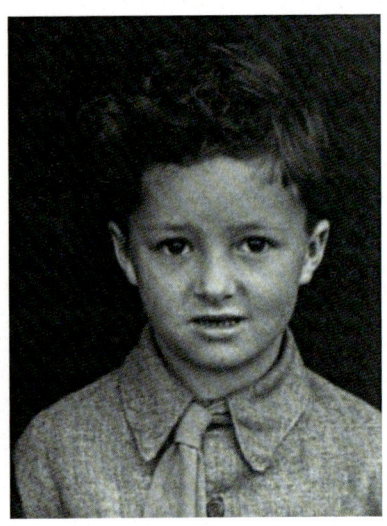

Starting pre-school (age 4)

Newborn sister Hilary, Birmingham (1948)

With Hilary (1950)

Stuart, age 7, Hatchford Brook Junior School, Birmingham (1951)

On holiday in Budleigh Salterton

Stuart (far right) as boxer Randolph Turpin, Queen's Coronation (1953)

Stuart (centre) with his first orchestra, Birmingham (1954)

Schoolboy boxing champion
(1954)

Working on the farm, during school breaks

Our playground (1949)

With Hilary, at the ghost-ridden 'Gobbins' (1955)

Mother (right) takes over The Red Lion (1958)

Clipston Old Grammar School (1957)

Stuart (centre) takes up woodwork, after being 'drummed' out of music class (1958)

Serving at The Red Lion (1959)

Tying the knot, in Foxton, Leicestershire (1966)

Fixing The Red Lion's gas lighting

Training for squash coaching

In disguise, ready for a rowdy Saturday night at The Red Lion

Daughter Emma (right) and cousin Sarah help
behind the bar at The Red Lion

Adopted daughter Kate

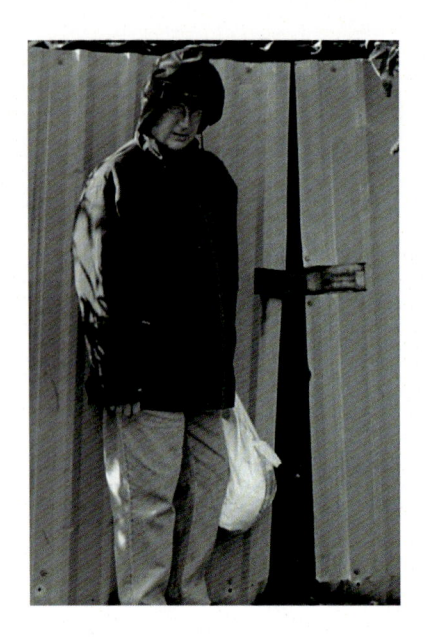

Roughing it in Shepherds Bush, London, late 1970's

From the streets, to successful businessman

Stuart (left) at a presidential meeting, the State House, Zambia (1990)

Receiving a State House reception from the president (1991)

With 'KK'

The African concert

Children entertaining at the concert

The president stars at the concert

Daughter Emma, with the president

Keshi Chisambi runs Stuart's project for the blind in Zambia

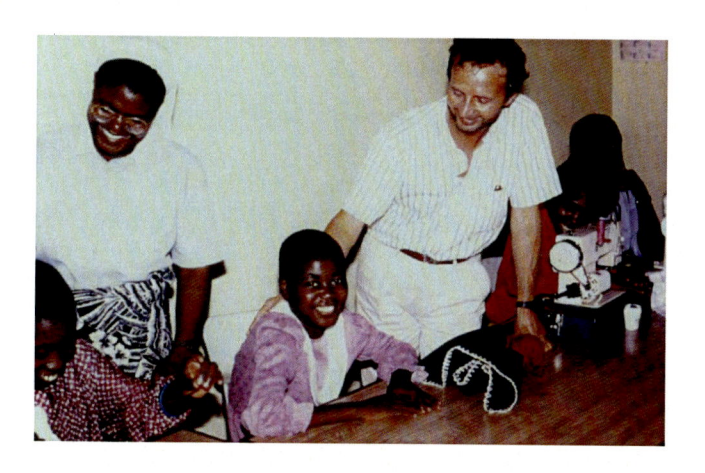

The terminal cancer unit in Zambia

Pop star Eddy Grant joins Stuart's mother (age 77) on her mammoth walk from Wymondham, Leicestershire to Wembley, for Nelson Mandela's freedom speech

Stuart and the team, halfway through the Great Spirit of Zambia Walk.
His mother strides out to lead the pack

Jeff Anderson and Louise Emmanuel ('Nowhere without You')

With the London Philharmonia Orchestra

Allan Wilson conducting the London Philharmonia Orchestra,
as they record the Angeli Symphony Opus 1

Captain Sharp

The squash coach

Flying High

Composing by Rutland Water (2011)

Stuart's mother Phyl; age 93

33. Fast Forward to Hell

1975

Family life hinged around the Red Lion Inn; though it was a slow, meandering existence. Even the snake-like streams and brooks pottered aimlessly along, in the close-by countryside. They reflected my inner being, and seeing them end, under the shadowy curtain of a gnarled oak, hurt me. They simply faded out. No one cared. No one remembered them. Every few years, an ox-bow cut-off would strangle the life out of them. They looked so pretty, but they were visibly decaying. Everything around me seemed set for the same fate. Our daughter Emma had brought meaning into this mundane miasma. She knew what was what, and could already find answers where I could not.

I was fascinated by her ability to play for hours with the crusty golden autumn leaves, which blanketed our back garden. Nature, of any sort, was her loving friend. She forced me to focus on these things. Emma had opened my eyes, and re-activated my sleeping spirit. For months, she maundered about the baby whom she would shortly be looking after. Emma would be the perfect little mother, but while she helped paint and decorate her old bedroom for the new arrival; the vivid vision of hell filled my night-time dreams.

No one should see, in such crucifying detail, how their own newborn would die. The 'snow people' had been right all along. They had tried to protect me, and I had dishonoured their friendship. The result was a headlong rush into an unstoppable future - but it would be good for me, they said.

I shivered, as cold sweat slid down my back. From the distant confines of my consciousness, I heard my wife's voice bringing me back to the real world. "Wake up, wake up," she urged. Slowly, my brain began to revive, and I could hear myself fighting with jumbled words to reply.

As my mind cleared, the demonic dream was left behind *thank God!* My wife's second pregnancy had not been of any major concern to her. Everything was going according to plan, even though she looked like a barrel balanced upon two thin sticks. I was normally happy to relate any of my fantastic night excursions, but this one was different. It had affected my whole being, and would not let go. It was mid-afternoon of the following day, and the invasive vision seeped into my consciousness at every turn.

My wife had been meticulous in planning for the birth, and was due at the local cottage hospital that evening. Emma had been born at a modern maternity unit, but Jo had found the experience disturbing and disagreeable; and vowed never to let it happen again. She had chosen the small rural clinic mainly because it was not a real hospital. It was more like a large home to her, and she had come to know the staff as friends over the past few months.

If the vision was accurate, I knew that she needed to be admitted to the main hospital in Leicester; where every emergency facility was available. Market Harborough, however, offered no such possibility. Knowing that she would view any attempt to divert to the Leicester Royal Infirmary as insanity, I nevertheless felt it vital to get through to her somehow.

"There's nothing to go wrong. Nothing at all," she replied to my observation and worries. "Even if you took me to Leicester, I'd get a taxi back, so don't even think of it." It was the end of the subject, and my concerned calls to the matron were met with similar short, but caring, shrift. It was simply impossible to relate my violent vision of death to her. We were sacrificial lemmings, ready to dive headlong over the cliff, on the ten-minute journey to Market Harborough.

Jo was as bright as a button, and planning her week with the baby, when we turned into the car park of the hospital. The matron was warm, welcoming, kindly, caring, portly and very sympathetic to my weighty worries. "Mr Sharp," she said, "your wife is in good hands here. Now stop worrying, go home, and relax. I'll call you in plenty of time."

I felt completely helpless. "Oh, Christ," I mumbled under my breath.

I shuffled and shivered my way around the garden, on that crisp December's night. I watched our home strangely change, as a mercurial mist licked the windows and outside walls. The moon's frosty glow created sinister shadows, and the once-friendly apple tree became an evil, grasping monster. I was scared of the future, and I could not believe it.

"Don't be stupid!" I yelled out loudly, and saw palls of breath pour profusely from my mouth, and lose themselves in the imprisoning midnight air. *I'm going to freeze to death out here*, I thought, and stormed into the house. I switched on every light, but bad vibes attacked me from every direction. I slammed myself onto the settee. Fighting eclipsing exhaustion was hurting me physically, and I slipped into an anxious sleep.

"The baby's dead! I knew it. I knew it!" I yelled. The phone rang, and the motherly matron had turned into a cold uncaring witch.

"I suggest that you make arrangements to have the body picked up as soon as possible," she said, with a wickedness that sent a chill down my spine; and I sobbed uncontrollably. In that hysterical moment, I heard the ringing tones of the telephone.

What the hell's up with the phone? How can it be ringing while I'm still answering?

I was dreaming again, and woke up in a sweat-soaked, heart-thumping panic. "Hello? Hello?" I garbled breathlessly.

"Hello, Mr Sharp," answered the kindly tones of the matron, "I thought you were never going to answer. I was a bit worried there, for a minute."

"Is everything okay?" I interjected quickly.

"Everything's quite fine," she said confidently. "If you get a move on, you'll be in time for the baby's arrival in about an hour or so. Dr Bennett will be supervising the delivery," she continued.

"Thanks, matron, thanks a lot," was my relieved reply. I hung up, and pondered the situation. "Got to be positive," I mumbled, before grabbing my coat, and flying out of the door into the minus ten greeting of a winter's evening. It was one of the coldest nights I had ever known. I sat in the car for at least five minutes, allowing the engine to defrost the beautifully crystallised windscreen. It was a long, freezer-cold wait. At 2:30 a.m., with the radio turned to full volume, I sang along to Cliff Richard's old hits. However, I couldn't seem to get warm, and the atmosphere in the delivery room added to that coldness *another really strange scene...*

Dr Bennett was leaning over the naked body of my wife, who was lying motionless on the slab-like operating table that doubled as a delivery bed. Cold shivers ran down my back, and bad vibes clawed their way into my soul. The room itself was frugal, uncomfortable, and devoid of any of the warmth that Jo had previously desired. It seemed isolated, and disconnected *maybe it's just me. Maybe I've become tuned into a different wavelength.*

Dr Bennett smiled his usual smile. In the past, it had put me at my ease; but this time it did not. I moved quickly to Jo's side, held her hand tightly, and brushed the dampened hair off her forehead.

"How are you, love?" I asked.

"This is hard work," she gasped.

"Er, Stuart," the doctor interjected, "do you remember the time between contractions when Emma was born?" (I found out, much later, that the contractions had stopped completely)

"No idea," I replied, curiously. Small, old, brown wooden speakers were attached to her, via equally old loose wires, to a sort of heart monitoring device. They were emitting irritating hissing noises, and became the doctor's prolonged focus of attention.

"We should get these replaced," he said, tapping the antiquated equipment with his fingers. His brow began to furrow as he produced a stethoscope, and proceeded with the more trusted method of listening to the baby's heart. For the first time since I had known him, Dr Bennett's smile disappeared; and he removed the instrument from Jo's belly. "I'm going to perform a forceps delivery, Stuart, so I'd like you to wait outside."

"It's okay, I'll stay here," I answered firmly, gripping my wife's hand.

"I said outside!" he said authoritatively. Moments passed, during which the doctor and I held each other's eyes. They were knowing looks; and he nervously prepared to apply the forceps, while waiting for me to leave. "Please," he implored.

I kissed Jo's forlorn forehead, and looked into her eyes. Gone, were the sparkle and fire. Gone, were the confidence and fight. Yesterday, she had brimmed and bustled with the good life. Now, her beams of light were reduced to darkness and despair.

The outside corridor doubled as a waiting room. I tried, vainly, to wrench up some hope from the pit of my stomach, but none was forthcoming. The passageway became a lonely, isolated island, and a place from which there could be no rescue. It was as if I had written the script.

Dr Bennett exits the delivery room in a panic... Rushes to the Matron's office... Picks up the phone to call the Leicester Royal Infirmary...

Two minutes later, it happened. "This is Dr Bennett from the Market Harborough Cottage Hospital, and I have a major problem with a delivery... I need help urgently!" There was panic in his voice during the conversation. A doctors' work-to-rule ensured that his request was out of the question. He was advised to acquire an ambulance locally, and get her to Leicester as quickly as possible. Jo was in shock, and staring aimlessly.

My soul was screaming at her *Why? Why didn't you listen?*

Apart from the strobe-like effects of the flashing blue lights, and the occasional wailing of sirens, the journey by ambulance was made in silence. I could only hold her hand, and project my love to her.

Entering the Leicester Royal Infirmary's maternity section, at this point in the history of hospitals, was like being sucked into the jaws of hell. Chronic chaos reigned everywhere. Floors were covered in blood, and shoeless nurses tiptoed through the congealing conflagration. Just one on-duty registrar was desperately dealing with several emergencies simultaneously, and screamed oaths at the pathetic plight of the ailing NHS.

It was an hour before someone decided that our baby was dead, and I was not allowed to see my wife. A terrible inner turmoil raced through my being, battering my soul into senselessness. At 6:30 a.m. I was craving for a morsel of news - any news, when the ragged, blood-spattered registrar appeared suddenly, like an extra from a Hammer horror movie.

"Mr Sharp," he said anxiously, "we have to get your wife into theatre quickly, to repair a little tearing. I would like you to sign this form, allowing us to operate." It was obvious, from his desperate tone, and exhausted exterior, that he was not ready for questions. It was action only, and I signed speedily. Dr Bennett had visibly greyed in the last few hours, and was unable to offer any crumb of comfort.

This should have been a great day; but it was my daughter, Emma, who now filled my thoughts. She had formed a unique bond with the new baby, during Jo's pregnancy.

At 9 a.m. I decided not to make any calls to the family, before ensuring that the operation had been successfully completed. "Mr Sharp," said one of the nurses, "I think you should go home, and call back at lunch time." It was as if blackness had descended upon everybody and everything, when I broke the news.

At 2 p.m. I made a number of fruitless calls to the hospital, but was not getting any feedback. "What do you mean, she's still in surgery? I enquired angrily, "how can it take over four hours to repair a small tear?"

Every minute, every hour and every day that passed, sank us further into a paralysing pit of darkness. I was not a churchgoer, and so had no idea what to expect. I sat in a pew, shivering, and waiting patiently for the local vicar to arrive. The smell of snow was in the air, and my lack of religious intent was about to catch up with me.

Maidwell Parish Church nestled nicely in the quietly effusive countryside of Northamptonshire. However, it belied the drama and dogma that was shortly to be unleashed on my soul. The altar loomed large, in the murky half-light. Stained glass windows exuded eruditious sprays of colour, as a figure emerged from the vestry. I stood immediately, as if the king himself was entering the chamber.

We shook hands, exchanged a few pleasantries, and I took to him immediately. However, the bottom line for the Rev. Hilary-Davidson was simple. Ben could not be buried in the main area of the cemetery. A spot near the back wall was the only possible option. The vicar was full of compassion, but the rules were not, and I sank into the depths of my own soul for sanctuary. "At the far edge of the cemetery, is a place where you can bury him. No white headstone, mind you. It must be black. If you're not happy with these arrangements, you can always try elsewhere," were his final comments for me to ponder *black - so we are in the non-believers' box*. The option felt ungodly *Ben didn't get a chance to be a believer, so why penalise him*? I had already been beaten into the ground, and was totally devoid of the energy necessary to fight further.

The grey, leaden skies slowly emptied their crystallised contents, and thick folding snowflakes fell over the cemetery. I held Ben's shoebox of a coffin under my arm. The vicar headed my paltry procession, and my mother was the only mourner *I am not doing this. It can't really be happening.* It was like burying a small bird. Everything was tiny, and one spit of earth covered the coffin *another small soul destined to oblivion*. The devastating impact crushed my inner self, and the surreal scenario was soon replaced with the bitter chill of reality. I wept from my heart, and became fearful of the future. I was instantly both mother and father to Emma. My customers were looking forward to their Christmas dinners that I would be preparing in an hour or two. Jo was clinging on to life at the Leicester Royal Infirmary, and desperately needed the sight of her daughter to inspire her back to the land of the living.

I did my job almost as if all was well. The Christmas dinner party, for local farmers, went off without them knowing of my nightmare. I did not want to spoil their one chance in the year to let their hair down. My mother and Aunt Pat held the secret, as they served behind the bar. Emma was not yet aware of the situation, and was sleeping peacefully. She could dream about her mother, with her new baby brother or sister, returning home shortly. Sleeping over at the pub gave me the chance to play both parents to her, during my stint in the kitchen; but it wouldn't last long *tomorrow, she must know the truth.*

At long last, the pub was quiet. Then the sadness set in. We all pitched in, to clean the huge mess created by Christmas mayhem. No one spoke. No one had an answer. We all felt the grim reaper gripping our souls. Tomorrow would mean taking control of our emotions, for Emma's sake.

I kissed her forehead. She looked so happy. I could almost see her dreams, full of excitement and wonder. I hoped to God that I could find the words to explain, but the night was far from over. I crept along the creaking corridor to the spare bedroom, my mind a morass of hurt and guilt, then gazed into the gloomy half-light, through the poky bedroom window.

I was three years old; sitting at the window in 1947, with the bedclothes wrapped tightly around my shoulders. I felt trapped again, inexplicably looking out of the open window into the winter's icy blast. Wispy waves of snow drifted into the bedroom. I breathed in deeply, and felt the flakes gently tapping on my face. For one moment, the scene brought me peace.

I reflected on the horror of the previous twenty-four hours, with maybe worse to come. I wanted to fall into someone's arms, and let them take over my body and soul. Exhaustion, with no time to grieve, is a cruel cocktail to anyone to bear. *"You will find the strength,"* Sally's voice echoed in my head, and I peered hard into the centre of the storm.

"Oh, thank God," I whispered, as James and Sally floated towards me *are they outside, or in my head?* I wondered. Either way, I was relieved that they had arrived to support me. They knew the future, and their words always inspired me. I trusted them with all my heart. I stepped back, and sat on the bed. It was a repeat of the past.

"Come with us," she urged, in a loving tone. *In a flash of light, I was back at Ben's graveside, holding a spade in my hand. It was the same winter's night, and the snow had created a protective white blanket over Ben's lonely plot.*

Sally pointed. "Over there, we've made a space for Ben over there. Now dig." Within a minute, I was staring down at his tiny white coffin, before carefully carrying it to a plot in an area reserved for 'believers'. This is where he should be, I knew. I dug furiously, though the thick covering of snow had kept the earth warm and soft. Soon, it was ready, and the 'snow people' stood quietly by the opening, waiting for the new ceremony to begin.

My heart pounded, as I laid Ben to rest for a second time. I felt a great rush of wind, and saw Sally and James with arms outstretched to the heavens. An immense vortex of light descended down through the snowy sky, and hovered above Ben's coffin. Am I dreaming? Whatever my state of mind, I was determined to stay with it, to witness the unfolding drama. The 'snow people' calmed my shattered spirit, and I had a duty to respect that.

Distant angelic music began to accompany the swirling light. It grew in infinite intensity, and I gasped as the spirit of Ben rose slowly through the coffin. I couldn't bring myself to see him in the mortuary - I didn't have the courage. Now, he passed before my eyes. He was alive and beautiful. "I love you, Ben," I whispered, and kissed his soft cheek. He continued upwards. Suddenly, a choir of angels descended from the heavens, and Ben was caressed into their collective care. I looked at the 'snow people'.

Sally turned her gaze from the angels. "Now, listen," she requested. I stood motionless, and in awe. My heart became quiet. The music heralding Ben to his new home was breathtaking, and it lifted my spirit to the heavens. A divine angel floated down, and gazed at me. There was silence between us. She looked at the 'snow people' and smiled. With the angelic symphony filling the atmosphere, she began to sing. It was a beautiful song, and it saturated my soul.

"Ben is safe. Now, we have a gift for you," she said, with great reverence. "You will remember everything from the past, and in the future."

"Thank you, thank you," I replied, with humility.

The vision ended suddenly, as tears flowed from my eyes. The bedroom window was wide open, and snow coasted its way in. I couldn't move, and just lay there, reliving the events of the night over and over again *how can I remember the future, when it hasn't happened?* The music had captivated my spirit. It had lifted me from the depths, and continued to play on in my mind.

Emma was simply incredible. She took the news with a maturity, and a sense of the inevitable, that shook me. It was as if she had known. She stayed calm, as only a child can, and just wanted to see her mother.

34. The Aftermath

1976-1977

NOTE: While surgeons in the USA, and other parts of the world, carry the title 'Dr'; in the UK they are referred to as 'Mr'.

Mr Gordon Smart was the consultant urologist, and was not given to verbosity; nor was he someone who tolerated inefficiency, or poor professional attitudes. "Mr Sharp," he said, with candour, "your wife has sustained some of the worst injuries I have ever seen in all my experience; and when you get to asking questions, just make sure you get the right answers!"

Two days ago, we were a happy family; with a future, and a new baby on the way. Today was different. In an instant, everything had changed. The baby was dead, my wife's life lay in the balance, and our nice world had crashed. Yesterday was light. Today was darkness. It was the day of reckoning, and there was no escape from the sentence that I had handed to myself. From within my newly-constructed, solitary, inner prison, I had time to reflect *if knowledge is power, then I'd had the ability to save my own child; so why couldn't I do it?*

I was allowed to hold Jo's hand through the oxygen tent, where she lay hovering in the perverse twilight zone between life and death. Somehow, I had to encourage her to live. I felt like a corner man in a boxing match, just before the final bell "Come on Jo, fight... fight!" I urged desperately. She looked desperately ill and, at this point, the Hospital Authority had retreated into silence.

"You should make an appointment to see the consultant," was the reply from the ward sister, to my request for any information. Mr Smart, once again, did not beat around the bush. "I was called in to save your wife's life, Mr Sharp," he said rather clinically. As he detailed the extent of her injuries, my mind flicked back and forth to the vision, and I could feel the blood draining from my head.

He took a deep breath, and continued. "We are now in a life-threatening situation. Your wife could not have sustained the kind of time in theatre, which I required to carry out further major surgery; so it was vital that I patched her up and get her out of the anaesthetic." Mr Smart was doing his best to tell me that the surgeons involved in the repair work had saved her life and, regardless of the outcome, the main objective had been achieved. "However," he continued, "in a few weeks, we will have to take another look at her, and assess the situation again." He was obviously preparing the ground for further massive and traumatic surgery, although I was numb throughout the entire insane interview.

Following the funeral, I revisited the Cottage Hospital in Market Harborough. The matron was quiet, subdued, and on the verge of tears. "Mr Sharp," she said, "I'm so sorry. It was the most tragic night we have ever had here… it's so very, very sad."

I could not answer; because everything I wanted to say was obvious in the emotion I generated. I was full up, and ready to burst, with grief. I walked slowly out of her office, and through to the very corridor that was my Judas on that fateful night. I stopped outside the doors of the delivery room, and something in my soul urged me in.

I stood there, in a tormented trance; building up the courage to open the doors, and confront the snarling beast that had so hungrily taken away our son. The room was empty and still; and the sacrificial delivery slab stood there in its solitude, holding the secrets of life and death. It was an overwhelmingly painful experience, and an inexorable, formidable force drew me to that cursed centre stage. Visions of my wife, struggling to give birth, flooded back. A torrent of tears gushed from my eyes, and saturated the fresh white pillow that lay waiting for the next patient.

Once again, weeks turned into months; and the interminable daily routines drained me to the point of desperation. Emma and I became a team, and she agreed to stay with friends and her grandparents on my busy nights. I forced myself on, as any sign of weakness or negativity now could burst the bubble of hope for us all.

At long last, Mr Smart called me into his office, with news of a plan for another attempt to restructure my wife's internal organs. "Mr Sharp," he said, "we are going to move a few things around internally, in an effort to get her working again…" *What?* His detailed explanation of the operation was horrifying, and a sixth sense told me that it was all wrong.

Somewhere, in my heart, it did not feel right. I had no good feelings, and let fly with my first volley.

"It's as foolproof as it can possibly be;" he retorted angrily, and continued, "we are creating a situation where the possibility of a successful outcome is thoroughly expected."

I was searching for a chink in his armoury of certainty, in his next feat of surgical supremacy. I found one in the word 'possibility'. In my situation, it was necessary to hang onto every wayward word, in an effort to foresee the future.

With two hours left on the countdown, Jo's phobic fear of the surgeon's knife saw her shaking uncontrollably. "What if it doesn't work? I'll be in here for ever!" she cried hysterically.

"It will work, Jo... Doctor Smart says it's a great plan," I responded lovingly.

The next three weeks of waiting served only to prolong the pain. Once again, her weakened body was savagely brutalised; and her recovery was slow. I was on my own, now, as the gravity of Jo's predicament meant that Ben's death was not brought up; with the funeral only being discussed in the most peripheral terms. Life was all about focusing on her recovery, and nothing else mattered.

At long last, the days of waiting were over and, after all the surrealistic surgery, we hoped to have the answer. I had timed my visit to the hospital to coincide with Mr Smart's final curtain call; and stood behind the windowed doors of the ward, viewing the scene; but something was very wrong. The consultant, with his tired team, were as a swarm of vultures smelling death. I could not feel the vibrant pulse of life, and a gut feeling started to pull, yet again, another veil of blackness over my eyes.

Abruptly, Mr Smart marched away from his patient, leaving his regalia of registrars in attendance. The ward doors flew wide open, and the gangling 6' 4" urologist blustered his way along the corridor, in a storm of anarchic anger. Through the doors, which were still open from the force of the surgeon's enigmatic exit, I caught a glimpse of Jo's reddened and distraught face. It was all over. Another operation had turned into a major disaster. I dropped my head in instant abject weariness, and felt my body slide into a nauseating numbness.

I slumped onto a chair, and waited for the assuaging abyss to swallow the dregs of my being. I could hear the quietly insistent tones of the ward sister, "Mr Sharp... Oh, Mr Sharp. I am so sorry," she said compassionately, adding, "Can you pull yourself together and see your wife... she really needs you now... come on, love."

I was physically and emotionally spent. *What good can I be to her, now?* I thought, as she hauled me through the doors to my wife's side. Jo was in the deepest depths of despair.

"They just left me. It didn't work... What the hell's going to happen now?" Our worst fears had been realised, and we both felt crushed and discarded by the system. Leicester Royal's 'Lord of the

Rings' had retreated to his holy hideout. It seemed as if we were in the vortex of a wicked whirlwind, being flung around in the epicentre of its centrifuge. There was no way up, and no way down; but the music in my mind was making things clearer. The 'Eureka' moment arrived like a bolt from the blue, but it left me on the horns of dilemma.

It was over a week before I could acquire an appointment to see Gordon Smart. For him it had been a major defeat. He had planned the new operation like a military campaign; he was the best there was; and he had failed. It had taken him a week to regroup, re-think and re-plan; but by now, I had lost all faith in his bespoke ability. My confidence had crashed, along with my faith in the faltering system. The nerve-jangling journey, to Mr Smart's consulting room, filled me with dread. He simply could not understand why it had failed.

"She really must have a very poor blood supply to the area, for infection to set in like this," he said coarsely, "but," he added, "I'm going to try and fix it internally; and if that doesn't work, in a few month's time we will..." At this point I switched off and, without a word of acknowledgement, gathered my tired and aching body together, and walked out of his office.

I will never know what made the staff nurse do it. Maybe she felt sorry for our situation. Whatever it was, she was about to put her whole future at risk for us. "Mr Sharp," she said quietly, "can we have a chat?" She was agitated, and wrestled with her words. "Let's talk in my office," she continued, and added, "I can't see you go on any longer like this, and what I am about to say will get me instant dismissal if you repeat it."

Once inside her comfort zone, she took a deep breath, and blurted it out. "They're experimenting on your wife. They're not sure what they're doing. My advice to you is to get a second opinion."

Her words galvanised my ailing spirit into action, and my next visit to Gordon Smart would be different. *Here we go again* the consultant had worked out a new modus operandi. His tiny office, hidden beneath the labyrinth of corridors, was beginning to get me down. I now understood the game. Things were to finally be on my terms; and I decided to act, and rid us of this hopeless hospital, once and for all.

He made an unashamed explanation, of the plan to attack my wife's defenceless body once more; but as his words blurred into a jumble of incoherent injustices, I stopped him in full flight, and ended his surgical project that was my wife. It felt good. I was in control for the first time, and I was going to get that second opinion at all costs. I put power and authority into my request, leaving him in no doubt that I meant business.

In what I considered the strangest twist yet, to our personal ongoing tragedy; something in him slumped, and he acquiesced immediately. The consultant's lofty supremacy set him above all his rivals, and it would have been a classical impudence for him to feel that he could charge in once again. But this time, it was not to be. The campaign needed a new general. For the first time, in nearly a year, I had become alive; and blood was running fast through my veins *something extraordinary is going to happen*.

He called St. Thomas' Hospital in London, and asked to speak to Wyndham Lloyd-Davies, their consultant urologist. From the moment I heard his name, I knew it to be a great mantle. It had all the right sentiments, and reflected compassion and erudite eminence. It exuded only good things, including a promise that we were not to be disappointed.

It was a year since Jo's traumatic trials at Market Harborough Cottage Hospital, and the cycle of seasons had completed. This was a new day, and a time to erase the previous twelve months from our minds.

He was the antithesis of the archetypal, cloistered consultant. Not towering; not glowering. He was a warm human being; who talked the language of love, and had a kindness that melted into every nuance of his voice. He was a pioneer, working on the very frontiers of microsurgery, and what he was about to say would shock us. The advance guard, of my wife's notes, had been received by the new great man in our lives; and he was well versed with the case.

"Well," he said, looking up from the notes, "This is a horror story," adding, "I just can't believe this is the same National Health Service that I work in…" He stroked his chin and continued, "The operations, the ones that you had in Leicester - they had already failed ten years ago. They were never going to work!" He paused. Wyndham Lloyd-Davies was clearing the decks, with a totally honest appraisal. We waited, motionless and speechless, for him to continue.

"Look, my dear," he said comfortingly, "I can offer you this. I can repair all the damage done in Leicester, and put you on the road to recovery; although I don't pretend it's going to be easy. Quite frankly," he continued, "if you like the look of the beast, you can stay here; and we can move quickly to resolve this dreadful situation. The object of the exercise last year was to produce a baby. Now, since that is never going to be possible again, have you looked at adoption?"

I was sincerely tempted to say, "Adoption? You must be joking!" My vision, of being able to adopt a child, had been heavily clouded by the situation into which we had been dumped, through no fault of our own. Therefore, I felt it to be our inalienable right. However, I had already written to every agency, including the Agnostic's Adoption Society, with no success. The local authority in Northampton had been the most sympathetic, and asked us to re-apply in the next five to ten years. I informed him of Northampton's response.

"Don't give up hope in that direction; but first things first," he chirped, We'll find a nice single ward for your wife, overlooking the Thames and the Houses of Parliament," he added compassionately. His meticulous preparations for the microsurgery made it appear that the operation had all the complexities and dangers of Man's first space flight. Even with his outstanding skills, Wyndham Lloyd-Davies still worried that the major internal scarring, which she had previously sustained, could upset the precarious balance of things to come.

Soft, gentle snowflakes were settling on the Houses of Parliament. Winter had arrived, and the tower of Big Ben looked strong and proud in its illuminated glory. The River Thames reflected past history; as it glistened its way beneath the hospital, and flowed under Westminster Bridge. I watched this prosaic picture for hours, from the insulated security of Jo's private ward; and I could hear the great clock preparing to strike midnight. Many people were hurrying and scurrying across the bridge, having revelled in pre-Christmas parties. *Lucky buggers!* I thought, as I looked down at my wife; now deeply unconscious, after surgery earlier that evening. Lloyd-Davies had done his stuff during the day, and I'd made the journey from the murkiness of the Midlands to be with her. Time was irrelevant, and I knew that our caring consultant would now be enjoying a party somewhere in London.

"Mr Sharp," echoed a voice, seemingly out of nowhere. I turned from my wondrous window view of Westminster, to see Lloyd-Davies looking tired and untrendy in his old raincoat. He smiled, and proceeded to check the various tubes and drips that were attached all over her body. "Everything's looking fine," he stated, and beckoned me to step outside the room.

These midnight ministrations of Lloyd-Davies proved, once again, that his concentrated commitment, displayed throughout this treatment, would continue. "Well," he said ruefully, "we just need a bit of luck now. I can tell you, it was a pantomime when I got in there, but," he sighed, "it's all gone well... I even closed myself."

It was the first time I had heard that something extra, in the form of luck, was necessary for the eventual success of his work. The day of judgement finally, and painstakingly, arrived; making it a crucial time for the surgeon and his team. He had put his reputation on the line. Having taken up a position outside the ward, I could see the consultant and his prodigies slowly and cautiously proceeding with what, they hoped, would be the final phase of their work. A quiet tranquillity fell over the room as he removed the lifeline of tubes, effectively putting her into freefall.

The registrar broke the silence. "There appears to be a little dampness here," he said, pointing to an area at the bottom of the long, vicious-looking scar. My heart stopped for a few seconds; then began again with beats that thumped in my chest, until I was forced to physically hold myself. Lloyd-Davies blotted the offending region, and replied belatedly, "It's from the outside incision... not a problem." Every second that passed, was good news. We were now five minutes into a 'go situation'.

As we hit ten-minutes, the hovering consultant and his team were still gazing intently at her abdomen. Lloyd-Davies ended the interminable silence. "Okay, we've made it, I'm sure," he said, with a positive professionalism. It was the greatest music in the world to my ears.

I could see delight creeping over the faces of the dedicated doctors who surrounded my wife. Wyndham Lloyd-Davies had done it. He had shown superb skill, and proved that he was the master. He had succeeded against a background of obsolete operations, which had instigated insidious internal injuries to my wife. He had also proved the staff nurse, at The Leicester Royal Infirmary, to be correct in her observations.

He was a hero; and he held Jo's hand, offering hard-earned congratulations. She had displayed incredible courage, throughout a nightmare of monstrous proportions.

Rivulets of tears streamed down her face, but this time they were of joy and enduring relief that, at long last, she could live again. "Thank you. Thank you," she whispered, from the bottom of her soul, "I don't know how to repay you."

"No need," he answered humbly, "We'll keep you here for a few weeks, and get you fit enough to go home," he concluded, smiling broadly. I was tempted to rush into the ward, and hug him; but to Lloyd-Davies, it was simply what he did. For Jo and I, it was so very different. He had released us from an ordeal of emotional torture within a dungeon of darkness. He was a crusader, whose courage and skill had rekindled our spirits, tended our wounds, and led us to a path of light.

Her discharge from St Thomas' was a day of true celebration, and with it came a final meeting with Lloyd-Davies. "Right," he said in a business-like way, "is there any more news about your application for adoption?"

"No," I replied.

"Right," he interjected, "the Northampton Authority owes me a few favours, and we certainly owe you some, so this is what you do." He was a consultant on a roll, determined to put the icing on a cake of wonder, for mere mortals such as us. He continued, "Go back, make a full application, and I'll do the rest!"

Those were the last words that we would hear from that unbelievable man. Our bond with two-week old Kate had been forged well before she was born and, somehow, fate and Wyndham Lloyd-Davies had ensured it. What a learning process it was, and special spirits had been flying all over the place. It had begun as a vision, showing Ben dying; and had ended with a new life coming into our own. Baby Kate had unknowingly waved a magic wand and, miraculously, Jo was happy again. It was almost instantaneous.

35. Reflections

1978

How can one go through such horror, then be fixed so quickly? One second flattened, and the next fine. Five pounds of flesh and blood, in the form of a newly adopted baby, had completely regenerated her. Surviving this experience successfully relied on trusting in the unknown. I still wondered how life would have turned out, if I had forced the issue; and taken my wife to the city hospital in the critical hours.

Jo had fought hard to recover, and her life seemed set fair. It meant all hands to the deck for Emma and Kate; and some sort of a routine was established. I reflected on our time together *the 'snow people' have got it right. This can't go on indefinitely.*

I was a cook, working night and day. Arriving home, at indecent hours of the morning, smelling of chip fat and smoke, was not the ideal image of a winner. Jo kept her countenance, but I knew that our marriage was descending into a dark period. Nothing had been said, but the vibes were not good. It could take years, to build up a catering client base that matched her vision of a successful partner, I mused; and working harder just didn't 'cut the mustard' *working smarter might…* Jo had been comparing me to local businessmen, and I knew that I was way down in the regional rankings.

The voices from James and Sally continued unabated, making it clear that good things would result. However, the transitional period was getting me down, and only my inner guides knew that ultimate success was there for the taking. Alcohol, however, was readily available, and I took to it like a duck to water. It made me happy, and it released the torrid tension of another night in the kitchen. Our aspirations, to knit together a normal life, were fading fast.

A wormhole was needed, to bridge the vastness of my time schedule to success. The music and visions had gathered momentum and, during Jo's absence in hospital, great symphonies and songs were now locked in my head. The 'snow people' had visited me with visions, regularly taking me on trips into the future. Journeys to London, Africa, America, Canada, France, Germany, Sweden, Afghanistan, Pakistan, Australia and others were indicated. It was almost laughable.

"You must go to London soon," said Sally. "The journey to find your respect starts there." This message had reverberated in my head for months. Sometimes James and Sally actually manifested; but at other times, only their voices were heard. Recently, it had been only the latter, and I learned to accept whatever method they used. Now, they had spiked me directly onto the horns of another dilemma. Every time I pondered a move into the future, I became fearful with trepidation. Every day I shook, just thinking about it.

I knew where I stood with my wife. I could feel it. On reflection, I had no idea why Jo had married me. She was sophisticated, academically inclined, and played the piano. I was not qualified to do anything, and inclined to labouring. Matchmakers, today, would have laughed at such a union.

I had thought about her constantly, after the fateful village hall hop when we were sixteen years of age. Being a pillion passenger, on my two-seater moped, was a bit of a hoot; but signalled a lowering of her transportation standards. I was surprised at her acceptance of my dating offer, and felt my immature ego inflate; but the runes were against us. Her teetotal parents were philosophically opposed to my unsavoury liaison with their daughter. My mother also had her own network of informants, and knew every move I made.

For entirely arbitrary reasons, I thought, she strongly advised me against dating Jo. "She's not your type," mother blasted, on more than one occasion. "You'll live to regret it." I'd scratched my head in confusion, but was delighted to be dating someone of greater intelligence than myself; so was preparing for a battle royal to keep her. It also gave me some standing amongst my peers, as I was levelling up at last *I need to prove them all wrong, so first things first*.

My seventeenth birthday was looming; and I was motivated to pass my driving test, acquire a highly paid drayman's job at the brewery at eleven pounds per week, and buy a car; to impress her. Our dating had suddenly ebbed away and, although I wasn't sure why, it was either Jo or nobody for me.

I had found solace at the hillside, where Joey had squawked his last goodbye. The enduring elements, in the changing seasons, filled my spirit with energy and enthusiasm. I could chatter away, unheard by anyone, to the forces beyond. It was a special place of safety and solitude. I was becoming comfortable with my own company and, even around many people, I felt detached *I may as well be from another planet*; but there was something special about Jo, that I admired. She was self-opinionated, stubborn, exciting, demanding, kind, caring, and full of hope for the future. It was a powerful potion, full of contradictions, courage and commitment. I could only hope and pray that the vision of our life together would manifest.

"Right, young man, pass your driving test next week, and you can start on the lorries." The brewery manager's sudden statement took me off guard. Working as an assistant in the warehouse had been sheer blood, sweat and tears; and I had witnessed, at first hand, exactly how much intense physical effort was required to be a drayman. The lorries were lumbering behemoths of machines, which created curse-laden tailbacks on any road they trundled along. Power steering was unheard of. This job had been my dream for months. Draymen were the pinnacle of the brewery staff, and the highest earners. With such a job, a car would be within my grasp.

I could also drive around her village and, purely by chance of course, stop if I saw her wandering around her habitat. *"Oh, hello, Jo. What a coincidence seeing you. I'm just passing through, on my way to Leicester,"* Might as well rehearse the line now because, as sure as eggs is eggs, I'm going to do it. "Thanks, boss," I replied edgily, "I'll pass."

36. Tying the Knot

1966

The wedding reception was more like the dividing line between heaven and hell. Jo's family glued themselves to the safety of an old wood-panelled back wall, in an effort to distance themselves from the Sharps. They looked, in nervous apprehension, at my alcoholic alibis of a family; who made the most of the gin and tonics that they'd smuggled in, via handbags and deep coat pockets; after an alcohol-free send-off had been planned. The Sharps were as ribald as the Dunmores were respectful; and the twain would never meet. It was the oddest of omens. Their daughter had married into the devil's own den. I was glad, and relieved, that she saw the funny side of it. Jo had spent her childhood in a puritanical place, and was now a rebel. I liked that. We'd had our ups and downs, in the previous four years of dating but, generally speaking, we got on well.

I tried hard to distance myself from the Red Lion, simply by not talking about it in her parents' company. I'd been elevated to the position of manager at the brewery, after years of driving beer wagons around the country; though I was surprised to have not lost my job on the first day.

From driving a tiny Triumph Herald, to heaving a two-ton truck around, without so much as a by-your-leave; was a disaster in the making. I lost my load of beer on the first roundabout, and flooded the road with a river of ale. Mountains of broken beer bottles poked through the developing frothy sea, and cut the main road off in both directions. I saw it all happen, as if in slow motion, in my rear view mirror; and the explosive impact was both impressive and frightening. I certainly made a name for myself within the company, and the incident ended up on the managing director's desk; as it cost the company over a thousand pounds.

As we drove off to our honeymoon, in Wales; I thought about the moment I'd passed my driving test. Without that bit of paper, we would probably not be married. I had originally been handed a real labourer's job; but became a top earner, and the car quickly became a reality. What a difference that, and a bit of cash, made. I smiled. We were going places fast. Jo's income, as a dental hygienist, ensured our first house purchase.

The 'snow people' were right - good things had resulted; but they had not visited for years. Maybe they felt that their job was over. Maybe they were jealous. Maybe they were waiting for the next trauma *I must stop thinking like this*. Mother had missed my company at the pub; and though we tried to visit at weekends, it eventually became a rare event.

They just stood there at the window, the moon's glow shining right through them. Jo was sleeping, and my sixth sense alerted me to their presence. I knew that, when I opened my eyes, they would be there *now we have a problem. They'll have a grandstand view of our night time activities.* I had to get a grip of my imagination. They did not speak, and disappeared in an instant.

Sleeping was now impossible. I reminisced about the time they had guided me to the whereabouts of my missing father, when I was eighteen. Mother was desperate for a divorce, but his signature was needed to finalise the details. The police had failed to find his lair, and so I took off to Luton on a whim *how do you find someone in a large town without an address? He might have left the country*. Nevertheless, I'd found mother's teeth, in a vast swelling ocean; and located Grace's eternity ring in a huge field.

With the help of the 'snow people', finding my father should be easy, I deliberated - and it was. I knocked on a door, which could have been any door. It opened, and a very nice lady presented herself. "Oh, hello, Stuart," she offered gently, "I've been expecting you." She'd recognised me instantly, from a picture father had kept of me when I was child. "You haven't changed a bit. How did you find us?" Inside the semi-detached council house, playing in the corner, were two small children. She pointed to them, "That one's your Dad's, and that one's mine."

"Mmm," I responded. "Fine." She desperately wanted me to hang on until he returned from work, as a welder somewhere in the city; but my job was complete. He had created a new secret family, and she seemed to be handling things very well, so there was nothing more to be said.

Mother got her divorce some six months later. My father attended court looking a dishevelled mess, and claiming poverty *smart move!* The judge gave him a severe ticking off; and awarded mother a pound a month, which she never received.

37. Cry for Help

1968 - 1969

It was another night of visions. *Mother was crying, and her hand was begging me to help her. She was in a fog, and I couldn't reach her. I didn't like the images, and forced myself to abandon the scene.* Married life had taken me further away from my mother; as it had done to Jo, from her parents.

This sea is too smooth. Everything had become like clockwork. Work, tend the garden, go to bed. I cut the grass to perfection, and Jo became a prima donna of plants. 'Work, tend the garden, go to bed' became strangely and uncomfortably predictable; and I missed the unpredictability of the pub life. We had agreed not to have children, as we were far too selfish for that. Well, that's what friends and neighbours happily concluded. I have never been sure of what changed; only that it came out of the blue.

"I want a baby," she exclaimed. I was perplexed and shocked, and no appropriate response came to my mind. The decision not to have children was the basis on which we'd married. It was a binding contract, which was suddenly about to be contested. All the 'buts' I could think of were shot down. *None of this makes sense,* I thought, as there had been no build up to her new feelings. They had simply arrived in the space of a moment.

Out on the distant horizon of our life, a storm was brewing. The calm seas were about to change. Squalls, and blustery winds, hit us in waves. A miscarriage was one of them; followed by another.

"What on earth is a retroverted uterus?" I asked, on her return from yet another trip to the consultant *this is why we were never meant to have children.*

The storm was gathering in intensity, when I received a devastating call from my mother. I held my head in disbelief. The Northampton Brewery Company, who owned the pub, had sold it to Watneys; and they, in turn, served notice on my mother to quit.

It was a loss-making venture for the new owners, and they wanted it off their books; twelve months' notice being all that they were required to provide. Her twelve years of hard grind was about to be destroyed.

A buyout was the second option offered by the brewery; but a cash sale price of four and a half thousand pounds was a mountain of money, not possessed by family members, so we were her only hope.

It was as if some kind of time warp had hit us. Seven years had been wiped out, but cash from the sale of our house purchased mother's pub; and we became joined at the hip, as partners with my family. It was much more than a financial sacrifice for Jo. The pub had declined since my departure, and needed a real boost of energy. The practical necessities, of providing a new way forward for the pub, pushed us on. I took the plunge, created a café atmosphere within the bar, and food became an option for our customers.

It was a revolutionary move, and quickly dismissed as a nonstarter by the locals. Pubs were for drinking and smoking, and they complained bitterly. They hated the smell exuding from the fish fryers, and drifted away to other establishments. The already pitiful takings dropped to almost zero. We had bought the pub, and saved mother from eviction; but I had destroyed what little trade they had survived on. Pat became hysterical. Bob was overwhelmed by the forces reigned against him. Jo found work in the local town, and we rented a cottage close by. Mother felt that I should stop the cooking facility; find work, as Jo had done, and become a sleeping partner.

A perfect storm had gathered, and now arrived with a vengeance. Suddenly, I became a figure of hatred. Jo saw my gamble begin to fail, and potentially damage our relationship. I promised her that I would create a successful catering business.

"This is only a short term setback," I explained; but our cosy existence had been shattered, and children were no longer a topic of conversation. Jo's trust in my judgement had taken a severe knock.

"You have to win them over." Sally's voice echoed, over and over again, in my head.

"Why can't I see you anymore?" I implored to the heavens. Then the visions started. The detail was extraordinary. I watched myself providing free meals to the locals, and becoming very successful. It was another 'Eureka' moment. *"Yes,"* I shouted to myself. *"I've got it; I understand what you are doing. Thank you."* However, the cold light of day always brought a chill of reality to the previous night's excursion into the future. Mother, Pat and Bob were depressed, and their body language became negative towards me. They did not have the vision necessary to move forward, in the way that I described.

"Giving food away is madness!" my mother exclaimed. "The smell alone is driving my customers away!"

The visions, brushed into my brain by the 'snow people', will be a tough assignment. This is going to be my first test, and it has to be done in bite-sized chunks. I wasn't used to working with a team; but if my plan was to succeed, I needed the whole family on board. What seemed totally implausible, required the full support of my mother to sell it to her customers. A loss leader, in the form of a basket of chips, was a concept unheard of in the area; and mother was the greatest salesperson I knew. She had a sparkling personality and 'brummie' sense of humour that crossed all barriers *if I can harness this, we're onto a winner.* The deal was done, and the trial would last a month. Failure meant that both food, and myself, would be off the menu for good.

Locals were steeped in obstinate cultural routines, and their farming lives were well-ordered. They lived by the good earth, and its never-ending clockwork efficiency. Food was always taken at specific times, and prepared by their slaves; but they had an 'Achilles heel'. Old Cooper was typical of the miserly, penny-pinching lives they lived. They exuded poverty, but owned great swathes of land. Their acreage was not viewed as a capital gain, because inflation was unheard of. It was simply a means to an end. Growing and producing things was their sole aim, but saving a farthing was an achievement to them.

I advertised the new, free menu on a blackboard in the bar. Cooper was the ringleader of the farming fraternity whose business barely kept the pub alive. If he fell for the idea, then the rest would follow. Hence, part two of the plan, which meant buying my potatoes from him. The purchase at retail, rather than wholesale price, made him a nice profit. As a bonus, he would receive a free basket of his own potatoes, fried to perfection, whenever he desired. It took three weeks for the scheme to click into action. During this period, we teetered on the edge of bankruptcy; as the farmers' counter-strategy, designed to freeze me out, started to bite.

Splitting their loyalties, between the Red Lion and the Bulls Head, meant a drive of three miles to the next village. After a night's drinking; the dark dusty road became dangerous terrain, and their insidious intention to boss our business was on the verge of success. Friday nights had gradually become tombstone territory for the pub, and it was a demoralising and depressing sight. Then, suddenly, it happened. The roar of vehicles arriving in the car park lifted our spirits. The farmers were back.

"Give me a basket of them there chips," Cooper blustered.

"And me! And me!" the cry continued.

I lost five pounds on the evening, but mother had doubled her usual Friday night's takings. I was back in business, but the trials and tribulations reminded me of why Hilary had planned and executed the perfect exit strategy from the pub, in her teens. Her marriage, to engineer Roger Hunt, sent a powerful message to the family. She would not go down the road of dysfunctionality, and her life from there on would be the antithesis of the madness that we had endured as children. I was envious of her ability to let it go, but my mother induced an inexorable force on my spirit. I was in awe of the 4 foot 11 inch lady's fearless ability to face the greatest of adversities.

Her lack of a formal education and social graces was a phenomenal asset for the pub life. She slapped strapping 6 foot 5 inch men if they got out of hand; and continued attacking them, as she chased them off the premises. Nothing, and no-one, intimidated her; and she brought every conversation down to the lowest common denominator. She held a poisoned chalice in her hand, and drinking from it would forever enslave you to her. She was one of those rare human beings who are instantly likeable; and the rich and famous, to the lame and lowly, loved her company.

38. Cooking the Books

1969 - 1970

The bank would not approve an overdraft facility. I pushed and prodded the manager, but he would not budge. I needed five hundred pounds to purchase professional catering equipment, but he saw it as a financial flop; stating, "The business is not viable."

A single frying pan was the sole contender for my burgeoning business plan. Producing fried fish, to accompany the fried chips, would be an expression of Einsteinian eloquence; but it didn't seem possible. There wasn't enough room in the pan for both the fish and the chips. Fish needed deeper oil than the chips; and the cooking times were different. It was a baffling conundrum. I was back in the farmers' good books, though, and had received my first paid order for two fish and chips to take away.

Then it hit me. I must take the chance of part-cooking the fish and chips before the evening's trade began. Once they sold, the same procedure would be adopted, although the operation would require precise timing. Anything left over, would be food for the family; I planned.

39. À La Carte

1971

It was a new record for a Saturday night. I had cooked one hundred three course meals, and counted every penny of the five hundred pounds with glee. Although I had been totally focused on the headlong rush to create this success, to the exclusion of my relationship, I expected to feel the love, by return, as a right. However, my immature, smelly existence of a day and night cook did not augur well with romance. My heart felt sad, but drowning my eviscerated emotion in alcohol only served to hold my head firmly down under the sand.

The voices had shown me the way to success, but the journey required great commitment and sacrifice. Mother, Pat and Bob, however, were overjoyed with the success of the business, and we began plans to expand. The bank manager was suitably embarrassed, but secretly delighted. The Red Lion became the talk of the town. Within two years, the pub had been transformed, and customers came from far and wide, to join in our own brand of 'Fawlty Towers' type fun.

40. Music Mayhem

1978 - 1979

The visions had become intolerable. Every genre of music, and the images of world travel, crowned every cell in my brain. Although the 'snow people' had long ceased to make appearances, they had not left me entirely unaided. Over the years, they had trained me to see the future as a movie. The grill in my kitchen became a video screen, and I burned many a steak as I was sucked into the sights.

There was almost no sleep. As I closed my eyes; I saw, clearly, the journey ahead, in great detail. It would not let me go, and alcohol only accentuated my dilemma. To tell, or not to tell Jo, became a game. I would try, and then give up. It came out in fits and starts. I made her nervous, with strange comments about becoming a composer and filmmaker travelling the world *if I push this too far, I could be sectioned.* Therapy was a suggestion.

I had died, unexpectedly. Jo found my body slumped at the front door. I had consumed two bottles of whisky during the evening; making it back to the house, but collapsing before I could enter. The local undertakers picked up my body, which fell apart in their hands. Clumps of skin were draped over the coffin, and lime was thrown over my emaciated corpse. "This is what sclerosis of the liver can do. I've seen it before." I was dead, but could hear the undertaker's pronouncement to Jo.

It was a visionary vignette, which drew a line in the sand; and I lay next to Jo, shaking. This was my future life flashing before my eyes. If I continued working at the pub, I would never live long enough to see Emma and Kate grow into adulthood. The time had come to leave for London, as the vision had required.

All hell broke loose; both at home, and at the pub. "Six months' notice?" my mother sobbed. We talked for hours, and I unburdened my vast vision to her. Then my mother remembered the visit to the clairvoyant in 1947. She worried about the business without me (I knew it would devastate them), but she just hugged me, and prayed.

Jo couldn't deal with my decision. "It's a journey into the unknown, with no safety net!" she exclaimed angrily, knowing that it would ruin our family unit. Both mother and Jo prayed for a change of mind during my notice period.

41. London Bound

1979 - 1980

London's North Circular left me lost and frustrated, and I turned off in desperation. I had never seen traffic like this, but I had never driven in London before. My old Ford Cortina estate held my few possessions and, while the November night was no time to become a homeless soul, I felt strangely at peace.

Jumping off the cliff, without a safety rope, was an exciting leap of faith. I was in freefall, and could feel the spiritual wind blowing through my body. My car was my new home, and I was now free to pursue my vision with some semblance of serenity. I also saw it as madness. I had one chance to turn back and become normal again, and one part of my mind desperately wanted to do this. The other part was stronger, and refused such a thought.

The Wembley Squash Centre came into view and, on an impulse, I swerved quickly into the car park and found a vacant spot behind the rubbish bins. *What a great stroke of luck,* I thought, before it occurred to me that it wasn't *I was meant to arrive here*. I strolled into the centre, which comprised over twenty squash courts, changing rooms, showers and a café/reception area. The car park was huge, and devoid of security. It was perfect.

I had left a cacophony of chaos behind. The pub went downhill, and was sold. Mother, Pat and Bob retired to Cornwall. Jo remarried, and I became a pariah. Following my impossible visions was equated with psychosis, which obviously required medical attention. My chance to totally trust the 'snow people' had arrived. The movie in my mind played over and over again, accompanied by wonderful music; but there was a missing piece of the puzzle. I prayed that the answer would come soon.

Being an actor, in my own film, was a thought that needed to be firmly strapped to my consciousness, and never released; but there was currently a gigantic gulf between travelling the world, as a successful composer, meeting presidents and pop stars; and living in my car in a pokey car park in Wembley, London *maybe I'm going mad*.

I broke down, and sobbed uncontrollably. Jo had given me every opportunity to return, get help, and restore the equilibrium; but it was not to be. I missed Emma and Kate desperately; and was crawling with hurt and indignation, knowing that they had integrated into a new family, with a sane and sensible step-father. I was no longer their father, or even a person. I was just a memory from their childhood.

These thoughts wounded and inspired me at the same time. Jo had fully committed herself to her new marriage, and it took a lot of courage for her to begin again. Although not required, my priority was sending cash to her on a regular basis, to help support my girls. I had free accommodation in my car, allowing any spare cash, from casual jobs, to be sent to them. Inevitably, though, the car's tax and insurance were ready to run out. The vehicle needed to be sold, and I gasped at the thought of living rough.

I rustled the two hundred pounds, in crisp ten-pound notes, in my hand, took a deep breath, and mentally assigned a hundred to Jo as I waved goodbye to the car now being driven out of the Wembley Squash Centre car park. This was a dark day; and I stood in silent thought, with a sleeping bag in one hand, and a kit bag in the other.

My squash playing skills had become a vital asset to my survival. Unbeknown to the management, I hustled business from unsuspecting low-level players for one pound an hour. The showers had a dual purpose. They kept me smell-free, and were a perfect place to wash my smalls. Their giant central heating system ran along great hot pipes, underneath the seating area in the changing room; and this became my drying area. The secret to my future survival in London lay in my ability to secure free accommodation.

Years were to pass, moving from one squat to another, and feeling more and more non-human. In exchange for occasional free accommodation, I supplied my services to a top squash coach. I offered to work for nothing, in exchange for a room at a pub in Shepherd's Bush. Living on the street was better, as it meant that I didn't have to barter for a room. I did not see myself as a vagrant - I was a composer, an author, an athlete, and a filmmaker.

Sitting on the pavement, opposite the BBC Television Studios in Wood Lane, writing out my vision, gave me a sense of self-worth. I stood out. People stopped, and chatted with me. "I'm writing a book, and composing music," I offered enthusiastically. *This is a vital chapter,* I pondered; while wandering aimlessly around the back streets of Acton, to pass the time, and think. My present squat was a derelict building, associated with a hostel for the homeless. I visited the hostel a few times looking for work, but the owner was a wealthy businessman, and difficult to track down.

I stopped at a second-hand furniture shop, where a guitar caught my eye. The manager claimed that one pound was a great bargain, so I offered the fifty pence I had left in my pocket. The assistant shrugged it off, and turned abruptly away *pity...* I also shrugged, and walked out. "Oi, mate, come back. You can 'ave it," was his almost belated cry. I was shocked, and ran back to the shop, where he blurted out "I shouldn't do this, but gimme your 50p quick..."

42. Two Years Later

1982

The complex multi-genre compositions in my head flowed out onto the guitar. I was mentally detached from my fingers, as they sped seamlessly from fret to fret *now this is a miracle!* I had never given up on my vision; and now had confirmation, for the first time, that it was real. The second-hand shop in Acton was a time-travelling Tardis, and another fifty pence bought me a tatty old tape recorder that was sitting on the sales bench. My heart sang with joy. I pressed the record button, and began. It was a double-sided tape, with ninety minutes duration, and the musical dream was about to be born. I can barely remember filling both sides of the tape with music and song. Most of what I recorded was a blur, as over thirty fully formed pieces of music magnetically attached themselves to the tape.

Two days later, it was back to heart-wrenching reality; as I found myself staring inanely at the BBC Television Studios once more. The pavement provided a thorny bed to rest my weary bones. I saw him out of the corner of my eye; his burly frame, and businesslike strident gait, belying the compassion to come. He stopped suddenly, looked down, and smiled. "What are you writing?" he asked. I was always happy to chat, but there was something special about this man. His tone was different, he was genuinely interested, and already felt like a friend.

Anthony Wade gave me an hour of his precious time. I have no idea why I told him my life story. It just seemed right, even though I risked losing his attention. "Hmm," he mused, before wishing me well, and walking on. He'd made me feel good, and I continued writing. I looked up with a start. He had returned, and stood over me like a giant. His offer caught me off guard, and I asked him to repeat it.

"I'll pick you up here in a few hours, and you can come and stay with me for a while." I was open-mouthed with shock. "I'm a jazz pianist. I'd like to listen to your tape," he offered. I happily agreed, and felt totally bemused as he left.

His generosity was overwhelming. His wife nervously prepared a bowl of soup, and tried to ascertain if I was musician or madman. She was not expecting a stay-over. This was supposed to be a session of music with her husband, and then goodbye. He was a night owl, and we talked into the early hours. With lights dimmed, he listened to all ninety minutes of my tape without a word. Picking out Angeli as his favourite, after a few more listens he proceeded to flesh out parts on his piano.

Eventually, he shook his head and stated, "If this piece was orchestrated, and recorded by a major orchestra, you'd have a masterpiece." He stroked his chin, and pondered the situation. "It's almost impossible to believe that you've written so many types of music, and laid it all down on tape in one continuous session… straight out of your head! It all needs to be recorded by top artists and orchestras; but that, my friend, would cost a fortune."

His wife was beside herself with worry, as I stayed almost six weeks as their guest so, inevitably, it was time to bid a grateful farewell. I made it clear that I would be back one day, with the cash to finance the artists and orchestras.

"Best of luck," was his parting comment. He dropped me off in Shepherds Bush, and it was back to the streets.

43. Hostel Bound
(...Seven Years Later)
1989

I finally met the owner of the hostel, and the timing could not have been better. His night manager had left without notice, and I was offered the job on the spot, with a salary of one hundred pounds per week plus a room.

I was floating on air. Khalid Javaid was tough, but a real gentleman. "You'll be on duty from 9 p.m. until 9 a.m., seven days a week. Your job is to keep good order, and make sure the clients don't steal anything, nor damage the property. At 7 a.m. you'll begin making the breakfasts," he rasped. This agreement meant that I could find other work opportunities, during the daytime.

"That's a wonderful song," Khalid applauded. 'Spirit of Africa' was another instant composition. I'd played and sung it to him, after he showed a genuine interest in my music.

"This is my charity song," I said. He reacted quickly, and suggested that he could present it to Panji Kaunda, one of the president of Zambia's sons. I looked at him incredulously. *He's a real dark horse,* I thought, and simply accepted that top businessmen knew such people.

44. Fast Forward to Zambia

1990

Arriving in Lusaka for the great meeting was all part of the dream, and stepping foot on African soil was one step nearer the vision. I could see my song leading a great concert, in a vast stadium, and attended by tens of thousands of people. Years before, I had met pop star Eddy Grant, a keen squash player, at the Wembley Squash Centre. After listening to my story, and vision of the African concert, he advised against it.

"It'd be difficult enough to hold such an event with a major budget; but without finance, I would seriously reconsider it," was his understated advice. It was actually a euphemism for 'You're totally nuts to think that your crazy dream could be acted out in reality'. His words reverberated around my head, as I walked the dusky, pot-holed streets of Lusaka; and headed for my meeting at the InterContinental Hotel with Panji Kaunda.

I was pulverised by the poverty in the country's capital *each one of these people would give their right arm to live, as I had done, on the relatively rich streets of London*. However, I felt oddly at home, as I empathised with their paralysing privation. Khalid had paid for my return ticket, and I had a hundred pounds in my pocket. My accommodation in Zambia was with Captain Eddie Lazzaro, of Zambia Airlines. The high priority meeting, with the president's son, would give me the opportunity to present my plans for the concert. However, two problems quickly arose.

The first was insurmountable; Panji Kaunda informed Eddie Lazzaro that the meeting with me was off. He owned a farm on the far reaches of Zambia, and suddenly did not have the time to consider my proposals. The knock-on effect was immediate.

My accommodation with Captain Lazzaro was curtailed to just one night. The message was clear, and Eddy Grant had been right. Without the connection with the president, Mr Lazzaro had dropped me like a hot potato. He apologised, and suggested that I make plans to return to the UK *this is not how it's meant to happen...*

I still had my song, which had been written to help the disabled; so I shook my head, and made my way to the offices of the handicapped, to make contact with a certain Keshi Chisambi. The three-mile walk, in the oppressive heat, was an eye-opener for me; as insects of all descriptions attacked my juicy, fresh face.

Eventually, on Leopards Hill Road, the salutary sign came into view, 'THE ZAMBIA COUNCIL FOR THE HANDICAPPED', and I breathed a sigh of relief. It was a tiny, dilapidated, naturally sandblasted structure, with a rusted tin roof. It did not show any signs of activity; so I knocked, and walked in. A small, rotund, middle-aged, ebony-skinned man in business attire looked up from his desk, and disfigured, unseeing eyes focused a strange gaze at me, "Yes, how can I help you?" he queried.

"My name is Stuart Sharp, from England. I've come to help you," I replied, to his gracious greeting.

"Come closer, Englishman. Come to where I can see you!" This odd, risible remark, from the little blind man, put me at my ease. He slid his knuckly hands over my arms and head, and slapped my empty pockets. "I cannot see your army, and you do not have any money!" was his correct conclusion. I liked this diminutive Zambian. He smiled suspiciously, and purported a very British sense of humour.

He was not surprised that my visit had turned sour, and explained how his country was bankrupt; before stating, "I think it is I who should be helping you and, by the way, did you know that our president recently met the leader of a third world country?"

I replied that my political knowledge was sparse on such a spurious point. "Prime minister Major, of the United Kingdom!" he responded raucously, and laughed uproariously. He continued. "Now what does a poor man, from a third world country, have to offer the handicapped of Zambia?" He chuckled again, and continued, "You are out of your mind, if you think you can come to our country, and put on a concert; on the basis of a song you have written, and without millions in your pocket"

"But I've seen it, Keshi... clearly!" I shouted, and explained in detail how the concert venue appeared in my vision.

"We have nothing like that in Zambia. Go home, Englishman. Your scheme is quite mad."

I couldn't leave. The 'snow people' had left me visions of the future, and they were always right. To give up now, would mean giving up on my life. I had sacrificed too much, and returning home unsuccessfully would have consigned me to the dustbin. I took a deep breath. "Right now Keshi, there must be someone who can talk to me about my plans."

"Talk to our president!" he replied sarcastically.

"Okay. Good idea! I will!"

Keshi's sightless eyes were incredulous; but he forced a smile, and slowly made it very clear. "You have proved two things to me, Englishman. One, you are crazy. And two, you are like me – poor."

"We should make a perfect team then," I retorted sharply. I was not going away, and quickly became a thorn in his side.

He drew his face close to mine, and whispered, "Let me look into your eyes, Englishman. Closer. Closer." His blind eyes glared into mine. "You really believe your own ridiculous words, I can see that. But I will give you some good advice. You will never see our president. Do not even try.

"Foreign governments, with good intentions, have not been able to help us. Visiting ministers are lucky to shake our president's hand. He will only sit down, and talk seriously, to foreigners who are heads of state. Have I made myself clear to an obstinate Englishman?" He motioned to a phone, which dangled from a single wire, on the back wall of his office. "I've been waiting for three years to get this repaired! We have a saying here, 'You cannot eat bread from grain you intend to grow'. Goodbye, Englishman."

I could not take Keshi's incredible philosophy seriously. There was nothing left to do, but hug the little man, "I love you, African man. You are the one. There is no doubt about that," I responded instinctively. His blind eyes fluttered in embarrassment. He smiled, and shook his head.

I was soon put in my place by the seedy halfway hotel, where dust-laden curtains contained the residue of every species of insect in Zambia. I woke up, feeling that a million invisible ants were crawling over every part of my body. My eyes were swollen from mosquito bites, and I felt exhausted from the heat. During this sleepless night, I played the concert movie in my head again, and examined the stadium in great detail *Keshi must be wrong*. Suddenly, a vision flashed before my eyes *hundreds of happy, smiling Zambian children in a shantytown enjoying squash lessons with me.* It was totally unconnected with my objective but, since I was a slave to my visions. I bucked up, and changed into my tracksuit.

The burly police officer requested my passport, and wailed a severe warning at me. I had transgressed a local law, requiring a permit to work in a shantytown. I had been summarily shifted onto the main road, and directed back to town. I was stunned; but the day had been a great success.

Walking into a shantytown had been a humbling experience.

Washed and drying clothes hung on makeshift lines, draped between mud huts. I soon found a hut wall against which I could hit a squash ball. It must have been the strangest sight the townspeople had ever seen. Great white eyes peered from behind doors and huts, although nobody ventured near me.

Children began to gather, but stood at a distance; unable to understand the figure before them. I stopped, and encouraged them to join me. The English language was a legacy the British had left in Zambia, and it helped my cause considerably. It took a strapping teenager to take the challenge and, within minutes, hundreds of exuberant children were joining in the fun.

The sauntering two-mile walk back to the hotel was a sobering experience. The beautiful browns and reds coloured a landscape that belied its poverty-stricken population; but I had never seen such happiness as the village kids hitting a squash ball for the first time. A distant sound, of typical African choral voices, cut through the sound of broken buses, which were belching thick smoke from their exhausts. The heavenly harmonies grew louder, as I continued my walk; and I felt drawn to the little church on my right, which reverberated with the excitement of the children singing.

I stood silhouetted in the doorway, and the choir ceased. A buzz of anticipation travelled through the congregation. Keshi Chisambi's pulpit sermon had been rudely interrupted by my presence, but I was surprised and delighted to see him giving forth to his flock. One of the children explained the problem, and the description of the interloper made Keshi brighten like a neon light. "Ah, we have an Englishman among us," he bellowed. "Welcome! Join us."

A wobbly wooden chair, which doubled up as a pew, was provided for a special place next to preacher Chisambi. "This man," he explained in hallowed tones, "has come to help us." The hushed atmosphere broke into instantaneous applause and halleluiahs. "I will ask the Englishman, Stuart Shap, to address us. That way we will have the benefit of hearing pure "Engleeesh." The snappy African accent on the 'a' in my surname made me smile. The 'r' had disappeared, and I had acquired the new Zambian mantle of 'Shap'.

A guitar, propped up in the corner of the room, set a new vision ablaze in my mind. I saw myself singing 'Spirit of Africa', with a great African choir providing the backing harmonies *this is my chance.* I grabbed the guitar, and joined Keshi at the pulpit. I nervously checked the tuning, took a deep breath, explained the song, and invited the children to join in.

The song took on a completely new meaning. All the children were natural harmonisers, and it ended with spontaneous and prolonged applause. *These are the children in my vision,* I understood, my spirit soaring. A chat with Keshi after the service, however, served to sink it to the depths. The news, about my escapades with the village children, had spread like wildfire. "You are creating major problems for yourself. The elders do not like you bursting onto their territory, without going through the proper channels. Imagine an African man turning up in your back garden, and using it as a football pitch!"

"Oh, God," I exclaimed, "I hadn't thought of it like that."

"Go home, Englishman. Go home." It was his last-gasp effort to convince me *if I have to go, I'll go out with a bang. There'll be no whimpering for me.* I had read extensively about Dr Kaunda's fight against the British in the fifties, and which ultimately resulted in him becoming president. Prison was the result of his early campaigns *but it's a great example to follow...*

45. Deported

1990

A Mercedes saloon and a police car had arrived, followed by a TV camera crew. I was hauled out of the village by police officers, and shoved into the Mercedes; leaving the children bemused and intrigued *I've really done it now...* I was given instructions to be at Lusaka International Airport at 10.30 that evening, and dumped back onto the main road *well, being thrown out of the country is going out with a bang, more or less.*

However, a TV reporter for ZNBC invited me for an interview on his early evening show. He'd had a tip-off about my squash coaching in the village, and arrived just in time to see my eviction notice being served. It was a reporter's dream, and I accepted his invitation readily.

Keshi jumped out of his seat, when I entered his office. "Ah, Englishman, you are here!" he yelled.

"I'm being deported, Keshi. How about that?"

His unseeing eyes flew open, and he shook his head. "Not unexpected, is it, Englishman? You have been making waves. That's very bad. Very dangerous. You are not safe here. The minister is doing you a favour."

"Don't you get negative on me, Keshi. I'm coming back, you know. And next time, I'll bring the cavalry. I've accepted the offer from the TV people, for an interview before I leave. I'm going to give them hell," I shouted.

"God be with you, my Englishman. But you are truly mad," was his sad resignation.

"I'll be back to say goodbye, Keshi," I responded, as I picked up my luggage, and left for the TV studios.

I had nothing to lose, and went on the attack. The reporter assured me that he was on my side, and believed in my efforts. As such, he allowed me to be as controversial as I wanted.

46. Change of Fortune

1990

I gave the example of their president, who was prepared to sacrifice himself to achieve the goal of helping his people. "Now, you have truly excelled yourself," was Keshi's strange comment. I turned up at his office for the final goodbye, and he was smiling; a rather unexpected response from the little man. "Yes, Englishman, you really have. Call this number now." I looked, perplexed, at the phone in his outstretched hand. "Quickly, call it." He was excited and insistent. "You will be talking to the president's son, Kaweche."

Nothing was making sense. I had maligned this country on national television; and the only result I could think of was prison or worse. Keshi's lack of information only served to confirm my worst fears. I dialled, with hesitancy between each digit.

"Kaweche Kaunda?" I blurted out, in the best African accent I could muster.

"It is I," was the very English response. "And this is Stuart Sharp, I presume?" he continued, with a bellicose laugh *nobody who intends to arrest me laughs like that*. "A car will be with you in ten minutes," was his final comment, and the phone went dead. I could only stare in wonder at Keshi, as he did at me. He was as much in the dark as I was.

47. The President's Son

1990

The Land Cruiser tore through the jungle roads in the waning light until, out of nowhere, a great lodge appeared. It was a heavily guarded retreat, and soldiers protected every inch of the grounds. It was a forbidding and formidable fortress, and the only creatures who had any freedom of movement in this area were monkeys.

After a passport check, and words with the driver, the vehicle was waved past the guard post; and I was ushered into the main entrance, which was adorned with leviathan lion skins. A large ornamental fan rotated slowly from the ceiling, wafting a soft gentle breeze. Then he was there. He was in his thirties, tall, well built, gracious, and courteous in his greeting.

My mind was working overtime *this doesn't feel like a hanging...*

"I've heard a lot about you. You are getting to be a familiar name in our country. I'm not sure if that's good or bad, but I would like to hear what you have to say in your own words." I was beginning to think my vision had finally made its first footprint in African soil.

"An interesting story, Stuart," he responded thoughtfully, after listening carefully. "Play me your song," he requested. He listened carefully to the tape, and made notes. "This is great," he responded enthusiastically. "You have captured the spirit of the nation like I have never heard before, and my father will love it. Now, here is a pen and paper. Write down, on one page, what you want to achieve in our country. Address it to my father, and keep to the point."

Oh, wow! Now I need James and Sally like never before. The blank page virtually wrote itself, and was filled within minutes *yes, they're still with me. Now I'm in the movie for real, and everyone will play their parts perfectly.* I hoped...

He quickly scanned my letter, and made more notes.

"Right, here are just some of the obstacles you will face, even if sponsors can be found to create such an extravaganza." The list was endless, and included: No electricity, stage, or public address system at the National Stadium. No public address systems, of the power required, in the country at all. In addition, the rainy season was about to arrive, and unleash itself for the next four months.

"And finally," he added, "you seem to have antagonised some very important people. We'll need to work on that."

I took a very sharp intake of breath. For every step forward, there seemed to be ten steps back.

"You've taken on an impossible challenge, Stuart, I think. Yes?" He tilted his head at me, quizzically, as he carefully placed my letter to his father into a state-embossed envelope, and sealed it

"Yes," I replied, "it is impossible; but it will happen."

"Only with my father's approval, it will; and even then, the weather could put a stop to it."

48. The President

1990

I was in a government Mercedes, on the way to see the president. It was surreal. Nevertheless, the movie was playing out according to plan; so I should just get on with it, and act out the role I'd been given. Proud, multi-coloured peacocks adorned the beautifully manicured lawns, and I became part of a quickly moving group of dignitaries. Nobody spoke or smiled. Various animal skins roamed the myriad of rooms, and antiquities blossomed everywhere.

The tightly packed group stopped, en masse, in front of a pair of enormous, intricately carved, oaken doors. We had arrived at the centre of government. The doors slowly swung open, revealing a giant, oval table where government ministers sat in silent anticipation *I've got to hold myself together, and remember my lines in the script.* It was the only way to get through this scene. Every face turned, to watch me make a few faltering steps into their domain, while my accompanying dignitaries appeared to melt into the woodwork. I was alone, and waiting for the star of the movie to speak his lines.

"Come in! Come in, my boy!" the president boomed. The ministers stood, in unison. At the head of this massive mahogany table sat President Kaunda, a tall handsome man in his sixties. He continued, "Welcome, the Spirit of Zambia. Come here, and sit by me. This young man is here in our country, with a plan to help our handicapped. He was on state television today, making various statements." He smiled, and nodded towards me.

Now it's becoming clear. He saw, in me, an ordinary person, with a ravenous and rebellious passion, who could promote the Zambian nation abroad. He read out my one page message, and commented on it in the most powerful way possible. I then explained the details of my expulsion order, in whispered tones. He was surprised and shocked, and took a few seconds to take it all in. He seemed unsure of what I was saying, as he stumbled over an apology. I stepped in to confirm it, and pointed out that the very man, who had executed those orders, was sitting opposite me. The president's towering, glowering looks in his direction demanded an explanation, as the meeting took a nosedive into embarrassment for all concerned.

Wavering words, from the minister responsible, were not

convincing. "Sir, it was all a mistake. There was a miscommunication. Everything has been resolved now. Our sincere apologies to Mr Sharp." Beads of sweat dribbled down his forehead, and I knew that I had made my first powerful enemy; which did not augment well for me, or my project.

Moving me into a government-protected house, reserved only for visiting heads of state, was his answer to my eviction notice. Margaret Thatcher had been the previous guest in 'Roan House'. I looked at the guestbook, and Tiny Rowland was emblazoned therein as the latest incumbent. Fortunately for me, he had completed his business, and was just moving out.

I was in a state of shock. The president had personally endorsed the concert, and had created a committee to make it happen. His top government ministers formed its nucleus, and I was provided with my own office. Francis Chelebase was his personal private secretary, and he became my link to the president. It was 26th November, 1990 and the concert date had been fixed for the 14th January, 1991. I had six weeks to create a multi-national concert, with all the obstacles that Kaweche had outlined. All of a sudden, I had became the general of an army, and the committee had swollen to one hundred strong.

Lusaka's Independence Stadium took my breath away. It was precisely as the vision had predicted. The army's engineers had been instructed to build the stage. The electricity board would pipe in the power. All the major public address systems from the copper mines were to be commandeered. Microwave links for communicating the concert live, to all parts of Zambia, were to be installed.

I was working hard, with the Zambian Union of Musicians, to orchestrate and choreograph my song; though finding the star to sing it proved to be a major problem. Without any recording equipment in the country at all, I was searching abroad for a sponsor; and had already called every major studio in the UK. I requested a tall, top black singing star to learn the song, and travel to Zambia to perform it. I also asked for a full recording studio system to be provided.

Their reward would be stunning and unforgettable. In exchange for such a commitment, they would receive a two-week holiday, including a safari, for their family as the president's personal guests. However, in each case, I did not get any further than a secretary or PA with the proposal. In most cases, the call was cut short in mid-sentence; and I was getting close to my wits' end. My genuine, long-planned, presidentially-backed concert was being casually dismissed by a click over the phone.

I was summoned to an extraordinary committee meeting, to present an update on the situation; which did not look good. With a month to 'C-Day', as we called it, we had a concert without a star. The rains had begun, and the committee was gloomy. They feared for the president's reputation, and I could see, from their body language, that the plug was about to be pulled.

"We are no longer able to accept any further instructions from the president in respect of your ill-fated concert." Their statement was simple and unequivocal. The managing director of Zambia Airways hammered in the last nail, "I will not approve the president's instructions to provide flights for your mother, or your children, to attend the concert."

The meeting lasted just one minute, and they left.

49. A Coup

1990

I feared for the president, since all of his instructions were being openly flouted. "I'm sure a coup is being planned, Kaweche." I suggested tentatively. He looked concerned, and contemplated my explanation of the new events overtaking me. He walked, and pondered. "They are hanging themselves," was his long awaited response.

Frederick Chiluba, a union man from the Copperbelt region, was gaining support throughout the country to crush President Kaunda, and he was acutely aware that the magnitude of the concert could promote the president on a global scale. Pressure from the west, for Zambia's first multi-national elections, was impossible to resist; and Chiluba was seen as Zambia's saviour.

He was determined to corrupt Kaunda's own men and, behind the political scenes, a feverish flow of intelligence was being exchanged. Rumours abounded, and it was widely thought that Kaunda's personal private secretary would be the first to fall. Counter-intelligence sources felt that he would be offered a post in Chiluba's government, if he turned double agent; but it was my concert that became a constant source of irritation for Chiluba and his campaign. As the gale force storms battered Kaunda's previously pristine, personal nine-hole golf course, set in the State House grounds; I was called to the presidential office

I peered out of his office window, and the forlorn façade reflected our precarious position. He looked up, and spoke slowly and clearly. "The concert will go ahead, and your family's flights have been confirmed." He turned, and watched the winter storm hack away at his windows.

"It will be okay on the day, sir," I humbly reassured him.

"God willing, young man. God willing," he responded. The country itself was under siege. The World Bank had confirmed a massive black hole in the Bank of Zambia's finances, and terrible troubles lay ahead. The president was in the 'last chance saloon', and I had two days left to find a star to sing my song at the concert. I also required a major amount of recording equipment.

By comparison with the president's political problems, the concert seemed so petty. However, it was clear that his authority was now at stake because of it. I was getting nowhere in my efforts to find a singing star, and outdoor recording studio equipment, at short notice; until a vision came to me, during my chat with the president in his office.

Making the call on behalf of the president, from the State House, was clearly indicated. Without the clarity of the visions, dead-ends were usually the result. The timing was now right, and the agreement with the president, to implement this strategy, was quickly in place.

50. First Assassination Attempt

1990

The monsoon lashed my government courtesy car. I was driving from the State House to the State Lodge, for a briefing with Kaweche Kaunda. The narrow track from Lusaka had become a ravenous river, and I became ludicrously lost. The rebellious road took on the mantle of the Zambezi; and a crossroads, that I'd previously known so well, now confused me. I stopped to get my bearings, and stared through the windscreen. Even going at full speed, the wiper blades could not cope with the torrent of water smashing down; and I worried that one wrong turn could be the end of my African adventure.

A sharp, loud crack on the side window startled me. African men, armed, and dressed in battle fatigues, surrounded the vehicle *this is unusual...* They pulled and tugged at the doors, which, fortunately, were securely locked. "GET OUT!" they screamed, "GET OUT!"

I sat in total shock, unable to move. Two men alighted on the front bumper, and the rest tried to force their way in. I had two options, I reckoned - get out, and be killed; or drive on, and be killed. I made a decision, pushed the accelerator to full revs, and released the clutch. The 240 horsepower Land Cruiser took off like a stone from a sling, two men flew from the bumper, and I held my breath for the bullets to smash through the back windows, before ripping into my body.

By pure luck, the vehicle veered off the road, and I smashed my way through deep floods at full speed *maybe they did fire, and miss!* The howling gale, and the crunching of the vehicle on giant, potholed, flooded tracks could easily have masked the shots. My heart pounded like never before, as I expected more bandits to appear from the bush. The recognisable, faint lights in the distance were like the gates of Heaven.

"Right, Stuart. From now on, you will need an armed guard," Kaweche bellowed. "It has happened before to my brother. He was held up outside Lusaka, stripped naked, and forced to walk back. You are an important man now. I will inform my father, and make the arrangements. It could have been Chiluba's men, or it could be bandits. Either way, they would not have shot you. Bullets are reserved only for our own countrymen. They would have robbed you, and then stabbed you to death. By tomorrow, you would have been a heap of bones, after a lion had made a welcome snack of you. You were very lucky. You made the right decision. There is a great deal of politics going on now, about your concert, and the opposition party is incensed; so we need to be very careful. They are capable of anything. My father says that it goes on."

The Zambian Union of Musicians had worked hard on African stars to perform at the concert, and had created a superb choir of children to sing the backing vocals for my song. The army was already building the stage, and many other services were being prepared and installed; but the star of the show, and the recording equipment, still evaded us. The first day at the State House, working to change my fortunes, was due; and travelling there with a security escort was unnerving. Suddenly, the power of the project hit home.

51. A New Vision

1990

Working at the seat of government was a shot in the arm, and I was energised to succeed. With only a few weeks to go, I was struck by another vision. Before starting all of his meetings, the president sang a wonderful old African folk song. 'Tiyende Pamodzi' meant 'Let's all cross the Limpopo River together, with one voice, in peace' *have I got the balls to ask him to sing it at the concert?* My vision went further, and I saw him inaugurating the event *I have to ask him, before my blood simmers down...* Working next to the president's office gave me a golden opportunity, and I went for it. He listened carefully, and checked his diary.

"Well," he responded, and hoisted his hand. His famous white handkerchief, held between his forefingers, fluttered like a dove. It was a symbol he carried everywhere at all times, and represented peace. He called in his PPS, and re-checked his schedule. Every minute in his diary was filled with vital meetings and travel abroad, except the 14th January, 1991. I had chosen the only date, for the concert, that the president was free this coming year.

There was much whispered banter between the two. The PPS was unimpressed by the possibility of his president being brought down, by attending a concert that probably would not see the light of day. His body language said it all. The key to the event was about to be decided. "Fetch my guitar," was the instruction to the PPS, followed by a scene which became increasingly surreal before my eyes. He played, and sang, his song for me, and I watched in awe. "I would have been a musician, had I not made the presidency," he smiled, after his performance. I was dumbstruck. A few weeks ago, I was being asked to leave the country; and now I was sitting in the president's office, being entertained by him.

I have the real star of the concert...

"I have never recorded it; you know, Stuart," he continued. My mind was in overdrive. This was the chance of a lifetime, for the president and myself. Now, I just needed him to say yes. He walked around his office, in deep thought. The opposition to the concert was growing amongst his own men, as well as the Movement for Multi-Party Democracy, headed by the diminutive Frederick Chiluba. He had the backing of the west and, although only a union official, was already flexing his muscles; and was pitching to become the new leader of Zambia.

Kaunda, however, felt under no threat. He had ruled Zambia for 26 years, and considered the Zambian people as his extended family. Zambia was the only country in Africa to have lived in peace during his entire term in office. The country was surrounded by hostile and warring nations, but Kaunda had kept his people safe. Kaunda felt that Chiluba was no more than an irritant; a fly to be swatted; and a total unknown; with no charisma, no connection with world leaders, and no experience of power.

"Right," said Kaunda, "we will do it."

I nearly fell off my chair. My heart beat so hard that it nearly burst through my shirt. I was instantly breathless. He called in his PPS, and pencilled the date in his dairy. The PPS backed out of the office, in typical African style; and took a long lingering look, out of the president's office window, at the staggering storm that continued to lash the windows and grounds.

There was an unspoken air of belief in miracles, which shuttled back and forth between the president and I. He was a devout Christian, praying several times a day; and I was gifted with a vision. It seemed that, between us, we had created the 'perfect storm'.

52. Final Call for Concert Sponsorship

1990

"Is this some sort of wind up?" By a stroke of good fortune, Ellis Elias, the owner of Red Bus Studios in the UK, had answered the telephone himself. His company was my last port of call. I had run out of options, since every other record company in the UK had dismissed my request as a prank. This conversation was rapidly going the same way.

"Sincerely, Mr Elias; I am calling from the State House in Zambia," was my almost pathetic reply. "If you can sponsor the recording, and find a star to sing my song, you will be the guest of the president." The fact that he was still hanging onto the telephone gave me hope. We had three weeks left, to pull it all together.

"Give me the State House number, and I'll call you back. I have to be sure," he commanded. I breathed a small sigh of relief.

"I have Mr Elias from the UK, Mr Sharp. Will you take the call?" was the State House operator's historic request.

I can't believe it. He's called back.

"So this isn't a wind up," he continued, "my engineers were planning a trip to Africa next year, to recording various African sounds, so maybe there could be an opportunity. Also, I'm making an album with Oliver Cheatham in my studio at the moment. He's a great soul singer from the States. Maybe he can sing your song, but I've many hurdles to overcome for him to travel to Africa at a moment's notice - and you need all my studio equipment to record the concert. Have you any idea what that would entail? There's tons of it!" I sighed heavily, took a deep breath, and prepared to close the deal.

There followed much sending and receiving of faxes between the State House, Mr Elias, and the Zambian High Commission in London. The amount of detail needed was unbelievable. Such was the tension, throughout the Zambian political elite, that nothing could be certain until the concert had been successfully concluded. On Christmas Eve of 1990, the agreement was signed. Oliver Cheatham would star, and the mass of recording equipment would be air freighted from the UK.

My ex-wife had received presidential invitations, for Emma and Kate to travel to Zambia as the president's guests. My mother received the same invitation. The managing director of Zambia Airways had issued all tickets under enormous duress. He was part of the movement for change in Zambia, and was vehemently opposed to the project. Then the bombshell exploded on my desk.

"Oliver Cheatham has been told by his manager, not to travel to Zambia unless accompanied by him." Ellis Elias had difficulty in spitting out the words. There had been no mention of a manager in our negotiations, and providing another ticket meant securing permission from the president once more, and incurring the ire of the Zambia Airways MD.

"Give me his name and passport details," I responded sharply. The name 'Joe Pyle' sounded very strange. "What kind of a name is that? It sounds like a gangster." I quipped.

"It is!" he responded, obliquely. I naturally thought that his retort was his idiosyncratic way of teasing me, and dismissed it from my mind.

53. The Concert is Close

1991

Keshi was circumspect about the concert. The rains had turned themselves off for a few days, and his meeting with the president had not thrilled him in the way that I felt it should. Driving Keshi in the government's Land Cruiser, to his poverty-stricken office, seemed somewhat of an anomaly. However, there was no time to think about the bizarre nature of the events unfolding before our eyes.

Outside his little office, he turned to the rolling thunderclouds on the horizon, and inhaled deeply. "I can smell it," he moaned, and pointed. "See, Englishman. No stars. Very soon now. And when it starts again, it will not stop for months." He opened the padlocked door to his office, and grabbed his battered old briefcase from the floor. A rolling roar of thunder, coupled with a stupendous flash of sheet lightning, turned us, Gorgon-like, to stone. The rattling rain on his tin roof was deafening, and it gushed through a leak in the ceiling. Keshi grabbed an old saucepan, which resided suspiciously close by, and caught the miniature waterfall; as he shoved papers into the briefcase. The pan was filling rapidly, and he brought it close to my face. "What do you hear?" he shouted.

I had no idea what he meant, and offered, "Rain pouring into your pan."

"Then you are not listening, because you are not an African man. This is the first monsoon in three years; and it is music to my ears. It is the only music I am going to hear for the next three months." The little man forced the pot against my face, and gestured. "Look. See all your dreams. They are being drowned. I need to go home. Come." The cascade of water was now flooding out his office.

I tried to guide Keshi to the safety of the Land Cruiser and my security staff, but he refused to get in.

His face dripped rain like the Victoria Falls. "Goodbye, Englishman," he shouted above the din.

"For God's sake, man. Get in the car!" I screamed.

"No, Englishman. Leave me alone," he responded, with a sad resignation; and plodded off into the curtain of cascading stair-rods. I was drenched and depressed. Keshi felt that the monsoon would scupper the show, and that his society would be left without funds. To see a blind man walk into a wall of water, and find his way home in the dark, is a sight I will never forget. It inspired me to a greater effort.

To the many opposed to the concert, it was a God-sent opportunity to persuade the president to cancel; before it was too late. Once again, the project had found itself in a perilous position. However, a vision of success kicked in, and my spirit soared once more; as I knew I had not come this far to fail now. Preparations for the arrival of the recording team and my family were well under way, and it deserved to succeed for Keshi's sake.

54. The Arrival

1991

A guard of honour lined the red carpet, as the giant Zambia Airways DC10 made a silky-smooth touchdown, and taxied proudly into place at Lusaka International Airport. The rains had stopped again; but ominous, deep black clouds jutted out from the horizon. The air was saturated with a damp mist, as a blazing early morning sun greeted the bedraggled concert troupe. They alighted wearily from the plane, to a reception normally reserved for visiting heads of state; and seeing Emma, Kate and my mother again, in such circumstances, was a joy for me beyond compare.

Ellis Elias and his team told a story of their Heathrow experience, which had almost put an end to their excursion and the concert. Zambia Airways staff had not been made aware of the ton of equipment to be transported. That was the duty of the High Commissioner in London, who was to sign the carnet documents at the airport before departure. It appeared that the MMD had got to him, too; and he did not arrive at the airport.

"We were within two minutes of returning to the studio," explained a tired and depressed Ellis Elias, "Only a last minute call from the State House in Zambia saved the day."

I shook hands with all members of the team, but when I came face to face with Oliver Cheatham's manager, my 'gangster' caricature was rapidly brought into sharp relief. Joe Pyle was the epitome of politeness and grace; but looked, every inch, the archetypal Italian Mafioso. His immaculate Saville Row suit, and ornate gold rings, gave the game away. But this was no time to investigate my mere machinations. He looked delighted to be here in Zambia, and to have the opportunity of meeting the president.

"'Av they got any gold mines for sale?" I was discussing Oliver Cheatham's forthcoming television appearance, to promote the concert; and the strange question came out of Mr Pyles's mouth in, what was for him, a natural and genuine way.

"No, Mr Pyle, they only have emerald and copper mines here," I replied, and hoped the subject would end. However, his interest heightened.

"Aw'right! I wouldn't mind a few o' <u>them</u>!" he replied, in typical

Cockney fashion *Oh, no! My feelings were right, and now we have a real gangster in our midst.* My current concern was keeping him away from the president. I had only seen characters like his in films and, true to form, he had an outwardly kindly and loving persona. He was a big man, with a gruff voice, and a face carved from the blades of victorious violent East End gang battles. He looked every inch the top dog. I took a step back, and reflected on the current state of play.

We had a concert, previously deemed impossible, yet to take place. The president was being besieged by political dramas. The Bank of Zambia was in a state of collapse. The IMF was insisting on multi-party elections. The MMD was fighting the president, and the concert, on all fronts. There were rumours of assassinations being planned, for the president and myself. Zambian CIA agents were tracking every move I made, and every word I uttered. A 24-hour armed guard was now in place for my family and myself. The director general of the ZNBC was opposing the broadcasting of the concert; and an overdue monsoon was threatening to return at any moment!

I took a deep breath. Flashbacks of wandering the streets of Lusaka, with only a dream in my pocket, and almost freezing to death on the streets of Shepherds Bush, now hit me hard *I have to be dreaming all this…*

55. Countdown

1991

Ellis Elias and his staff were incredible. They set up their recording equipment in the stadium, in conjunction with the army, the electricity board, and ZNBC. I introduced Oliver Cheatham and Joe Pyle to the school choir, who were to provide the backing vocals for my song. The president introduced Emma and Kate to the nation on national television, and my mother began planning a walk for Zambia, when she returned home. Everyone kept an eye on the weather. With 48 hours to C-Day, a major frontal system was developing off the central west coast of Africa.

The Zambian Met Office made furious calculations. "It is a major storm, and it will hit Zambia on the day of the concert," said the Met Office manager. "It is a deep depression, and could lash the country uninterrupted for months," he forecast.

It's a depression, alright The consequences of his words were just the kind of ammunition the opposition forces needed to attack us with a vengeance *Keshi could be right*.

I had to pull myself together, and send out positive vibes. A final meeting with the president, on the 13th of January, ensured that he and I were on the same wavelength. We believed that we would make it, before the weather had its wicked way. Preparations throughout the country, to receive the historic pictures of the event on television, were in place. Artists and musicians arrived from all parts of Africa to participate, and rehearsals at the stadium were in full swing. I looked up at the greying clouds, and felt the cool breeze on my cheeks. "Don't do this to me now!" I screamed. "Have some pity, for God's sake!" Many were hoping for the gathering storm to smash the concert to pieces; but a minority, including the president, were praying for its success.

It was impossible to sleep. I scrambled out of bed, every half an hour or so, opened the window, and sniffed the breeze *so far, so good*. At exactly 5 a.m., the windows began to rattle violently. My heart skipped a beat, then began banging hard in my chest. I didn't recognise it as rain - it was far too loud for that. I forced open a reluctant window, and was simply stunned.

This was not rain. This was the Victoria Falls itself, having transported itself to Lusaka, continuing to cascade its waterfalls over the city. I slammed the window shut, and fell back onto the bed, shaking with fear and trepidation. The monsoon had arrived in its complete, passionate, and all-consuming embrace.

At 6 a.m. I received the first call, and I knew that I was about to be hung, drawn, and quartered. The work of hundreds of people, from all over the continent, was about to be destroyed.

The president was advised to withdraw from the concert, to save his embarrassment; and to heap the full responsibility onto my shoulders *this can't happen! The vision can't be wrong. Not now! It's never been wrong.*

The president, however, was unflappable, and simply refused to capitulate. We both agreed to give the weather one more chance, and review it at noon. By 11 a.m. the roads had turned into rustic rivers, and the stadium had flooded. Hundreds of crew and concert entertainers huddled at the Ridgeway Hotel, courtesy of Richard Chanter, the accommodation sponsor. Oliver Cheatham looked desperately despondent. It was a scene of complete and utter desolation.

Two minutes before midday, the storm eerily abated. I ran out of Roan House, followed by my armed guard, and peered unbelieving at the parting clouds. The sun, in all of its baking glory, shone its searing rays directly over Lusaka; but the city was still surrounded by the majestic monsoon clouds, leaving the oddest sight imaginable. A great shaft of burning light hovered over Lusaka; and even the most hardened atheist could be forgiven for thinking that the universe itself had come to the rescue.

The capital city had turned into an instant steam bath. The president's inauguration and song was scheduled for 2 p.m. Then, as if a powerful producer had pressed the play button of a scene that had been previously put on pause, the soggy deadness instantly became a hive of frenzied activity. Within an hour, the waterlogged stadium had dried out, and everyone was busily engaged in the work that they had come here for.

Tens of thousands of bedraggled shantytown dwellers began the march to the Independence Stadium. The crew and entertainers piled into the buses, which had been provided free by the mayor of Lusaka. The president, and his enveloping entourage, prepared themselves; an armed escort rushed Oliver, Ellis, and the recording team to the stadium; and the entire city became mobilised. It was an incredible sight, with 75,000 people packed into the stadium, and thousands more locked out.

The sun continued to radiate its splendour over the concert for the next three hours. The president gave a star performance, Oliver Cheatham's rendition was electrifying, and it required the army to keep the audience from mobbing the stage. The whole event was a spectacular success, and it finished on time at 5 p.m.

Within a few minutes of the president's departure, the black clouds rolled back over Lusaka, drawing heavy drapes across the skylight, and the monsoon continued from where it had left off, with full and furious ferocity.

"It was indeed a miracle, Stuart," said the president, at the State House reception the following day. Keshi smiled broadly for the first time, and remembered my words when we first met. "I agree with the president," he said. "It has been an unforgettable and unbelievable experience."

Emma and Kate took an incredible story back to their school in Baschurch, Shropshire. My mother began to prepare for her walk from Leicester to London, and I became consumed with turning the next part of the dream into reality.

If I can be instrumental in making such an impossible event like this happen, the rest of the journey should be a piece of cake... I now had footage of the great event, to prove my case to those who had doubted my determination *what would their response be, now?* From my experience with my father, I knew that sceptics would not see the miracle, in the midst of the Dark Continent, as anything but pure coincidence.

However, from my point of view, at the actual scene of the event, I felt that not only had a higher power protected me from an ignominious death in a jungle ditch but; with the help of a handful of people, willing to believe in an impossible dream, had brought about a major success against incalculable odds. This gave me the spiritual strength to continue my journey, whatever the tempests of life would throw at me.

56. The Follow Up

1991 - 1995

The president embarked on a countrywide campaign, to ensure victory in the forthcoming elections. Within weeks, I chalked it up as one vision down, with three to go. The movie in my head was finally synchronising with reality *I have to keep going...*

Recording all the music that was in my mind, with the world's greatest orchestras, was the next monumental challenge. Back in the UK, Khalid Javaid offered me more hostel work, for which I was grateful. However, to fulfil the vision, I needed to become a millionaire. Finding commissionable work, with Sky as the limit, was the only way forward. I already laboured all night, and now I knew that I must toil all day, too.

I planned to work 20 hours each day, for seven days a week. Four hours rest a day, I reckoned, would be enough to sustain me. I made a military style strategy, to visit all the developing businesses in the Shepherds Bush area. My business plan offered working for nothing, to increase their business profit, and accept a commission on the results.

Owners and managers laughed at me, and six months of footslogging ended up with a nil result. Businesses had become highly technological, and I needed to be a master of the emerging IT systems. I immersed myself in the new technology and, after a year of battering my brain into studious submission, I felt ready to try again. I was proud of myself, after having become a first class student. My guitar skills had also improved significantly. With a business card in my hand, a smart suit, and a neat haircut, I set out to become the model of a successful salesman.

Danny Edgar owned a developing property company, and he was one of the first to brush me off. He was a big, rough, and tough man who seemed to talk to ten people at the same time, but I instinctively liked him.

I saw a warrior, with a disarming twinkle to his eye. I looked beyond the gruffness, and saw an honest and compassionate soul. My experiences in Africa could now stand me in good stead. He took no prisoners; but I felt that, given a chance, I could make a decisive difference to his company.

A year later, I arrived at his offices again, this time armed with a written proposal. He was suitably impressed with my persistence, and I even managed to get in two words every minute or so, as he answered many telephone calls simultaneously. He was an aggressive, positive, successful businessman, who worked an eighteen-hour day; and there was something about him that I admired and understood.

I needed to be around successful people, and it was important for me to learn their skills. He threw my proposal into a filing tray, looked at me, smiled, and nodded towards the door. My interview was over. No words had been spoken, but some form of acknowledgement had taken place. I had made him a clear-cut offer; one which involved no cost to his company, and ensured that I would work very hard to create even more success for him.

I had my first major sale working for a company selling diesel generators, and earned almost three thousand pounds commission in one week; which really fired me up. The same occurred with a TV production company. It was a small start, on my way to millionaire status; but it was already a giant step away from my origins.

57. A Call from On High

1991

The call, totally out of the blue, took me aback. "The old man wants to see you in Zambia, Stuart," was the summons from the High Commissioner in London. I stared at the phone in amazement. "When can you travel?" he continued. I was flustered, unsure of what to say, and torn between two important, but conflicting, interests. I was on a roll with my financial objectives, and felt that one more push would see Mr Edgar on my side. However, when the president of a country calls, there can be only one decision.

I joined him, and his family, in Kasaba Bay; on the shores of Lake Tanganyika for Christmas. It was a stunning spot; which doubled as his holiday home, and a quiet place to prepare national and international strategies. We sat on the old wooden veranda, overlooking the sea-like lake. Hippopotami lolled around aimlessly, nudging each other; their grunts echoing ominously before they disappeared beneath the water.

"Can you prepare a marketing plan for Zambia?" He came right out with it. "Once I am back in power, I will need you to work with me to get my country on its feet. I have prepared an office, in a protected house. Can you do it in a week?"

This was headhunting, African style... To be considered for such a task was a truly great honour. I knew that the concert had been a miracle of marketing, and had given him much to consider. Such a proposal, from so high up on an international stage, sent my confidence soaring. "Take a trip around Zambia, and get a feel for what is needed," he continued, graciously.

Dr Kaunda was the most humble man I had ever met, and his love for Zambia knew no bounds. He felt that any ministers, who were not towing the line, were just his family behaving badly; and that love would overcome their problems in the end. His strong Christian beliefs were never once used to coerce me into his faith.

I believed in a higher power, if one could just connect to it. I felt that there was a correlation between this power, and our own efforts and energy. Maybe this higher power was called 'God'.

Sally and James had long gone. Maybe they had been figments of my vivid imagination, and I had somehow been connected to this higher source all the time. Whatever it was, it had guided me to the president of Zambia. It had allowed me to produce one of Africa's most successful concerts, with my own music. This, alone, was an impossible achievement, whichever way one viewed it. The president had recognised this.

Once again, I was confronted with bad vibes coming from many of his ministers. I was certain that they were involved in double-dealing, and the president just could not see it.

"How do you see the election going, sir?" I inquired politely.

"A landslide, Stuart. A landslide, 80-20 in my favour!" he laughed confidently. However, my tit-bits of unconfirmed information, garnered from ordinary people, did not bear this out. Many had openly expressed to me, that his huge confidence-boosting rallies were no more than 'rent-a-crowd' scenarios, specifically designed to give him a false sense of security. The wind of change in Africa was gathering momentum. I sighed heavily in my heart, but outwardly showed a positive reaction. He continued, "I'm travelling to all four corners of Zambia, starting today, so I will leave you in the very capable hands of my ministers" *Oh dear, the kiss of death is imminent...*

"So, Stuart, be my guest, and I look forward to seeing your report shortly."

I thanked a real gentleman of power. Maybe, for the last time.

58. A Prison Sentence for the President

1991

I was summoned to a ministerial meeting, prior to the old man's departure for his campaign, and without his knowledge

"This is not going to happen." Their words were harsh, and harsh in delivery. I was unwelcome, and should leave their country as soon as possible. The message was clear. The president's days were numbered *I wonder what they'll tell him about me?*

My efforts to contact him again were constantly thwarted, and my every move was monitored until I finally departed the country. I did write a marketing plan, and left it in the State House office; but I did not expect him to ever see it.

His election campaign was highly publicised in the UK and the rest of the world. With the army generals loyal, he had the ability to retain power even if the election went against him; which was the normal practice of other African leaders. It was expected of him, also. I had dallied with the ultimate power in Zambia, but felt the downdraught of the approaching political hurricane.

In some respects, I felt relieved to be back in the UK. I am certain that the forces reigned against the president were reassured, too; as a dead charity worker in their country would not have augured well for a new Zambian democracy, despite the fact that that my body would never have been found.

I hung onto my vision, made contact with Mr Edgar, and worked hard on the road for financial success. The phone rang, and I let it ring until the last second while I tried to feel the vibes it carried. It was the evening before the Zambian election results. To answer, or not to answer, that was the question. I felt my heart quicken, and snatched up the handset. The international squawks and scratches on the line meant only one thing. "How are things looking in the English press, Stuart?"

The president's son, Kaweche, was calling from the State House in Lusaka. I couldn't lie. "It's looking bad, Kaweche. 80-20 in favour of the MMD." I expressed the news sadly. He laughed.

"Watch the news tomorrow morning, and you will see my father win by a landslide." Apparently, the whole Kaunda family had gathered at the State House, ready for the country's celebrations to welcome the father of the nation, Dr Kenneth D Kaunda, being returned to power. It was the first multi-party election held during his reign, Zambia was a one party republic, and he was the head of UNIP (The United Independence Party), which had governed for 27 years. He was the longest serving African president in history, but he was also blamed for destroying the Zambian economy.

He was labelled, by the West, as a murdering dictator. The western media conveniently failed to mention the oil price hike, in the early seventies, which decimated the Zambian economy. The country was landlocked, and depended on imported oil. Western governments had encouraged Kaunda to borrow from high street banks, at exorbitant interest rates. The UK made tons of money doing deals, like this, with many other third world countries; and when the pot ran dry, they decided to pull the plug.

Kaunda turned to Iraq and the 'friend of the west', President Saddam Hussein; whose closeness with the UK meant full support for the Iraqi dictator. High-ranking UK government ministers regaled Hussein at every opportunity, since he was fighting a proxy war on behalf of the Americans.

Hussein loved Kaunda. They were both rebels in their own way, but there were light years of difference. Kaunda would never kill, or even think badly of, any of his citizens; for simply uttering an anti-government expression. Despite this, Hussein shipped tons of free oil to Kaunda. Unfortunately, it was never enough to pay the capital and interest back to the UK high street banks.

By 1991, a hole as big as a Centurion tank opened up in the Zambian finances, and the nightmare began. Poor Zambians bore the brunt of the nation's spiral into bankruptcy, and Frederick Chiluba had Kaunda's head on a plate. The leader of the MMD offered Zambians a European way of life, if they voted for him. They threw cash at the crowds, and convinced them of a bright new future. It was no contest; but my poor old friend, the president, blinded by his trust in his own men, could not see it. How could he not trust people that fought with him against the British, and spent time in jail with him?

"I will, Kaweche, and send my best wishes to your father," I replied. It was 8:30 on the morning of the 31st October, 1991. Along with millions of others, I watched history being made in Zambia. It was Africa's most peaceful transition of power in history. The MMD posted 74% of the vote, and Dr Kaunda's party 25%; with the 1% remainder going to minority parties. Kaweche had been right about the landslide, but not about the direction that it took.

Frederick Chiluba, the insignificant little union man from the Copperbelt, had beaten the goliath. He quietly took the keys of office, and was courteously shown around the State House by the former president. The West was appeased; and new funding would now flow into Zambia, subject to the structural changes agreed by Chiluba. For him, it was a sweet victory, and long coming.

Those he trusted most had misled Kaunda, and his close supporters and family members fled to South Africa during the night. The ANC, and particularly Nelson Mandela, had been very grateful for the unswerving support of Kenneth D Kaunda. He had put his country on the line to give sanctuary to the ANC, and now it was time for their help. The news pictures saw the old man in handcuffs, being unceremoniously carted off to jail on charges of embezzling the country's coffers. Chiluba's vendetta had the support of the nation. 'Where had the billions gone?' was the question on the lips of the incoming government, and Chiluba hired the UK's foremost legal and financial investigators to find out.

My vision had not included becoming the marketing manager of Zambia and, so this was not a loss to me. I could only watch the saga unfold on television, and reflect on my time with a man of honour and belief, in a stunningly beautiful country.

59. Back to Reality

1996

"Okay, I agree with your proposal." Finally, Danny Edgar took me on. Money was coming in from sales orders that I had produced for other companies, and I was able to purchase my own flat. I finally had my foot on the property ladder, and intended to become my own developer. My target was half a million pounds in the bank, and a property worth the same amount. This was my pitch to John Peat, the bank manager of the Royal Bank of Scotland. He raised his eyebrows somewhat, but signed me up.

I must achieve these targets, and track down Anthony Wade It was a tough challenge. I could focus on earning eight thousand pounds a month; and watching the movie in my head, of orchestras performing my symphonies, kept me highly motivated. I now knew every instrument, and every note they played. My first piece of business for Mr Edgar took twelve months of hard slog to procure. I learned how councils and planning committees worked. I studied environmental health. I made it my business to know the top dogs of each local governmental department. I worked round the clock, for three main companies, and success begat success.

Two years later, I had achieved my goal. I sat with my bank manager and gloated. "I told you I'd do it," I stated, excitedly. He put me on the list of his best customers, and I was invited to all the bank's special events. It was time to reflect again. Within a square mile of the bank, I had previously been a squatter and a penniless vagrant. Now, before tax, I could call myself a millionaire. It was near enough for me, and I could afford myself a big pat on the back.

I walked past the BBC Studios in Wood Lane; and looked at the pavement opposite, that I had once called my home. "I'm a millionaire!" I would blurt out to anyone in that area *London's great! No one takes a blind bit of notice of anyone talking rubbish to themselves, nor anybody else.* It felt wonderful, and I danced on air. Now it was time to make the call, for which I'd waited fourteen years.

"Oh my God, I don't believe it!" he cried. Anthony Wade was alive and kicking. Now, it was payback time. I was going to enjoy this. I could put cash in his pocket, and offer him paid work to start the process of extracting the musical files from my head.

"The object, Anthony, is the Philharmonia Orchestra. Nothing else will do, and I don't care what it takes."

He was bowled over. I showed him my bank statement, and his eyes stuck out like chapel hat pegs. "Well, you son of a gun, you did it!" he exclaimed. By now, he had a production partner, Kevin Stoney, who also turned out to be a godsend. He was the best 'put it in - take it out' man in the business. "It'll have to be the Stoney-Wade partnership to get the ball rolling," Anthony explained.

I had three parts in my head, and all were complex and powerful. They were full of mountains and valleys, hills and dales, main roads and back alleys, winter storms and quiet summer days, sadness, joy, and love; but never hatred. The problem was where to begin. A small studio, it turned out, off Tottenham Court Road, was where. The recording times were constrained by neighbours and excessive noise, but this restriction gave me another vision. My own studio would be the way to go. But for now, we would start.

I had kept my old tapes, and those fleshed out on the piano by Anthony, all those years ago. Since my last meeting with Anthony, he and his business partner had become prolific composers for television, and had made incredible demos for film companies. They had studied, and had a good knowledge of orchestration. It was the perfect time to meet up again, and the reunion was full of high expectations.

I split my day into twenty-four hours. Eight earning money for the project; eight for the taxman; four composing, and producing the Angeli music; and four trying to rest. It was a daunting schedule.

I had the basic melody, but we needed to create a replica of the orchestra in my head. It also had to be planned in reverse order. Opus 2 and 3 would be first, because there was still something missing from Opus 1, and it had not yet arrived in my head. All this confusion came with an accompaniment of time-consuming frustrations. I could hear and feel the music, but I needed to find a means of translating it into comprehensible ideas, for the two producers to work on; and as I hummed and sung the various parts, it became a slow, laborious task.

I felt that getting the intro spot-on would give the piece a solid opening. The computer had a good range of orchestral samples and, after several weeks of hard work, we began to close in on the first minute of music. I could finally see many years of intricate ideas evolving at a snail's pace. I commanded myself to keep calm, and stay on track. At every moment, and at every turn, I willed Sally and James to manifest. Once again, I needed proof that they had not been figments of my imagination.

60. Back in Africa

1992 - 1996

Meanwhile, Dr Kenneth Kaunda languished in a Lusaka jail, alongside thirty ordinary prisoners. 'KK', as he was affectionately known, feared nothing. He was a lion of African politics, and prison meant nothing to him. Kaunda had once locked up Chiluba, and this was his revenge.

The old man had been in and out of prison since handing over power; and he constantly berated the new president as corrupt, and ruinous to the country. He refused to lie down, and announced to the world that he would be fighting the next election. Chiluba promptly changed the constitution, barring any president from serving more than two terms in office. Another assassination attempt on Dr Kaunda made no difference, because to die for his country would have been a blessed sacrifice for him.

I write this because, on release from prison, his intermediary called me, requesting that we meet in a London hotel. Dr Kaunda needed to know how the forthcoming election was being rigged, and it had been five years since I had last seen him. I was finally able to inform him of my desperate last meeting with his ministers, before he left on his ill-fated campaign tour. I brought Danny Edgar along to the meeting, and we had further meetings at Danny's home in Hampstead.

If we could prove that the next election was an intended fraud, then Chiluba could be cast out of office. There was much talk of the new president salting money away in Swedish banks, for his own predicted demise; and whispers abounded of expensive houses, being bought in third party names. Between us, we began our own covert investigations, and reported back to the old man on our findings. On the face of it, Chiluba had already rigged the next election. More new laws were brought in, banning anyone from becoming elected if their parents had been born out of the country. Everything possible was being done to thwart 'KK's' return to power.

He returned home, at the helm of UNIP and, with the help of other smaller parties, boycotted the 1996 elections. However, when Chiluba walked back into office, things went downhill fast. When their son, Wezi Kaunda, was brutally gunned down; Kaunda's wife, Betty, felt that things had changed, and that her husband's campaigning for the presidency again was no longer safe in the face of such opposition.

After the assassination of his dearest son, and unwilling to play dirty, he finally retired from active politics, leaving Chiluba to get on with it. At seventy seven years of age, he had done his best for his country. He had been president of his party for forty years, and now enough was enough. I saluted a friend.

It was a strange interlude in my film, almost as if it didn't happen. Danny was overjoyed to meet the president of a country, and play host to him. It was something he would never forget, and it brought us much closer.

61. The First Version

1997 - 1998

It took almost three years of blood, sweat and slaving over a hot stave to complete a more or less accurate electronic version of Opus 2 and 3 of the Angeli Symphony. Anthony's colleague and friend, Allan Wilson, was a well-known film score conductor, orchestrator and arranger. Anthony had primed Allan about my story, and arranged for me to meet him at Abbey Road Studios. It was incredible to be in the place where the Beatles, with George Martin, made the world sit up, and take notice of their music *maybe I can do the same…*

Allan Wilson was a master of music; but to obtain his cooperation, I needed his positive opinion of my demo tape. He was a very busy man, and extremely sceptical of my story and music. I saw that he did not have time to get into it, and the handover was a brief affair *now, I'm in the hands of the vision.*

I ran the movie through my mind, again and again; and it clearly showed the world's greatest musicians recording all three parts of Angeli. Before we could contemplate another three years, developing Opus 1, it was vital that Opus 2 and 3 were successfully recorded. It all rested on the judgment of Allan Wilson, and he was taking his time to respond. I found myself constantly sighing, and banging my desk, with frustration. A week went by, and Anthony discovered the conductor had not yet listened to it. His scepticism must be getting the better of him, I imagined. The call took another two days to come.

"Well, Stuart," he exclaimed, "you've composed a masterpiece! If the best orchestra records your symphony, it'll be stunning. I am truly amazed." He continued, "I was fearful about listening to the tape, and telling you that it wasn't worthy of the best musicians, knowing the time, money, and effort you'd put into it. Now, I understand what your vision is all about. I have to tell you that the piece needs a full orchestration and arrangement, before we can think about booking an orchestra. This will require a great deal of work and expense. How are your finances situated?" Allan was excited, and concerned.

"We should be fine," I offered, gingerly.

"Well, what you're trying to achieve is firmly in the domain of film and music moguls, with huge budgets. I understand that you have another part to the symphony; but if it's anything like Opus 2 and 3," he paused, "it will be a unique moment in music history; but there is a very long way to go. I'll work out a detailed budget, covering orchestration, arrangement, score copying, conductor fees, orchestral recording studios, engineers, choir, choral arrangements, post-production, rehearsals..." I removed the phone from my ear, as he carried on.

"Right, Allan, right," I interrupted, "I'll pay fifty percent upfront right now. I just want to get on with it. Can you gather together the world's best musicians?"

"Coordinating up to a hundred people, to put it all together, is a major task in itself, and we should allow another year to the point of recording," he offered.

"Okay, let's go," I replied positively. It was truly a colossal challenge for me; and I felt like a jump jockey, riding a potential national winner, and clearing the first fence. I wondered if I had the physical and mental strength, to finish the course and win.

By simply thinking the thought, I had brought on disaster to myself. I regularly kept myself fit by playing squash with Rahmat Khan and Mo Yasin, two of the great squash-playing Khans. They kept me on my toes, and made sure that my physical condition was the best it could be for my age. I was probably one of the fittest 50-year olds in the country.

Mo dropped the ball short in the right hand corner and, as I stretched to play a wrong footing forehand boast, my right hip cracked. The noise echoed around the court and I fell, poleaxed, to the floor. The pain was indescribable, and I was unable to move. I knew, instantly, that I was badly injured.

The x-rays clearly showed that the joint had disintegrated, and it would have been all too easy to slide into negativity. This was when surgeon Derek McMinn came into my life. He had successfully operated on the British squash champion Jonah Barrington, and had him back coaching squash within one year.

I didn't have one month. I was totally incapacitated, but needed to continue bringing in big money each week. I had appointments booked all over London, and I needed to see each one urgently. I also needed my hip operation without delay.

The taxman's decision to take almost fifty percent of my earnings, because none of my musical expenses could be offset against my tax liability, had been an enormous financial shock. I had a potentially disastrous problem. Tens of thousands of pounds were already disappearing into the music machine, and I had only started to scratch the surface. Allan's 'music moguls only' warning echoed loudly in my mind. My tax liability was growing exponentially. Half a million pounds, that I had put aside for the project, suddenly became a quarter million; and this meant working even harder.

My brain went into overdrive, and I could feel it starting to burn. I used my extension bath shower unit to drown my head in cold water, in order to think. The pain in my hip was excruciating, and I could not walk, drive or sit down.

I had urgent sales that required close attention before the looming Christmas holiday period, and so the sight of two burly Afghan asylum-seekers, carrying a crippled salesman into crucial meetings, was a vision company owners found beyond belief. They were astonished at such commitment; and my business, oddly, increased because of it.

It was an instantaneous idea that had worked. Two six-foot immigrants, looking for work, were the ideal body carriers. I lay on a mattress in the back of a van, was driven to each appointment, and lifted bodily up steps, into elevators, down corridors and into offices. You couldn't have made it up...

Arriving at Anthony's studio, in this condition, caused an uproar. We were back in 'Fawlty Towers' territory again. Cash for Keshi, in Zambia, was sent regularly. He was now a priority, along with Emma and Kate. My daughters both needed cars and cash. I enjoyed giving away money, since I didn't need it for myself. Many Arabs, who became wealthy through oil, remained living in tents in the desert. They did so in preparation for the oil running out. My money was like their oil. The street was my desert.

"You must not drive for six weeks," warned the hospital management team. The operation to metallise my hip had gone well, and the pain had disappeared instantly after the operation. I reduced the six weeks to six days, and my crutches became a useful tool to cross the manic roads of Westminster. We were about to begin Opus 1, when the news broke. Kevin was planning a move out of London, and he had put his flat-cum-studio up for sale.

"Okay, Anthony, I'll just have to buy one of my own," I shouted, to convince myself to visualise such a possibility, now that even more large amounts of money were required. "I'll employ you permanently to work on the music," I continued, in the same bluster.

Within weeks, we were in our own fully equipped studio, ready for the onslaught; and Anthony was fully committed to the project. The coordination, of all the requirements laid down by Allan Wilson, was in full swing. Opus 2 and 3 were on the way, and I was convinced that Anthony was a maniacal genius.

He had the ability to translate my graphical descriptions, of each musical phrase, brilliantly. He could reach into my mind, and see what was going on. He was a natural orchestrator, an intuitive interpreter of my music, and kept me going with an enhanced zany form of humour. However, the air became blue with profanities (mostly mine), whenever he stepped into the area of adding his own touches. It was a monster musical jigsaw puzzle; and if I felt that one piece was not fitting into place, I would start on another.

Allan was beavering away, on my demand for the world's best musicians to form the orchestra for Opus 2 and 3. "What about Caroline Dale for the cello?" he asked.

What about Caroline Dale? She was only the BBC's Young Musician of the Year, at 13 years of age, in 1978. She played the cello in the film 'Hilary and Jackie', depicting the life of legendary cellist Jacqueline du Pré *and what about her performance in Anthony Minghella's Truly, Madly, Deeply?* "Yes, yes, please try and book her," I yelled. Creating such an orchestra, to gel on one date in the future, was an almost impossible task. Finding the pianist, who could play the critical crescendos and softest of whispers, and be available on such a specific date, would be an equally onerous task. I'd already spent a thousand pounds on a session pianist, simply to see if the piano part worked at all. Allan was a Trojan, a true gentleman, and a top professional. I knew that the project would be safe in his hands.

However, it was becoming less safe in my hands. I had vastly overspent on people and items that were not in my original budget, and the taxman was preparing to pounce. The awesome tenor and musician, Malcolm Banham, led the choir. Their part in the score was vital, because they were the angels. Finally, after much searching, rehearsals with Nigel Clayton convinced me that I had the piano soloist we needed.

Slowly, the orchestra came together, until suddenly; we were within two weeks of the recording, at Sony's magnificent Whitfield Street studio. Mike Ross-Trevor was the world-class studio engineer, ready to take on the recording reins. With films like 'Hilary and Jackie', 'There's Something About Mary', 'The Fifth Element' and 'The Wind in the Willows' to his credit, I knew that we had the right man for the job.

The bombshell arrived right on cue. The taxman was knocking at my door, with a bill requiring instant payment of almost one hundred thousand pounds. I felt the punch rip right through my body. They had no concept of my work, nor did they care. They had thrown out my music expenses, as irrelevant to my business.

"How could you think that employing great orchestras was a personal expense?" I screamed to the air. The Government Gestapo was threatening to bring my project to an instant halt, and I had just seven days to come up with the cash. It was the taxman, or the recording; and somehow, I had to do both. My call to John Peat at the bank dripped with urgency, and he knew it. I had come up with a plan to raise the tax from the house.

"It's impossible to turn a re-mortgage around in seven days," he answered, almost apologetically.

"Right, what about getting a valuation and, if the equity is okay, loan me the hundred thousand until we can finalise the paperwork?" was my riposte. There was a polite pause.

"Even getting a valuation in seven days would be difficult," he continued, in his beautiful rolling Scottish accent. "Leave it with me, Stuart. I realise the pressure you're under, and I'll get back to you."

Seven days later, £100,000 was deposited into my bank account, and snatched away immediately by the taxman *not only is the government unsympathetic to my project, but they are downright cruel. One day, they'll be made aware of their attitude and actions.* John Peat had come through with hours to spare but, in the intervening days, I had felt my life racing towards a heart attack.

62. Date with Destiny

1998

Assembling a full orchestra, of the world's best musicians, for a 10 a.m. start, seemed a truly mammoth challenge. It would only take one key player to do a no-show, and we would have been in serious trouble. "They're all travelling separately, from every part of London," Allan quipped, as we sipped a cappuccino in a nearby café *that was a piece of information I did not need to hear.* It was 8:30 a.m., and Allan and I had arrived to see the preparations in full swing at the Sony studio. "Don't worry," he continued, "They're the greatest musicians your money can buy," he smiled. "They'll all turn up, you'll see."

Anthony Wade and Kevin Stoney arrived. That made four of us *just a hundred more to go...* At 9 a.m. the studio engineers and staff arrived, and started setting up the astonishing amount of recording gear. Seats for each member of the orchestra, with accompanying boom microphones, remained alarmingly empty. At 9.45 a.m., a few of the great musicians, looking more like stragglers from a previous night's party, strolled in. My heart began to pound again, and I wondered just how much pressure I could take, before it shot out of my chest and landed on the mixing desk.

Mike Ross-Trevor looked cool, and was ready with his team. Allan was unworried, and smiled as he took up his conducting position. Caroline Dale was next arriving; and I started to believe that it was really going to happen. I could not take my eyes off her. This was the musician who was in great demand by the world's top composers; and who was now tuning up her cello to play my first composition.

A nervous flashback took me back to my squat in Acton, where I had tentatively plucked at the strings of a cheap second-hand guitar. Next, to hit my tearful eyes, was my home on the pavement, opposite the BBC Studios in Wood Lane, dreaming of this moment. Then, the numerous occasions in which Anthony and I had screamed at each other, when things were not working out. I blinked and, as if by magic, every seat on the orchestral floor was filled; and Allan was making his opening remarks.

"The piece you are about to play was composed by Stuart Sharp."

He gestured towards me, and the orchestra nodded collectively at the 'great composer'. "He is not a musician, as you will find out when you begin to play…" *Oh, my God. What are you saying, Allan?*

Laughter filled the air, as my cover was blown. I sat next to Caroline Dale, and she blushed, unsure of what she had let herself in for. Allan knew what he was doing, though, and went on to explain the story behind the music. *Whew, I'm saved. Now, however awful they think the piece is, it won't be quite that bad…*

The baton was raised, and I heard my Angeli for the first time. It was like witnessing the birth of a first child - a miracle. Life was being created, from the tiny black dots that had been shackled, for years, to musical staves. Suddenly, they danced, tiptoed, trotted, cantered and galloped across the manuscripts. They were finally being released from a lifetime's imprisonment on paper, and I could see that they were happy at last. Hours went by like seconds, as each section of the score was repeated, until I was completely satisfied.

Anthony bellowed through the talkback microphone on many occasions, "Stuart says it doesn't sound right, maestro." *That's not how a great composer would normally address the world's finest classical musicians.*

A lot of good-hearted sniggering took place. But it worked. I had the honour of talking to the first violinist, and humming how I felt that it should be played. He knew immediately what was required. A quick chat and rehearsal with the violin section and, voila! it was perfect. Their final run-through, from top to tail, sent me into heaven *this was why I had to have the world's best!* One level lower, and the whole point of the music would have been lost. All the terror and torment of the years, that I had spent visualising this moment, now evaporated into Angeli's air. *I'm a real composer now,* I realised.

It was an unforgettable day. The cello solo was rendered with the touch and sensitivity of a virtuoso, and totally connected with the piece. Caroline was both humble and wonderful. Nigel Clayton's masterful interpretation of the piano solo sent my spirit soaring *if my heart were to give out now, I truly would not care...*

I wondered how long this feeling would last, before the cold light of day hit me again. Opus 1 now had a reputation to live up to, before even being orchestrated. Once again, I found it difficult to see myself as anything other than a poverty-stricken vagrant.

I had once walked the streets, close to the recording studio, without the wherewithal to buy a coffee. It was an unbelievable juxtaposition. As Angeli unwound itself from my mind, and onto orchestral scores, it left a plethora of space for other music, which had been waiting in the wings, to fill the void. The music was integral to the film in my head, and the two were inseparable. Now, the search was on for the producers. A thought struck me. *It was not for me to find them. It was for them to find me.*

63. My Father

1998

All of a sudden, I thought about my father. *Look what he's missed,* I thought, sadly. He would have been astonished, and proud. He was the only member of our family who could actually play an instrument, and I remember him tinkling the ivories at our first pub in Shepshed.

My mother received the call. My father's daughter, from his second marriage, had tracked her down, in order to pass a message on to me. My father was dying in a Bedfordshire nursing home. Forty years had elapsed without a word, and he requested to see me before he died. My instinct was immediately against such a visit, and many negative emotions flashed through my head. However, in the final analysis, my better judgement as a humanitarian took over. I made no arrangements to visit, as I was unsure if I would change my mind at the last moment; so it had to be when the feeling took me.

It actually took me by surprise, one Saturday morning. "Okay, go now" were the words that blasted into my inner hearing.

"Ah, Stuart, I'm so glad you made it," were the first words from the nursing home manager, who greeted me at the door. I was taken aback, having never seen the woman in my life. "Don't worry, you haven't changed a bit. Your picture is hanging on your dad's bedroom wall. Come in. Your father is sitting among the old folk over there."

It was a depressing sight. Several very elderly people were languishing in motley old chairs, in various states of soporific slumber and senile stupor. My father, head drooped, his hands trembling from Parkinson's disease, was dribbling into a plastic cover wrapped around his neck. Unusually, although in his late seventies, he had a good head of jet-black hair. I stood in front of him, holding back my tears. His head rose slowly, and we made eye contact.

It was an incredible moment. Gone, were the years of bitterness and hatred. Gone, were all my negative questions. This was a picture of my father, dying before my eyes, and I felt nothing but love for him. "Hello, Pop," I offered quietly. His hands stopped shaking, and tears started to run down his cheeks.

He was wheeled to his bedroom, and I sat with him for hours. We chatted about the 'good old days', which in fact were the atrociously bad old days, but I still remembered them fondly with him. He did not shake, during the time we spent together, and I said silent prayers for his peaceful transition to the next life while he talked. His eyes closed, and a smile appeared on his face.

He was happy, and I felt joy in helping an old man to face his demons, and finally conquer them. He died shortly afterwards. Hilary and I attended the funeral, and finally met our half-sisters; which completed a circle of uncertainty. My mother could not bring herself to forgive him; and refused to attend.

64. Opus 1

1997 - 1998

Keshi was organising a seminar for the blind, and urgently needed funds; so a trip to Zambia, to sponsor the event, became necessary. The president had warned me not to travel to Zambia under the present regime, as they would 'greatly embarrass me', as he put it. In other words, I would be arrested, and jailed.

This was not a pleasant thought, as I had seen Zambian jails. They were horrific places to visit, and being an inmate would be unimaginable. It was a big decision, but the journey would have to wait until Opus 1 of Angeli had been safely recorded.

The air had turned blue in my studio again. A major introduction was missing from the opus, and it still hadn't arrived in my mind. Continuing without it put the score out of sync, but we forged on nevertheless.

Months of devotion had ended. It was orchestrated, and arranged; and further orchestrated, by Allan; but the whole point to Angeli was missing, and there was a totally empty space in my head.

"Okay!" I yelled, finally, to Anthony, "You do the intro!"

Two weeks later, he played me his work. It was stupendous. "Right, Anthony, it's wonderful."

He interrupted quickly, "But. But. But. I can feel the 'but'!" he screamed. "You mean it's crap!"

"No. No. It's great. But it's not right for Angeli." I replied gently, and with enormous respect for his day and night work to produce this stunning intro.

"What's wrong with it?" he screamed again.

"I don't know. It's just... not right; that's all I know," I responded, with sad resignation. Rehearsals for Opus 1 had been booked, with a major orchestra in Bratislava, and we had no choice. We had to go with it as it was; although Allan felt that it was a great score.

The piece was performed by the Bratislava Radio Symphony Orchestra, and received enthusiastic applause from the musicians, and even the recording engineer; but I was glum-faced. All the struggle, and all the cash flowing like a river over the symphonic waterfall, had ended in disappointment.

"What's wrong with it, Stuart?" Allan asked, compassionately.

"I don't like it. It's not what's in my head; and we don't have an intro," I sighed wearily.

"Everyone else likes it, Stuart. It's really wonderful," he offered.

"It's not good enough. We have to start again," I cried.

Starting again meant grinding it out on the interminable London streets, looking for more sales. The Philharmonia had one available recording date left in the calendar year, and I booked it. This left me six months to correct the score, and find an intro. 'Find' is the wrong word - it had to arrive. I was exhausted, from years of continuous moneymaking, and working three days a week for the taxman. It was draining my spiritual batteries, with no chance in sight for recovery.

I knew what was wrong with the score. Authentic Uilleann Irish pipes were essential for the centre section; but it was far too late in the day to consider this problem, as there were many other minor adjustments that needed to be made. It was ten o'clock in the evening, and I lay on the bed, staring at the ceiling that doubled as my personal video screen. The introduction to Angeli must be in my mind somewhere; so I started to focus, to the exclusion of my whole being.

I had been lying motionless for three hours when, from the left side of the ceiling, I saw a trumpet player coming into view. He was standing on a hill, dressed in Roman costume, and playing to the sky. Then, from the depths of my soul, an audio fader, connected to my inner hearing, was brought up gradually. It built and built, until angels appeared from the heavens, with a glorious choral response to the beckoning trumpet.

It took my breath away, and I knew the missing piece had arrived.

Allan answered. "Yes, Stuart? Why such a late call?"

"Just take this down fast! I haven't got time to explain," I yelled. The part was fresh in my mind, and I wanted to be able to sing the parts, and describe it graphically, before it disappeared.

"Hang on, hang on!" he shouted, "I'm trying to transcribe onto a manuscript. "Sing it again, slowly." After an hour of singing, and yelling, and describing, and huffing, and puffing, he had it all down.

"That's fantastic!" he yelled again. "This is it! This will set the scene for the whole piece. Wonderful! Well done!"

We were ready for the Philharmonia.

Déjà vu. Sitting in the same old café, with the same old sunlight streaming through the same old dusty blinds, the same old cappuccino, the same old Allan Wilson, the same old lovely smile, the same old street, and the same old time. It was 8:30 a.m. again; but this time was different.

We awaited the arrival of the world famous ensemble. This was it. I could hear it in my head, and it was magnificent. The Uilleann pipes, and the choir, would be required after the recording. An entourage of supporters, including my mother, arrived by 9 a.m. The atmosphere was building. I had just employed one of the world's greatest orchestras, and the flashbacks struck again.

I was back at the pub, serving pints, and cooking steak and chips. I was being beaten by my music master, and wore the class dunce's hat. I could hear him screaming at me.

"Sharp, you are wasting my time, you are wasting the school's time, and you are wasting the class's time!"

He was still with me, sitting in the café next to Allan. He was grinning, and ready to make some snide comment; but I beat him to it, and grabbed him by his tie.

"Now, you bastard, come into the studio with me and listen. Just listen to one of the world's greatest orchestras, playing my composition. What are you going to say about that, now, eh?" *I poked him in the stomach with my free hand.* It gave me a good feeling to imagine it.

The quiet was intense. The orchestra was ready. Allan raised his baton. The trumpet began, heralding the Angeli introduction. It took my breath away; not because it was being played by one of the world's greatest trumpet players, but because it sounded exactly as I'd originally heard it.

It was perfect. The angels had no choice at all. They would have to descend from the heavens, following such a call. The performance transcended my vision of its majesty. It was a day without end, the atmosphere was exultant, and I had a major realisation. The music was the umbilical cord of my existence. It fed my spirit; drove me on; and without it, I would die.

Malcolm Banham, and his wonderful singers, joined the team in the studio two weeks later, to overdub the choir parts. Their voices were subtle, powerful, and magnificent; as they became the true angels. We were nearly there.

65. Tommy Keane in Galway Bay

1998

Months later, the whole team was on its way to the home of Tommy Keane, the great Irish pipe player. Costs were escalating, and I had committed myself to visit Keshi in Zambia with enough cash to keep him and his family going; so my head was spinning with sales plans, to feed the fiery furnace that was consuming my diminishing bank account.

My vision had seen the Irish pipes being recorded live in an ancient pine forest. Then, lo and behold, such a wood appeared behind Tommy's beautiful pink house, on the shores of Galway Bay. Once again, every detail of the visions had come to pass. Allan had contacted Tommy months before, and he was well prepared to play the interlocking piece. The rain rushing in from the Irish west coast was ready to pounce, and flashbacks to Africa now flooded my mind.

"We need to cut the niceties short, Allan. We must get it done now," I whispered. The tall pinewoods shrouded Tommy in a spiritual mist, inducing the perfect atmosphere, and the world-class Celtic pipe master played with the haunting genius for which he was renowned.

Finally, all the pieces for Opus 1 of Angeli had been recorded. Now, much post-production awaited, to integrate the soul-stirring pipes and choir.

66. Time to Reflect

1999

Whilst asleep, a dream transported me to Ben's grave, to meet Sally and James again. I made the journey to his grave every few weeks, and then travelled to the hillside to meditate. *I could see myself haymaking. I could smell the grass roasting in the baking sun. I saw myself finding Grace's lost ring, on the old dirt track. At the graveside, Sally and James looked directly into my eyes.* "What am I to do next?" I asked Sally.

"Write the book," she replied. I kept a diary containing thousands of notes, but writing a book was the job of an author.

"You know how to do it, you've done it before. You will remember," she assured me.

The dream ended suddenly, and I awoke with a start. I juggled with strange thoughts. What if the 'snow people' were simply figments of my imagination, as my father had professed? But then, I thought, they had guided me to achieve impossible things. If I had not believed that they were real, I would not have followed their advice.

There seemed to be no answer. Writing a book was another challenge beyond my capabilities, and expecting to convert over twenty years of notes into a book was too daunting a prospect. I decided to wait until the spirit took me by the hand, and provide me with the right words, at the right time.

67. Cash Flowing to Africa

2001

My bank statement arrived. I was stupefied, and stared in disbelief, almost petrified. It was ten pounds overdrawn. Not a lot, in normal circumstances; but in my case, it meant that hundreds of thousands of pounds had flown the financial coop without my knowledge.

The bank manager must have thought I had lost my mind. It was just too difficult to explain my vast vision. It was simply not possible to get out and earn more cash, in the volumes I needed. *The house has to go*, I realised, as Africa beckoned.

Anthony, and his colleague Anji Zantboer, accompanied me on my visit to Zambia. The words of the ex-president rang out in my mind. I could be arrested, on some trumped up charge, and there was absolutely nothing that I could do about it; but I had to face the beast. My name came up on the immigration computer in Lusaka. The officer looked down at my passport, and pointed to his superior. "Move over there," he pointed

I was manhandled into a back room. "We know who you are," he greeted me, smiling sarcastically. "So, you are helping the blind. Well, let me tell you something. Since you brought them to the attention of our president, they are better off than us." He moved around the dusky room, nodded to himself, and slid his hand over the dusty table. "Yes, much better off... hmm, I may have to confiscate your baggage."

The message was clear. To get through customs, a bribe was necessary; and that might not be the end of it. He placed my passport on the table. "It needs stamping," he whispered. Luckily, I had five thousand kwacha in cash in my wallet. I sighed, and swiftly placed it in the passport. He turned slowly, picked up the document, and walked out. "Follow me," he said sternly.

"Go back in line." Anthony and Anji had already gone through, and were watching helplessly from the other side *if President Kaunda was in power, this guy wouldn't dare...* Now it was obvious, that to stay clear of major problems would cost me. I was a marked person, and Kaunda's enemies had long memories. I had successfully thwarted their plans to disrupt the concert, and survived several assassination attempts. I intended to finish my project in Zambia, and if it meant another confrontation with the dark forces of political power, then so be it.

"What the hell was all that about?" Anthony queried. I couldn't tell him. Such a story would have terrified both him and Anji.

"Nothing, just a backhander to get our baggage through. Let's go." Soon, the smiling face of Keshi and his team came into view, at the airport entrance. It was a wonderful reunion, and sponsoring a seminar for the blind, in Ndola, was a way of bringing us all together again.

The crazy cratered roads, that connected the various townships in Zambia, now battered my body. I had forgotten how bad they'd been, but now they were much worse, since Chiluba's promise to re-metal them had never materialised. Twelve hours, on the old cratered Chingola Road, in a truck with shot suspension, eventually took its toll.

Kabompo, on the Angolan border, was going to be a township too far. We hit a massive pothole, three feet wide and almost as deep. My metal right hip survived, but my left took the full force of the impact, and I screamed in agony. I knew that the left hip had gone the same way as the right, and that I was in deep trouble. Anthony and Anji looked on in astonishment at my sudden outburst, which I quickly brushed off, while holding my breath. I could not let them know of the problem that had so suddenly devastated me. The sun was setting fast, we were running out of fuel, and Kabompo was several hours drive away.

Every creak of the truck, as it manoeuvred the patchwork of potholes, sent riveting pain through my body, and I knew that I would not make it. A sign announced that the Chimfunshi Wildlife Orphanage was off to the right. "Driver, go down there," I shouted.

"But, sir," he replied politely, "you cannot go there after dark, and it will be dark in minutes." Anthony and Anji were also devastated by the journey, and were showing serious signs of exhaustion. It was no more than a jungle track, and recent rains had created deep floods directly in front of us.

"Go for it," I insisted. "It can't be far." The driver sighed, as the truck sank deeply into the flooded track, and leech-infested water slopped into the cabin *Oh, no! This could be the end of us...* The deep-throated echoes of lions on the prowl reverberated everywhere, as the vehicle swished and swashed its way out of the flood.

We all breathed a simultaneous sigh of relief. However, the petrol gauge was showing empty and, although we had a spare can of diesel, no one was going to step outside to re-fuel the tank. The track got narrower, and great prickly bushes smacked into the truck, gauging their way blindly along the windows. The darkness was intimidating, the noise was sharp and sinister, and the smell of fear was amongst us.

An opening appeared in the distant clearing, and our headlights caught the outline of a hodgepodge of buildings. I held onto the pain in my hip, and prayed for a good Samaritan to emerge from the buildings.

Suddenly, the truck started to sway, as if we were a ship caught in an ocean swell. Anji screamed, and the driver shouted, "It's a hippo!" A giant black hippopotamus had arrived on the scene, like a stealth bomber out of the darkness, to attack this invading predator.

In an instant, lights flickered on in the buildings; and an infuriated inhabitant ran to the truck, holding a lantern. It was an amazing sight, particularly as he showed no fear of the hippo. "You people!" he screamed, in a definitive British accent, "Get off my property now. No one is allowed here after five o'clock!"

The lantern lit up his craggy old face, which was fluffed up by a white beard. We all knew that we were going nowhere, no matter what this incensed little man wanted.

Then a woman, of a less pernickety nature, joined him; and began to pat the hippo on the head, as if it was a kitten. "It's okay, Billy, there's a good boy," she whispered quietly in his ear. We were all transfixed. 'Billy' immediately quietened, and stood like any good hippo should, by his masters.

"Now, what brings you here; when there are signs on the main road saying, quite clearly, 'No visitors after five p.m.'?" We had struck lucky. They were British *Thank God!*

"Do you take in badly injured animals after five p.m.?" I asked, with a grin. After a stony silence, she looked in the truck for such an animal. "No. It's me. I'm the injured animal!" I exclaimed, and pointed to my side. "It's my left hippo!" I continued, jokingly, but in a great deal of pain. 'Billy' took in every word, the nice lady eventually understood, and saw the funny side of the situation, the grumpy old man continued growling his indignation, and we were allowed to follow them into their own little 'sleepy hollow'.

"Now keep this side of Billy, otherwise he might eat you!" said the very nice lady. By chance, we had arrived at the home of David and Sheila Siddle. Once inside their 'cottage in the jungle', their hospitality was overwhelming. After food, and Anthony's ability to make the old man laugh, we were treated to a history of their work.

Chimfunshi Wildlife Orphanage was founded in 1983, when a game ranger brought a badly wounded infant chimpanzee to their cattle ranch. David and Sheila had lived along the Zambian Copperbelt since the 1950's, and nursed a chimp, nicknamed 'Pal', back to health. In the years that followed, they created an international reputation, building one of the world's foremost sanctuaries for chimpanzees. Billy, the hippo, was an exception. He was another orphan rescued by the Siddles, and brought up from a baby; making him the only tame hippo in the world.

Their hospitality extended to sleeping huts; in the vast, open and, frankly, scary compound. Anthony and I shared and, with a torch rapidly running out of energy, we watched giant spiders hang from the ceiling, with their great eyes peering down. It was impossible to sleep, knowing that huge baboon-sized arachnids were waiting to pounce. We took it in turns to do spider watch, while the other slept. The pain in my hip intensified, and I knew that it would be impossible for me to travel another kilometre in the old truck. Monkeys dancing on the roof at dawn created a deafening din, but heralded our survival.

Sheila Siddle arrived at our door at 5 a.m. to plan our escape back to Lusaka. Our old truck, having been battered into submission, would not budge. It had miraculously brought us to the Siddles, but was now on its last gasp. Without a telephone to the outside world, Sheila put out a Mayday call via her short wave radio transmitter. I needed a four-wheel drive Land Cruiser, at minimum, to endure the crippling crater-strewn road back to Chingola. "That's the best I can do," she said. "The message should be picked up in South Africa, and relayed back to Chingola."

How on earth this intrepid British couple could have lived a jungle existence, under such circumstances, for 50 years was beyond my comprehension. The Zambian authorities would have found it an impossible task, to lay telephone lines deep into the jungle for the Siddles. More messages were sent, from her crackly transmitter, and a successful outcome was now in the lap of the gods.

I stood on the concrete viewing area, by the fortress-like walls enclosing the chimp compound, and pondered the future. Anthony and Anji breakfasted on fried eggs and elephant steak. My days of earning vast amounts of money were now numbered. I needed to move fast, around the London metropolis every day and, for the second time, I was becoming a cripple. I felt exhausted.

The film in my head was complete, and I was both the actor and the audience. I enjoyed both experiences, and it was an excellent production. The soundtrack was breathtaking, and the theme song, Angeli, which was launched to promote it, was a major hit. The money rolled in, and I built Keshi's centre for the blind; but the truth always slapped me in the face, as the cold light of day dawned.

Sally's voice rang out in my head. "Look up. The answer is in the sky. That's where you must be."

"Sally," I yelled, as my heart pounded. Sheila was feeding the monkeys, and looked up with a start. She shook her head, and carried on. God knows what she must have thought. So many long years had passed, without any communication with the 'snow people'. "Sally, please don't go, what do you mean?" I whispered. There was no response. I was deflated, and frustrated. I watched the chimps playing, screaming, and beating each other up, when I heard a low drone in the sky.

A small plane flew overhead, and I wondered if Sally's words were connected in any way. It didn't make any sense, so I continued to ponder. I wondered who would make the film, and who would record the theme song. It all seemed a long way off. Then out of the clearing, as if by magic, a stunning Land Cruiser came into view.

Sheila dashed over and called me. "There you are," she said. "Not bad for jungle communication."

Her Mayday call to Johannesburg in South Africa had been relayed back to Chingola in Zambia, and then on to an air charter company who supplied the Land Cruiser. We glided over the potholes as if they didn't exist. There was something about this air charter company, and their incredible service, that was almost spiritual, and I made it clear to their PA that I would be seeing them again one day.

"The owner is British," she replied. "You should meet him for sure."

"I'll come back to thank him personally," I responded, gratefully. We took one of their planes back to Lusaka, to join Keshi for the final meeting. I fought back the pain, as the institutionalised deprivation and suffering of the Zambian people made my personal inconvenience seem insignificant. Thinking about their fortitude, against terrible odds, always gave me strength.

I looked out over the vast African savannah from the aircraft, and saw how quickly one could travel between the townships by air. The vision of the small plane flying over Chimfunshi struck me, and Sally's words echoed in my mind. Then I was struck by another thought. *Even the smallest plane can hop around this vast wilderness with ease.*

I moved to the captain's cabin, and requested to sit in the jump seat. "Be my guest," he replied. The controls fascinated me, and I studied his airmanship *I need to become a pilot.* My mind wandered into pure fantasy. *The film and music were doing so well, that I became the pilot of my own plane in Zambia, and flew to all destinations.* I was jolted back down to earth, as the wheels of the aircraft greased the runway.

The trip had gone well, I'd avoided being locked up, and the meeting with Keshi was almost at an end. "How are you going to raise the seven million pounds that we need, to build the centre?" asked Keshi, almost nonchalantly. He was referring to the project that we had costed, to create a fully staffed sports stadium for the disabled, with doctors, a surgery, and all 'mod cons'. It would double as a national, fully equipped sports centre, which would put Zambia on the map for international sports events, and this figure would cover its running costs for the first ten years, long enough to get it established.

"I'm not going to raise it Keshi, my friend, I'm going to earn it!" I responded, positively. As I moved, the pain in my hip, which I had tried so hard to conceal, sent me a reminder, which seared right through my brain; causing me to cry out in agony. A silence pervaded the dusty little office, as all eyes focused on me.

"What the hell was that?" Anthony shouted. "That's the second time you've screamed out."

"Nothing. Nothing at all. Just a bit of cramp," I replied quickly.

"How're you gonna carn seven million pounds?" repeated Anthony.

"Remember, it's me, Anthony. It's what I do," I quipped.

However, every step I took now had become agonising, causing me to scream inwardly. I knew that I was never going to earn that kind of money by working as I'd done before. My previous, prolific, profit-making career was over; but now I had the music and the film. They were done, dusted and successful - in my mind, at least. I had eleven hours to meditate on the problem, and at 35,000 feet I was cruising. All sounds in the plane disappeared, and my mental video screen activated.

I replayed the movie, repeatedly, in my mind. I went through all the support given to me by the 'snow people'. Sally's last communication, 'the answer is in the sky' baffled me *the screen's blank. The future's blank. I don't know what to do.*

'The music for the film is not finished' was the first caption to splash across the screen. It came in a flash, and disappeared in a flash *what does this mean?* Before I could take a breath, another caption followed the first. *'Write the script, then write the book.'* Oh my God.

I wasn't a scriptwriter, nor was I an author. I had already done all the hard work, and now felt that this was a job for professionals.

Then a cold dose of reality hit again. *How would anyone write such a script?* They would need a book, from which to work. However, this was a major new undertaking, and I was down to my last few pennies. As the greyness of Heathrow beckoned from 5,000 feet, I finally had the answer. I would sell up, downsize, and pray that the money raised would see me through to the end.

As we disembarked from the plane, the pain in my hip was agonising, and it was all I could do to put one foot in front of the other.

68. Selling Up for Music

2001 - 2003

The 'For Sale' notice went up, and the house was sold within days. "I have cash. I'm not messing around. When can you move?" was the buyer's startling statement. I rekindled my black hole of a bank account, and looked out for a much cheaper property. Within six weeks, I was living close to my mother. After Bob and Pat had passed on, she had moved to a picturesque village, back in Leicestershire, making the circle complete. I did not downsize, but instead, descended downmarket. I walked with the aid of a stick, and rattled with painkillers.

It was back to the drawing board. I had reviewed the movie repeatedly, and now heard all of the missing incidental pieces. The new music totally contradicted the majestic Angeli Symphony and theme song. It was raucous, down, and dirty. I produced rough demo recordings on my guitar, before seeking out a new local recording studio. I'd been led to believe that all the great producers worked in London, and that nothing creative existed north of Watford; but I needed a great producer within spitting distance.

The conundrums, careering around in my mind, kept crashing into one another. I was in the middle of nowhere, crippled, and without any musical contacts. Yellow Pages was the first thing delivered to my door *okay, that's the first sign*. I ripped off the wrapper, and searched under 'Recording Studios', where at least fifty tiny backstreet facilities were listed. "Come on, Sally, or James," I mumbled, "which one is it?" Speed was of the essence, as my finger scrolled down the list. At that precise second, 'Deadline Studios, Leicester' appeared. "Okay, that's it," I told myself.

Adam Ellis, the young owner and producer, was quietly spoken, but his self-effacing style belied a genius. He brought together an assembly of top rock and pop musicians to work on my music. They included Tony Robinson and Gary Birtles, from The Beautiful South's line-up; and drummer Tim Browne, and bass guitarist Tom Westmoreland, completed the band.

Tom was a stalwart, who played with the sword of cystic fibrosis hanging over his head. 'Rock 'n' Roll Revolution', 'Guilty', 'Killer Touch', 'Ku Ka Zama' and 'Date with Destiny' were some of the film's incidental tracks. Adam arranged, and sung tight harmonies, himself. He played wonderful rhythm and lead guitars, and produced the music to a world-class standard.

I spent over two years in his studio, working up to twelve hours a day. However, the tracks were missing a top-notch lead vocalist, who knew the songs intimately, and could do justice to the varied and complex tracks.

"Okay, Adam, until we get one, I'll do a guide vocal." The band sort of sniggered. It was all good-humoured, and I hobbled into the sound booth to transform into 'Rexford the Rocker.'

What came out of my mouth was not me, or certainly not what I thought I was. I had discovered another self. Without a singing lesson to my credit, I blasted forth, and hit top notes that I could not believe. Each song was completed in one take.

"My God," said Adam, "you've nailed it. There's no need for a lead singer. No one could do better."

The rest of the band were delighted. Adam went on to sing 'Mystery Man', 'Dirty Doggin'', 'Love is a Word' and joined me on 'Date with Destiny'. Before long, all of the songs for the soundtrack were completed; and the three-year programme, to produce the tracks, had ended. I felt elated and, with the CD in my pocket, took a journey home that I had never made before.

69. Plane Spotting

2003

The traffic was gridlocked in Leicester, and I turned onto a country road instead. Leicestershire village roads have their own spaghetti-like peculiarity, and a mistake took me along a back road to nowhere. Confused, a sign for Leicester Airport came into view, and I took it for no apparent reason. I parked up, and watched all the light aircraft buzzing around the airfield.

As I sat silently, I was back at Chimfunshi in Zambia, and Sally's words, 'The answer is in the sky', came back to me. I watched the students circling the airspace, and bouncing the planes on landing. *Not so easy*, I imagined, but my mind was on fire. I could now see why I had found my way to the airport, and this was not a coincidence. Nothing was a coincidence *I was meant to be a pilot.*

I went to alight from the car, to seek a better view, and screamed in agony. My dream was destroyed in seconds, as my crippled hip anchored me to the seat.

70. Derren Brown

2004

Thoughts of taking up flying disappeared into a deep tunnel of pain.

"I can't make it. I can barely walk, and getting into the De Monfort Hall, let alone sitting through the show, will be impossible."

Adam had a spare ticket for the Derren Brown Show. "If you can drive there, the band will help you into the hall. Try and make it, somehow. It'll be incredible," was Adam's insistent response. My hip operation was in two weeks' time, and would put me out of action for six months.

"Okay, I'm coming; meet me in the car park." Stuffed with painkillers, and grateful for the automatic gearbox in my car, I made the journey. I squirmed, and sweated profusely, as Derren Brown plied his amazing talents to a Leicester audience; though I whispered to Adam that I could not possibly return for the second half of the show.

"Someone is about the leave before the interval. Please do not leave. During the interval, write down the name of a loved one who has passed on, come back, and something amazing will happen to you." Derren Brown's sudden and out-of-context statement shocked me.

Adam smiled. I wrote down Ben's name, and returned to my seat, in agony. The grinding pain pulsated through my body, causing sweat to drip down my forehead, and my heart to race. Thirty minutes into the second half, something strange was happening with the pain. I felt a slight easing, and my heart rate slowed. The sweating stopped, and I pondered Derren's words. Fifteen minutes later, the pain had disappeared completely, and I could sit upright and normally, for the first time in many months. Toward the end of the show, Derren looked in my direction, and talked about the amazing incident that would take place. I skipped out of the hall, free of all pain, while Adam and the band were stunned.

I waited for an hour, at the stage door, for this wonderful man to appear, and thanked him for the miraculous cure of my crippled hip. "I did nothing," he said, "you did it all yourself, but I am very pleased for you."

Of course, he was right; but he had been the catalyst. Mr McMinn was astonished, as I jogged into his consulting room. A new x-ray showed no improvement in my hip. "You should be crawling in here, with a hip like that." My explanation of complete freedom of movement, when there should be none, met with a great deal of scepticism. "There's no logical explanation, Stuart; but I suggest that, while you're in this state, we postpone the op until the pain returns; because for sure, it will."

71. Plane Sailing

2004

My next port of call was Leicester Airport; even though winter had arrived with a vengeance, and was not an auspicious time for a novice to be flying *I must train for my pilot's licence, while the going's still good.*

Dave Darley was my tutor. "It's gusting 35 knots, and the cloud base is 600 feet. We can do low level circuits, if you're game." I was enthusiastic to fly, whatever the weather. My experiences in Africa had freed me from all fear, and it was hands on from the word 'Go'.

I taxied the little Cessna along the taxiways, into the side field, and back again *Oh my God, why the hell don't they have a proper steering wheel?* Guiding the plane with your feet seemed so unintuitive. We took off, and all of a sudden I became so petrified that my throat closed up, and I couldn't speak or breathe. "We have to land," I gasped, "I can't do this!" *So much for fearless Freddie*, I chided myself, as we sipped coffee during the debrief.

Dave assured me that, if I stuck at it, and turned up for a lesson every week, I would be fine; but I could not see it. Watching him set the plane up for landing looked so simple, and I would never look at pilots in the same way again *how can the answer be in the sky?* I asked, over and over again. It did not make sense; but I had always followed the guidance in my head, regardless of the outrageous content, or the possible outcome.

My body shook, every time I travelled to the airport for a lesson, and it did not seem possible to get beyond the simplest of tasks, such as taxiing the plane in a straight line. Learning to fly the plane, it turned out, was only a small part of the programme to acquire a licence; and as I scanned the thick manuals on each subject, all the theory exams, plus learning radio-telephony, looked impossible. I had always had difficulty studying academically and, now, at 58 years of age, I had no clue as to how to approach these vast subjects.

My hip was still fine, and I was able to start exercising again on the squash court. This was a miracle; so I saw it as a sign, and forced myself to the airport for each lesson. One part of my brain shouted, *"Why are you beating yourself up for no reason?"*

The other part said, *"Go for it. The answer lies in the sky."*

I was constantly taking deep breaths, and trying to stay calm.

"No, keep it level!" Dave screamed, as he grabbed the controls and forced the plane down. "Are you trying to get us killed?"

I just didn't get it. Keeping the plane at an almost level trajectory after take-off seemed counter-productive, when the object was to climb. "Do what I tell you to do, not what you think you should!" shouted Dave again. I was mortified, and could not touch the controls again. He landed the plane, and I was convinced that I did not have the capacity to commandeer the complex cockpit controls.

72. In the Cockpit

2004

I'd had fifteen hours of flying instruction, and still could not land the plane without bouncing it like a balloon. My timing on the 'flare out', and keeping the nose in the correct position, was abysmal. Most students had perfected this manoeuvre after seven hours, and Dave was getting bored. "We're going to be doing circuits like this forever, if you don't buck your ideas up," he said, jokingly.

My mother was in her late eighties, and enjoying a pub lunch. Taking her out and about was a joy, and always made her happy. "I've always wanted to sit in the cockpit of an aeroplane, and fly around the sky," she confessed to me, one day. I thought for a moment. *Maybe this is my chance to make her dream come true.* I noticed that she was beginning to cough a great deal, and this concerned me *I'd better get my act together quickly.*

She'd chain-smoked all her life, but had stopped in 1993. I was sure that, nonetheless, it was catching up with her, and had a feeling that she would not be with me much longer. This reality check jolted me into action. Unless I could land the plane perfectly, ten times out of ten, I would not be allowed to progress to the next stage of lessons. I called a friend, who was an ace fighter pilot, and explained my problem.

"Right," said he, "it's easy. When you've flared the plane, just relax, enjoy, and the plane will land itself."

Mmm, that sounds a little too relaxed...

73. Flying Fingers

2001 - 2004

I started to write the book. My fingers swept across the keyboard, but it didn't look right. I stopped, and saw that it was more like a script, full of dialogue and descriptions *wait a minute, what's going on here*? I continued writing for weeks, and concluded that I needed a professional screenplay writer to help me. Allan Wilson was aware of my dilemma, and contacted a colleague who could provide the assistance I required.

Craig Clyde was just the man. He was well qualified, and actually taught the subject. The only drawback was his location. Salt Lake City, Utah was not exactly round the corner. I gave myself a challenge, and a reward - land the plane perfectly, ten times successively, and I would allow myself to make the journey to America. I placed a chair in front of a long mirror in the bedroom, and visualised it as a cockpit and a landing strip. I focused on relaxing, as I pulled the power back, lifted the nose, and waited.

"Right," said Dave, "it's now, or never." The pressure was on, and I took a deep breath as I turned into the final approach. I trimmed the plane at 65 knots, and had the perfect angle for landing; although Dave was ready to pounce on the controls, expecting another disaster. The wheels greased the tarmac, and the plane held steady. I'd achieved a perfect landing.

"Okay. Full power. Go around and do it again. Great! Well done." Dave was delighted, and relieved. An hour later, I had achieved ten perfect landings. I almost believed that I could fly a plane (nothing could be further from the truth), but I had got over the first hurdle.

"We'll arrange for your first solo, as soon as possible," my intrepid instructor shouted over the engine noise, as I stepped out of the plane.

"See you in two weeks, Dave. I'm off to America," I replied.

Landing in Los Angeles for the first time was exciting. America was bright, and bustling with energy. Meeting 6ft 4in Craig Clyde, and his wife, Vaunie, was a joy. I came fully armed with my script notes, and music.

"I need to hear the story from your own heart first," said the big man with an even bigger heart. It was an intensive two weeks, and

Craig offered to write a first draft, from which I could work. "I'll try to be as English as I can, but I can't promise," he smiled.

I arrived home to dullness. I had not noticed the pandemic negativity in the UK before. America was 'can do', but the UK gave off 'can't do' vibes; and the depressing scepticism here contrasted with the positive optimism of the States.

Emma and Kate had moved on with their lives. Both had partners; and Kate had a daughter, Maddie, now aged six - my first grandchild. Mother's cough was getting much worse, and I feared for her. I needed to press ahead, become a good pilot, and take mother flying in the cockpit before it was too late.

I stepped up my flying programme, and the long trek towards writing the book began. I adopted a professional approach to study and my flying skills; and with the assistance of an air traffic controller from East Midlands Airport, began a three month course in radiotelephony.

74. Going Solo

2004

It was time for my first solo, and Dave sprung it on me without notice. Assuming that I'd opt out, if I knew in advance; he had arranged for the Chief Flying Instructor to join me after a circuit. "Okay. Off you go. You're on your own," came his quickfire remark, as he left the aircraft *Oh my God, are they mad putting me in charge of the plane?* I found myself taxiing to the holding point, and could not believe what was happening. There was no one to help me - if I messed up now, I could end up dead. For the next thirty minutes, I flew flawlessly around the airport. It was the greatest experience of my life.

"I can fly!" I shouted. I called my mother, and she was even happier than I was. But there was still a long road ahead, before I had my licence; and the next twelve months were gruelling. I passed all my theory exams, and was ready for the final test of flying skills. Newly qualified pilots explained to me how nerve-wracking, and exhausting, these three to four hour procedures were. The instructors could not make them any more difficult if they tried, but this was understandable. They wanted to be convinced that their students were competent aviators.

I had worked hard for this day, and was lucky that the weather was mild. It was all a matter of flying to places that you'd never been to before, finding them without GPS, controlling the plane, making all the correct radio calls, simulating Maydays, flying the plane in many configurations, having a simulated engine failure, preparing to land in a field, and landing back home; using varying degrees of flaps. There was absolutely no room for any error. At this level, such a mistake would mean re-taking the test, and relearning a manoeuvre. I was determined to focus, and pass; as I had to fulfil my mother's dream urgently.

I alighted the plane with the CFI looking on, and walked almost silently back to his office. My heart began to beat faster as he sat down. I just stared at him. He was signing papers, and I couldn't wait any longer. "Well, have I passed, then?" I blurted out.

He looked up in surprise. "Oh, of course you've passed," he replied, offering his hand, "Well done. You did very well. Your licence will be sent from the CAA very soon."

I was in a state of shock. I was now a fully qualified pilot. I couldn't wait to break the news, but booking a flight for mother came first. I raced home in the car, feeling as high as a kite.

'The answer lies in the sky'. These words flashed into my mind again, and I was no wiser *but now, I'm getting closer.* Mother was deteriorating, and complained of being unable to move her foot.

"It's like a lump of lead," she complained, but was determined to fly with me.

Craig Clyde continued to work on the first draft of the screenplay and, finally, after one year, it arrived by email with a note: 'Your story is so big it was difficult to know where to start, and where to go with it. I've written 164 pages, which is far too long for a script, but you can work with it as a template'.

On reading my own life story, in script form, I saw all the problems involved in writing a screenplay. Every bit of dialogue would have to be changed; but the generous American had pointed me in the right direction.

75. Screenplay Writer

2005

My next challenge was to become a screenplay writer, and I could see that it would be a long and arduous task. However, overcoming my previous impossibility, in gaining my pilot's licence, had energised me for the challenge ahead; and every night, I visualised the 'snow people' arriving in a dream, to give me the answers.

It was 4th December, 2005 and the thirtieth anniversary of Ben's death. I made my way over to his grave, and had my usual word with him. I felt that he was happy that I had not squandered the angels' gift. I talked to Ben regularly, and imagined him as a handsome six-footer in Heaven. Then it was back over to the hillside, as I retraced my steps home.

Ominous grey clouds, with their austere mountainous peaks, juddered their way towards the slope; and silvery snowflakes made their first appearance of winter. I shivered, my face freshened by the northerly winds. I stared into the gloom, closed my eyes, and contemplated how long it would be before mother and I joined Ben. I wondered if I would ever complete my mission in Africa.

In the distant reaches of the snowy scene, Sally and James appeared, floating toward me on the cusp of the crispy clouds that wended their way to the hillside. Then, in an instant, they dissipated into the void. No words or thoughts came into my mind. For the first time, I was not frustrated with the lack of communication. I simply assumed that they were happy that everything was on course.

76. A Dream Comes True

2005

Getting my aged mother into the car, for her journey of a lifetime in the co-pilot's seat, was fraught with difficulty; as her undiagnosed illness was taking its toll *how on earth is she going to climb onto the wing, to get into the plane?* But she was resolute, and I loved her indomitable strength of mind. The president of Zambia said that I had inherited her spirit and, without it, I could not have achieved what I had done. She looked up at the wing, made up her mind and, together, we got her onto it.

"Grab onto the side," I shouted, quickly jumping up, and guiding her towards the open door. It is not an easy task for an able-bodied person to slide into the seat, from the wing. Getting my mother in, and strapped down, was a major operation. We both gasped, and I prayed that it would work out. I set a course to fly over her Leicestershire cottage, as she wanted a bird's eye view of the village. I descended from 5,000 feet to 1,500 feet, and circled the area she'd requested.

"I can't stay here for long, or we'll get complaints," I shouted.

"Bugger them," she replied. "I want to see what they are all up to." I banked the plane to 60 degrees and she saw, for the first time, views of neighbours' back gardens that were unavailable to anyone else. "I always wanted to see the bigger picture," she cried.

"Say again, mother?" I asked, incredulously.

"Are you goin' deaf, or are you testin' me?" she responded sharply. I didn't ask again, but she had just given me the answer to Sally's conundrum. I was excited.

"Thanks, mother. You've just given me the answer!" *The higher the flier, the bigger picture they can see. My film would need people of a higher calibre; people who could truly see, and create, the bigger picture.*

My mother was too absorbed with the view, to listen to my cryptic comments. We would never again make such a journey together.

77. Crippled Again

2007

I turned over in bed, and shouted out loudly with pain. The magical spell had ended. My heart pounded, and I was immediately depressed. Mr McMinn had said that it would not last, and it hadn't. But I had been given a three year reprieve, during which time I had gained my pilot's licence, recorded all the incidental music, and made a great start on the book and the screenplay.

"You must only get involved with producers who have a genuine interest in your film, and what your objective is. You must never relinquish control. You are the only one with the passion to see it through. Most will only be interested in what they can get out of it. There are plenty of multi-millionaire producers in this business, who have never made a film. Be very, very careful."

These words, from Michael Eisner, one of the most important characters in the entertainment world, stood me in good stead over the years to come.

My mother's innocent statement in the plane, while flying over her village, was the key for any filmmaker wishing to take on my story. My second new hip was a walk in the park. My whole body was now free of pain, but I had gained many, many insights from such an experience. I could feel every cell in my body regenerating; and I was back, ready for the fray.

78. The End of an Era

2008

Mother was frail, and heading for her 94th year. "You make sure you finish the job now, because I may not make it," she croaked, and coughed, horribly. She died in my arms a few weeks later. I was devastated. She was a great-hearted soul, and I would miss her terribly. It was the end of an era. Now she would join Ben, and I redoubled my efforts.

The script re-write was a major undertaking. If I could do a good job, it would form the template for the book. A year later, I had finished the final producer's draft. It was another year of no visions, no dreams, no voices, and no advice. I re-took my CAA flying check, and passed.

Flying high, over Draycott Water in Oxfordshire, I remembered mother's wonderful words. Then I remembered Sally's words *what will happen next*? I had slavishly followed the advice of the 'snow people', and so many times the journey had taken me to the darkest places, before the light appeared. I had lived in my own strange world for the past thirty three years.

79. Beyond the Silver Lining

2009

It was a bitterly cold January day, and winds gusting to gale force were lashing Leicestershire. Pitting myself against the winter elements was spiritually elevating as I headed for the hillside, after visiting Mother's and Ben's graves.

The storm was now seriously battering the countryside, and I held onto the old, crooked fence that overlooked the great promontory. Low, black clouds, looking like beasts in the skies, blew by me and clawed at my face. The gale tried its best to rip me from my mooring, and carry me, airborne, to the ends of the earth. I held my ground, and stared into the beautiful abyss. The trees swayed violently, the wind became a turbulent ocean, and I closed my eyes.

Eternity stood before me. Slowly, and imperceptibly, the storm-battered hillside became calm. It was a wonderful summer's day again, and I was watching myself haymaking with old farmer Cooper. I could smell the heady aroma of the freshly cut grass, crispening in the midday sun.

The aura of peace and tranquillity that surrounded me contrasted profoundly with the relentless, raging roar of the storm.

I looked around and there, standing curiously by the great old oak, were Sally and James. The sun's rays shimmered through the green, leaf-covered branches, and cast a golden glow over my old friends. My heart filled with joy, as they beckoned me to join them.

"This journey is nearly over, and another is just beginning," Sally said quietly, and with purpose. James, as always, looked on happily.

"Look around. What do you see?" she continued, rhetorically. "You see the sun, the fields, and the horizon. Beyond the horizon, bigger pictures of the future lie before your eyes. Remember. Remember everything. All will become clear, when it becomes clear."

In an instant, and as usual, they had disappeared into the ether. The sun-kissed day turned cold, and the balmy breeze became a tempest.

I opened my eyes, and the battering wind threw me against the trunk of the ancient oak. I held onto the fence, as if my life depended on it, and inched my way back to the sanctuary of the car.

Sally's parting words, delivered with intense passion, now echoed through my mind, "Finish the book, Stuart. Finish the book!"

There and then, a new determination took hold of me. I could not, and would not, let her down. "Our dream goes on, Sally" I whispered, as I started the engine…